Early praise for this new edition of *Web Development Recipes*

If you are a front-end web developer, *Web Development Recipes* is a must for your bookshelf. This book is a ready reckoner for developers at all levels.

➤ **Shreerang Patwardhan, CSM**
Technical Consultant, GSPANN Technologies, Inc.

The second edition of *Web Development Recipes* continues its status as a veritable grab bag of interesting front-end web development tips, tricks, and techniques that will be of particular use to those new to front-end development, those developers who've missed the HTML5 and CSS3 wave so far, or anyone ready to try out a few new things to make their projects better. *Web Development Recipes'* real skill is in giving you enough ammunition to try new things and to then inspire you to explore and take things further on your own.

➤ **Peter Cooper**
Editor, *JavaScript Weekly*

Web Development Recipes is a reference book, a training manual, and a technology guide all in one and should be included in every developer's library. The authors are seasoned experts who have separated the wheat from the chaff and brought you the best examples of modern web development to learn from and use immediately in your work.

➤ **Steve Heffernan**
Author of Video.js

A really thorough explanation of good web development solutions.

➤ **Todd H. Gardner**
  President and Co-Founder, TrackJS

Whether you're just getting started with the web or looking to expand your skill set, this updated version of *Web Development Recipes* provides crisp, clear, and concise examples across a variety of the latest web technologies. No fluff, no frills. Just solid, practical advice on how to leverage these tools to work for you.

➤ **Kevin Gisi**
  Senior Staff Engineer, Mashable

I believe the recipes in this book will rekindle your joy of coding, as they have for me. This book is designed to suit novices, intermediates, and ninjas, with recipes that combine code snippets with superb explanation. With its diversity of topics and real-world examples of tasks you face daily, the book will be a favorite that you go back to as a reference time after time.

➤ **Nouran Mahmoud Marouf**
  Front-End Engineer, Tarifah

Web Development Recipes
Second Edition

Brian P. Hogan
Chris Warren
Mike Weber
Chris Johnson

The Pragmatic Bookshelf

Dallas, Texas • Raleigh, North Carolina

Many of the designations used by manufacturers and sellers to distinguish their products are claimed as trademarks. Where those designations appear in this book, and The Pragmatic Programmers, LLC was aware of a trademark claim, the designations have been printed in initial capital letters or in all capitals. The Pragmatic Starter Kit, The Pragmatic Programmer, Pragmatic Programming, Pragmatic Bookshelf, PragProg and the linking *g* device are trademarks of The Pragmatic Programmers, LLC.

Every precaution was taken in the preparation of this book. However, the publisher assumes no responsibility for errors or omissions, or for damages that may result from the use of information (including program listings) contained herein.

Our Pragmatic courses, workshops, and other products can help you and your team create better software and have more fun. For more information, as well as the latest Pragmatic titles, please visit us at *https://pragprog.com*.

The team that produced this book includes:

Rebecca Gulick (editor)
Potomac Indexing, LLC (index)
Eileen Cohen; Cathleen Small (copyedit)
Dave Thomas (layout)
Janet Furlow (producer)
Ellie Callahan (support)

For international rights, please contact *rights@pragprog.com*.

Printed in the United States of America.
ISBN-13: 978-1-68050-056-1
Printed on acid-free paper.
Book version: P1.0—July 2015

Contents

Acknowledgments

Thanks for picking up our book. We really appreciate it, but you should know that although we wrote the book, many other awesome people helped make it what it is.

When we shipped the first edition of the book, we relied on our experiences as professional web developers working in a wide range of industries. With this edition, we thought we could come in quickly, update things, drop things that don't matter anymore, and call it good. But it's never that easy. Our editor, Rebecca Gulick, offered just the right amount of great advice and prodding to push us all in the right direction.

We're all extremely grateful to Dave Thomas and Andy Hunt for giving us the opportunity to write for the Pragmatic Bookshelf. They've built a system that puts readers first but gives authors all the support we need to meet their expectations. We're better people because of the work they've done. In addition, we're thankful to Susannah Pfalzer, who offered some great feedback and support along the way.

Thanks to Joel Andritsch, Kevin Gisi, Nouran Mahmoud Marouf, and Shree-rang Patwardhan for their help reviewing this book for technical issues. Joel and Kevin were especially helpful with their deep dive and awesome insights.

Additionally, we want to thank our other business associates, including Erich Tesky, Austen Ott, Jeff Holland, and Nick LaMuro, for their support and feedback throughout the process.

Brian Hogan

I love learning about code and showing other people how to use it, and it's great to be able to share that with Mike, Chris, and CJ. It's always a pleasure working with these gentlemen on any project, but it's great to have them join me on a book like this where there are so many different technologies. We each have areas that we focus on, which makes it much more manageable. Thank you for your help, guys.

I can't write books without my wonderful wife, Carissa. Sometimes I wonder if she should get credit on the cover too for putting up with the writing process, which mostly revolves around me lamenting the fact that I can't get something working. She always assures me it'll work out. Thank you, Carissa, for your support and love.

Chris Warren

I can't thank my awesome wife, Kaitlin, enough for her support during the writing and editing of this book.

Thanks to Brian, Mike, and CJ for sharing in this experience. I've known these guys for a long time, and it was great to get to do this with friends.

Mike Weber

I'd like to thank Brian Hogan for being my mentor over the years and for getting me started as a web developer. Without him, I wouldn't be where I am today.

I'd also like to thank my other coauthors, Chris and CJ, for helping me and for their effort. I'm lucky to have such hardworking associates.

And, finally, I'd like to thank my wife, Kaley, for putting up with my late nights writing and revising so we could finish the book.

Chris Johnson

To my wife, Laura, thank you for supporting me every step of this journey. You gave me strength to work on this project, and your love and support fueled me all those late nights. To my daughter, Kenzie, I hope you see this some day and realize that no goal is too big to accomplish.

To my parents, thank you for teaching me to work for things I want and to never give up.

Thanks to Brian, Chris, and Mike for collaborating on this; you have made me a better writer with your constant feedback and support. You guys kept me going when sections got tough, and I really appreciated that.

To my colleagues at both Getty and Madison College, thank you for your support and feedback.

Preface

It's no longer enough to know how to wrangle HTML, CSS, and a bit of Java-Script. Today's web developer needs to know how to write testable code, build interactive interfaces, integrate with other services, and sometimes even do some server configuration, or at least a little bit of back-end work. This book is a collection of more than forty practical recipes that range from clever user-interface tricks that will make your clients happy to server-side configurations that will make life easier for you and your users. You'll find a mix of tried-and-true techniques and cutting-edge solutions, all aimed at helping you truly discover the best tools for the job.

Who's This Book For?

If you make things on the web, this book is for you. If you're a web designer or front-end developer who's looking to expand into other areas of web development, you'll get a chance to play with some new libraries and workflows that will help you be more productive, and you'll get exposed to a little bit of that server-side stuff along the way.

If you've been spending a lot of time on the back end and you need to get up to speed on some front-end techniques, you'll find some good recipes here as well, especially in the chapters on workflow and testing.

One last thing—a lot of these recipes assume you've had a little experience writing client-side code with JavaScript and jQuery. If you don't think you have that experience, read through the recipes anyway and pick apart the provided source code. Consider the more advanced recipes as a challenge.

What's in This Book?

We've included a bunch of great topics to get you started on the path to more advanced web development. Each recipe poses a general problem and then lays out a specific solution to a scenario you're likely to encounter, whether it's how to test your site across multiple web browsers, how to quickly build and automatically deploy a simple static site, how to create a simple contact form that emails results, or how to configure Apache to redirect URLs and serve pages securely. We'll take you through both the how and the why so you can feel comfortable using these solutions in your projects. Since this is a book of recipes, we can't go into a lot of detail about more complex system architecture, but you'll find some suggestions on where to go next in each recipe's Further Exploration section.

We've organized the recipes into chapters by topic, but you should feel free to jump around to the topics that interest you. Each chapter contains a mix of beginner and intermediate recipes, with the more complex recipes at the end of each chapter.

In Chapter 1, *Eye-Candy Recipes*, on page 1, we cover some ways you can use CSS and other techniques to spice up the appearance of your pages.

In Chapter 2, *User Interface Recipes*, on page 35, you'll use a variety of techniques to craft better user interfaces—including use of JavaScript frameworks like Knockout and Angular—and you'll look at how to make better templates for sending HTML emails.

In Chapter 3, *Data Recipes*, on page 121, you'll look at ways you can work with user data. You'll construct a simple contact form and do some work with charts, and you'll take a peek at how to build a database-driven application using CouchDB.

In Chapter 4, *Mobile Recipes*, on page 163, you'll take user interfaces a step further and look at ways you can work with the various mobile computing platforms. You'll spend some time with jQuery Mobile, look at how to handle multitouch events, and dig a little deeper into determining how and when to serve a mobile version of a page to your visitors.

In Chapter 5, *Workflow Recipes*, on page 193, you'll discover ways you can improve your development process to produce quality code while being more productive in the process. We'll investigate how Sass can make your life easier when you're managing large style sheets. And we'll explore CoffeeScript, a language that produces JavaScript that works everywhere but lets you take advantage of more modern language capabilities.

In Chapter 6, *Testing Recipes*, on page 241, you'll create more bulletproof sites by using automated tests, and we'll show you how to start testing the JavaScript code you write.

Finally, we'll turn our attention to moving into production in Chapter 7, *Hosting and Deployment Recipes*, on page 277. We'll walk you through building a virtual machine so you have a testing environment to try things in before you set up your production environment, and we'll cover how to set up secure sites, do redirects properly, and protect your content. We'll also show you how to automate the deployment of websites so you won't accidentally forget to upload a file.

What You Need

We'll be introducing you to many new technologies in this book. Some of them are fairly new and somewhat subject to change, but we think they're compelling and stable enough to talk about at an introductory level. That said, web development moves quickly. We've taken steps to ensure that you can still follow along, by providing copies of the libraries we use in these recipes with the book's source code where appropriate.

We've tried to keep the prerequisites to a minimum, but you'll want to familiarize yourself with a few things before you dig in.

HTML5 and jQuery

We use HTML5 markup in our recipes—you won't find any self-closing tags in our markup, and you'll see some new tags like <header> and <section> in some of the examples. If you're not familiar with HTML5, you might want to read *HTML5 and CSS3: Level Up With Today's Web Technologies [Hog13]*.

We'll also use jQuery when it's appropriate. Several of the libraries we introduce in these recipes rely on it, and it often results in code that's easier to understand. In most cases, our code examples will fetch jQuery from Google's content delivery network. In a couple of cases libraries will require specific versions of jQuery, and we'll be sure to point those out.

JavaScript Coding Conventions

To ensure that JavaScript doesn't block the page from loading quickly, we'll place all of our JavaScript code in the body of the page, right above the closing <body> tag. This also eliminates the need for us to use any checks to see if the document is ready.

As a convention, we'll prepend any variable names that reference jQuery objects with a dollar sign so we know when we're referencing jQuery objects vs. regular variables. This makes these variables easier to identify when we're reading the code later:

```
// jQuery object
var $images = $("#images");
```

```
// not jQuery
var options = {fx: fade};
```

Finally, we'll enclose all of our JavaScript inside an Immediately-Invoked Function Expression (IIFE) to avoid polluting the global state:

```
(function($){
  // Our code goes here.
  // All variables within are local to this function expression.
})(jQuery);
```

This also can have an impact on performance, as JavaScript can reference the variables directly in the IIFE instead of having to look in the global scope.

The Shell

You'll work with various command-line programs in these recipes whenever possible. Working on the command line is often a huge productivity boost, because a single command can replace multiple mouse clicks, and you can write your own scripts to automate these command-line tools. The *shell* is the program that interprets these commands. If you're on a Windows machine, you'll use the Command Prompt. If you're on OS X or Linux, that's the Terminal.

Shell commands will look something like this:

```
$ mkdir javascripts
```

The $ represents the prompt in the shell, so you're not meant to type it in. The commands and processes you'll use are platform-independent, so whether you're on Windows, OS X, or Linux, you'll have no trouble following along.

Node.js

Several recipes in this book require that you have Node.js installed. We'll be using some tools that require Node.js to run, such as Grunt, Enfield, Coffee-Script, and Sass. Visit the Node.js website[1] and install the version for your operating system.

QEDServer

Several of the recipes in this book make use of an existing product-management web application. You can work with this application by installing QEDServer,[2] a stand-alone web application and database that requires minimal setup. QEDServer works on Windows, OS X, and Linux. All you need is a Java Runtime Environment. Whenever we refer to our development server, we're talking about this. It gives us a stable web-application back end for our

---

1. http://nodejs.org/
2. A version for this book is available at http://webdevelopmentrecipes.com/.

demonstrations, and it gives you a hassle-free way to work with Ajax requests on your local machine.

The examples in this book will run against the version of QEDServer that we've bundled with the book's code examples, which you should download from the book's website.[3]

To use QEDServer, you start the server with server.bat on Windows or ./server.sh on OS X and Linux. This creates a public folder that you can use for your workspace. If you create a file called index.html in that public folder, you can view it in your web browser by visiting http://localhost:8080/index.html.

A Virtual Machine

Several chapters in this book use a Linux-based web server with Apache and PHP. You'll learn how to set up your own copy of this server in Recipe 39, *Setting Up a Virtual Machine* on page 282, but we've provided a virtual machine that's already configured, which you can get from http://www.webdevelopmen-trecipes.com/. You'll need the free VirtualBox[4] application to run the virtual machine.

Online Resources

The book's website[5] has links to an interactive discussion forum as well as a place to submit errata for the book. You'll also find the source code for all the projects we build. Readers of the ebook can interact with the box above each code excerpt to view that snippet directly.

With all that out of the way, we're ready to jump in. We hope you enjoy this book and that it gives you some ideas for your next web project!

Brian, Chris, CJ, and Mike

---

3. http://webdevelopmentrecipes.com
4. http://www.virtualbox.org/
5. http://pragprog.com/titles/wbdev2

## CHAPTER 1

Eye-Candy Recipes

A solid application is great, but a couple of extra touches on the user interface can make a huge difference. If they're easy to implement, that's even better.

In this chapter, we'll use CSS to style some buttons and text, and we'll do some animations using CSS and JavaScript.

Recipe 1

Styling Buttons and Links

Problem

Buttons are an important element in user interaction with our websites, but each browser has its own idea of what a button should look like. On top of that, sometimes we might want links to look like buttons. For example, if we have a form on a page, we may want a button that submits the form, and a link that cancels the process and takes us to another part of the site—and we want those elements to match visually. Additionally, it'd be great if we could control the look of form buttons without having to create a new graphic with new text each time we need one.

Ingredient

- A CSS3-compliant web browser, such as Internet Explorer 9 or higher, Safari, Opera, Firefox, or Chrome

Solution

Using CSS to style form elements or links is common, but by using a single class and a few CSS rules, we can create a style that makes links and buttons match. This gives us a consistent style across our elements without resorting to using buttons for links, or links to submit forms. Best of all, we can override the default styles that vary among browsers and operating systems.

Since we want to achieve a common appearance for both links and buttons, we start by creating a simple prototype HTML page containing a link and a button:

cssbuttons/index.html
```
<p>
  <input class="button" type="button" value="A Button!">
  <a class="button" href="http://pragprog.com">A Link!</a>
</p>
```

Note that we assign a class of button to both elements. We'll use this class to style both the link and the input elements so that you can't tell one from the other on the page.

As we set up our button class, many of the attributes that we set apply to both the link and input elements, while a few serve to make them consistent with each other.

First we apply the basic CSS attributes for both:

```
cssbuttons/css-buttons.css
.button {
  border: 1px solid #282727;
  background-color: #DBC73C;
  display: inline-block;
  font-weight: bold;
  font-family: "Verdana";
  text-transform: uppercase;
}
```

We use display: inline-block to ensure that both elements can have proper widths and heights. On modern browsers, buttons already have this property set, but links don't. The result looks like the following figure:

With these basic attributes, we already have some consistency between the objects, as the preceding figure shows, but we're far from done. The font sizes don't match and the padding is different, so it's easy to tell that these are not the same type of element. So, we tweak those values in the .button rule:

```
font-size: 1.2em;
line-height: 1.22em;
padding: 6px 20px;
```

By setting the font-size, line-height, and padding on the class, we override any values already set on the <a> element and input elements. Now our buttons look a little better:

We still need to address a few inconsistencies that give away that these two elements aren't the same. When you hover over a button, the cursor doesn't change from an arrow to a pointer, as it does when you hover over a link. So we have to choose the behavior we want and apply it to both. Additionally, links pick up the default link color on the page, and linked text is underlined. So we unify those as well:

```
cursor: pointer;
color: #000;
text-decoration: none;
```

Zooming in on our buttons in the Firefox browser reveals that, although they're close to the same height, the link is slightly smaller. This discrepancy is enough to be noticeable, so we want to address it. Firefox adds a little extra padding to its buttons, but we can override that by specifically targeting buttons in Firefox like this:

```
input::-moz-focus-inner {
        border: 0;
        padding: 0;
}
```

And in Chrome, when you click the first button, you see an outline around the box. To remove that outline, we can add this style:

```
input.button { outline: none; }
```

This removes the last discrepancy between our two buttons, allowing us to focus on their overall look. We can improve that by rounding the corners and adding a bit of a drop shadow, by adding this code to our existing .button rule:

```
  cursor: pointer;
  color: #000;
  text-decoration: none;
➤ border-radius: 12px;
➤ -webkit-box-shadow: 1px 3px 5px #999;
➤        box-shadow: 1px 3px 5px #999;
```

Our buttons now look like the ones in the following figure:

All modern browsers support the border-radius property, but notice that we're adding two lines to our style sheet for box-shadow. The second line is enough for most modern browsers with CSS3 support, but by also including the -webkit prefixed property, we provide support for older versions of Safari and the Android browser. The -webkit prefix is for WebKit-based browsers such as Safari, Opera, and Chrome. (Chrome and Opera use the Blink rendering engine, which is a fork of WebKit.)

As a final touch, let's add a subtle gradient for texture. We'll use this to our advantage shortly when we set the look of the buttons when they're clicked. First, we add this to the end of our .button rule:

```
➤  background: -webkit-linear-gradient(top, #FFF089, #DBC73C);
➤  background:         linear-gradient(to bottom, #FFF089, #DBC73C);
}
```

And with those lines added, our buttons look like this:

> **A BUTTON!**   **A LINK!**

Once again, two lines achieve the same effect across multiple browsers. In this case, we're not only prefixing a rule. The syntax that WebKit-based browsers use is slightly different from the standard.

Finally, we want to add some CSS associated with click events so that a visual indicator shows that the button was clicked. Users expect that indication, and its absence can be disconcerting. Although we have numerous ways to convey that the button was clicked, the simplest is to reverse the gradient:

```
.button:active, .button:focus {
  color: #000;
  background: -webkit-linear-gradient(top, #DBC73C, #FFF089);
  background:          linear-gradient(to bottom, #DBC73C, #FFF089);
}
```

We can reverse the gradient in several ways, but the easiest way to do it consistently across browsers is to swap the colors at each end of the gradient. By setting this background on .button:active and .button:focus, we ensure that the excepted changes happen, whether the link or the input button is clicked.

CSS-styled links and input buttons allow us to style otherwise disparate elements and use them in the appropriate manner—links for navigating between pages and input buttons for submitting data—while presenting a consistent interface. By not relying on JavaScript to make a link submit a form or a button outside of a form redirect to a page, we avoid breaking functionality in older browsers, and we make it easier to understand how the page is working.

Further Exploration

We've chosen the colors for the buttons in this recipe, but you'll probably want to change them for your own projects. If you need help getting your own gradients right, check out http://www.westciv.com/tools/gradients/.

If a button isn't available to the user, you can remove it from the interface. Or you can add a disabled class to it and style it appropriately, making it look more faded out. Once you have a disabled-button style that you like, what else must you do to truly disable it? Form inputs have a disabled attribute, but for links you'll need to use JavaScript to apply the disabled class.

Also See

- Recipe 2, *Styling Stand-Alone Quotes with CSS* on page 6
- Recipe 30, *Building Modular Style Sheets with Sass* on page 213

Recipe 2

Styling Stand-Alone Quotes with CSS

Problem

Quotations from experts and praise from customers carry a lot of weight, so we often want to draw attention to these quotations visually. Sometimes we offset the margins a bit, increase the font size, or use large curly quotation marks to make the quotation stand out. On a website, we want to do that in a simple and repeatable fashion while keeping the presentation of the quotation separate from the markup.

Ingredient

- A web browser that supports HTML5 and CSS3

Solution

We typically use CSS to separate our presentation from the content, and styling quotations shouldn't be any different. Modern browsers support some more advanced properties we can use to make our quotations stand out, without adding much additional markup to the page.

We've been asked to add some short customer reviews for the product pages of our store. They're only a couple of sentences long, but each product page will have several quotes, and we want them to stand out from the product descriptions. First, let's look at the HTML and CSS techniques we'll pull together to make this happen.

We want to have a solid foundation to build our CSS upon, so we start by setting up our HTML structure. Using the <blockquote> and <cite> tags makes sense for wrapping the quote and the source, respectively:

```
cssquotes/quote.html
<!DOCTYPE html>
<html lang="en-US">
  <head>
    <meta charset="utf-8">
    <title>Quote</title>
    <link rel="stylesheet" href="basic.css">
  </head>
  <body>
```

```
<blockquote>
  <p>
    Determine that the thing can and shall be done,
    and then we shall find the way.
  </p>
  <cite>Abraham Lincoln</cite>
</blockquote>
</body>
</html>
```

Now that we have good semantic markup for our quotes, we'll start styling them. First we take a simple approach: we put a border around the quote and increase the size of the text, while putting a bit less emphasis on the author's name and sliding that to the right. The quotes look like this:

> Determine
> that the thing
> can and shall
> be done, and
> then we shall
> find the way.
> *Abraham Lincoln*

Here's how we make that happen:

cssquotes/basic.css
```
blockquote {
  border: 1px solid black;
  padding: 5px;
  width: 225px;
}

blockquote p {
  font-size: 2.4em;
  margin: 5px;
}

blockquote > cite {
  color: #AAA;
  display: block;
  font-size: 1.2em;
  text-align: right;
}
```

In this basic style, we give the <blockquote> a width and a border. We then use a direct child selector on the <cite> tag to make sure we're styling it only if it's a child of the <blockquote>. We change the color of the author's name, adjust the padding to line everything up as we'd like, and end up with a simple but good-looking quote.

Now that we've established our basic quote style, we can start to get fancier. Rather than using a border, let's surround the quote with large styled quotation marks. First, we style the quote itself. We add some space on the left using a left margin so we have some room for the quote:

cssquotes/quotation-marks.css

```
blockquote {
➤    margin-left: 50px;
➤    padding: 5px;
➤    position: relative;
➤    width: 225px;
}
```

Then we adjust the paragraph inside the quote. We want to place the quotation marks behind the text, so we need to pull the paragraph out of the normal flow by setting its position and z-index properties:

cssquotes/quotation-marks.css

```
blockquote p {
    font-size: 2.4em;
    margin: 5px;
➤    z-index: 10;
➤    position: relative;
}
```

Next we add the quotation marks:

cssquotes/quotation-marks.css

```
blockquote:after, blockquote:before {
    position: absolute;
    z-index: 1;
    font-size: 12em;
    color: #2ABBD5;
    text-shadow: 2px 2px 0 #DDD;
    font-family: serif;
    height: 0;
}

blockquote:before {
    content: "\201C";
    top: -30px;
    left: -55px;
}
```

```
blockquote:after {
  content: "\201D";
  bottom: 30px;
  right: 0;
}
```

To achieve this effect, we use the :before and :after selectors, which let us insert content into the document when the specified tags are encountered on the page. Using the content attribute, we can specify what that content should be, whether it's open-quote and close-quote codes, a specific character code, or a string. Although open-quote and close-quote are the standards, not every browser understands them, so we're using character codes.

The text we add can be styled like any other element. Here we adjust the color, font family, and font size of the quotes, and we add a text shadow to make the quotes pop a little.

Pay attention to the z-index attribute that was added, as well as the position:relative; attribute on blockquote p. Using the position attributes plus z-index lets us place the quotation marks behind the quote, so we don't need any extra space for the marks; plus, it looks cool to have the text overlaying them. We also position our blockquote:after along the bottom so that no matter how long the quote gets, the closing quotation mark stays at the end.

Finally, we add a dash before the author's name, using the same technique we used for the quotation marks:

cssquotes/quotation-marks.css
```
blockquote > cite:before {
  content: "-- ";
}
```

When we're done, we get something like this:

❝ Determine that the thing can and shall be done, and then we shall find the way.
-- Abraham Lincoln
❞

And that's pretty nice. And we didn't have to make any modifications to the markup.

For our last style, we'll go all out and style the quotes to look like speech bubbles. Our goal is to create something that looks like the following:

> Determine that the
> thing can and
> shall be done, and
> then we shall find
> the way.

Abraham Lincoln

Thanks to CSS3, we don't need images to put our quote inside a speech bubble. We can use a combination of the techniques we've used so far to get the same result. We start by setting a background color on the blockquote. This will be displayed in all browsers, even ones that don't support the CSS3 effects we're applying. Next we use the linear-gradient attribute to apply a background that has a gradient, and then we round the corners of the element by using the border-radius attribute. Now we have this:

```
cssquotes/speech-bubble.css
blockquote {
  background-color: #FAF205;
  background-image: -webkit-linear-gradient(top, #FAF205 20%, #FFFC9C 100%);
  background-image: linear-gradient(#FAF205 20%, #FFFC9C 100%);
  border-radius: 20px;
  padding: 15px 30px;
  position: relative;
  margin: 0;
  width: 225px;
}
```

As you learned in Recipe 1, *Styling Buttons and Links* on page 2, because different browsers use different syntax for linear-gradient, we must use multiple lines of code to get the same (or similar) effects across browsers. Although current versions of Safari and Chrome no longer need this special prefix, we're including it to support some older Android and iOS devices that still do.

We place the unprefixed linear-gradient, which covers all of the current web browsers, after the prefixed ones.

We need to make a few changes in the blockquote p and blockquote > cite styles:

```
cssquotes/speech-bubble.css
blockquote p {
  font-size: 1.8em;
  margin: 5px;
  position: relative;
  z-index: 10;
}

blockquote > cite {
  bottom: -70px;
  left: 50px;
  display: block;
  font-size: 1.1em;
  position: absolute;
}
```

We change the size of the paragraph text slightly, and we use absolute positioning to push the citation down, away from the quote.

Finally, we create the bottom triangle of our speech bubble by using block-quote:after:

```
cssquotes/speech-bubble.css
blockquote:after {
  border-color: transparent #FFFC9C;
  border-style: solid;
  border-width: 0 15px 50px 0px;
  content: "";
  display: block;
  bottom: -50px;
  left: 40px;
  position: absolute;
  width: 0;
  z-index: 1;
}
```

We set the content to an empty string because there's no need for actual content here; we want to create a new content element so we can style its borders. By setting the border widths to different thicknesses between the top and bottom, and left and right, we create a triangle. Multiple values can be set on any CSS attribute that can specify values for each side, in the clockwise order of top, right, bottom, left. We use this to set the sizes of the borders as well as the border-colors, with transparent borders on the top and bottom and color on the right and left.

Further Exploration

We focused on styling quotations in this recipe, but the techniques can be applied in many other situations. For example, by combining the CSS you wrote with the code in Recipe 8, *Swapping Between Content with Tabbed Interfaces* on page 47, you can further customize the style of our different examples, tweaking colors to help distinguish between different sets of data. You can also apply the ideas in Recipe 27, *Using Sprites with CSS* on page 190, to add background images to your quotes or examples.

What other styles can you come up with for quotes? In our final example, we created a speech bubble. Swapping a border from right to left on the block-quote:after flips it on the vertical axis, but what would we have to do to move the author's name and the triangle to the top of the bubble?

We can use these same techniques to create other kinds of irregular shapes that can make design elements stand out, including stars, hearts, and the infinity symbol. The CSS-Tricks site has some great examples of these different shapes;[1] you can experiment with the examples there and see what else you can come up with.

Also See

- Recipe 1, *Styling Buttons and Links* on page 2
- Recipe 27, *Using Sprites with CSS* on page 190
- Recipe 8, *Swapping Between Content with Tabbed Interfaces* on page 47
- Recipe 30, *Building Modular Style Sheets with Sass* on page 213

---

1.   https://css-tricks.com/examples/ShapesOfCSS/

Recipe 3

Creating Animations with CSS3 Transformations

Problem

Flash used to be the go-to tool for developers wanting to add animations to their sites. But as Flash animations become a distant memory, we have a new, built-in tool for animating content with CSS3. However, we may still run into sites that rely on Flash and need to be modernized.

Our client's website originally had its logo done in Flash so that a "sheen" could be seen crossing the logo when the user loaded the page. He just noticed that his site looks different on his phone, and he's not only frustrated that his animation doesn't display, but he's even more concerned that his logo doesn't show up at all. While the missing effect doesn't break the entire site, the missing logo removes some of the site's branding.

Ingredient

- CSS3

Solution

We'll replace the Flash logo with an image so it appears in all browsers. And we'll add back the animation for browsers that support CSS3 transformations.

Since the advent of CSS3 transitions and transformations, we've been able to add animations to sites natively without resorting to plug-ins like Flash, or even having to rely on large JavaScript libraries. The animation we'll add will be visible to all users except those who might still be using Internet Explorer 9 or older.

Let's start with the markup for the header that contains the logo. We add an ID of banner to our <header> element and a class to the <img> tag so we can access them from the style sheet later:

csssheen/index.html
```
<header id="banner">
  <div class="sheen"></div>
  <img src="logo.png" class="logo">
</header>
```

To get the effect we're looking for, we can create a semitransparent, angled, and blurred HTML block that moves across the screen after the Document Object Model (DOM) is loaded. So, let's start by defining our header's basic style. We want a blue banner that crosses the top of our content. To do this, we give our header the desired width and position the logo in the upper-left corner of our header:

cssheen/style.css

```css
body {
  background: #CCC;
  margin: 0;
}
#banner {
  background: #436999;
  margin: 0 auto;
  width: 800px;
  height: 150px;
  display: block;
  position: relative;
}
#banner img.logo {
  float: left;
  padding: 10px;
  height: 130px;
}
```

With our basic layout in place, we can add the decorative elements for the animation. Let's first create the blurred HTML element. Since this is an extra effect that has nothing to do with the content of our site, we want to do it with as little extra HTML markup as possible. We use the <div> with the sheen class that we defined in our markup:

cssheen/style.css

```css
#banner .sheen {
  height: 200px;
  width: 15px;
  background: rgba(255, 255, 255, 0.5);
  float: left;
}
```

In the current state of our page, as shown in the preceding image, we see that we've added a thin, white, transparent line that's taller than our header.

We're off to a great start. Now we want to blur the sheen element and reposition it so it starts left of the header and is slightly angled. To change the angle of the rectangle, we need to add a browser-specific prefix to our transform style. Browser-specific prefixes were created to add "new" CSS3 features before the CSS3 specs were finalized. As of the writing of this book, the CSS3 specs are still in development, but not nearly as many prefixes are required. Because browser prefixes are a bit of a moving target, we recommend referencing David Hund's site[2] to find out which prefixes are still necessary. While it won't hurt to add prefixes to styles that used to require them, maintaining these styles can be tedious and error-prone.

csssheen/style.css
```
#banner .sheen {
  position: absolute;
  left: -100px;
  top: -25px;
  box-shadow: 0 0 20px #FFF;
  -webkit-transform: rotate(20deg);
  transform:         rotate(20deg);
}
```

With our styles in place, we're almost ready to animate our sheen. Next we add the transition declarations, which we use for controlling the animation:

csssheen/style.css
```
#banner .sheen {
  transition: left 2s ease-in-out;
}
```

The transition definition takes three arguments. The first tells the browser which CSS attributes should be tracked. For our example, we only want to track the left attribute, since we're animating the sheen as it travels across the header. (This can be set to all to control the transition of any attribute changes.) The second parameter defines how long the animation takes, in seconds. This value can be a decimal, such as 0.5s, up to multiple seconds for a longer transition when slower changes are desired. The final argument is the name of the timing function to use. We use one of the default functions, but you can define your own. Ceaser[3] is a tool that we could potentially use to define our own function.

Next, we need to add a style declaration that defines where we want the sheen to end up. In this case, it should end on the right side of the header. We *could* attach this to the hover event:

---

2. http://shouldiprefix.com
3. http://matthewlein.com/ceaser/

```
header:hover .sheen {
  left: 900px;
}
```

But if we do that, the sheen will revert to its starting spot when the user hovers away from the header. We want to make this a one-time deal, so we need to use a little bit of JavaScript to change the state of the page. We add a special class called loaded to our style sheet; this class positions the sheen all the way at the end of the logo:

cssssheen/style.css
```
#banner.loaded .sheen { left: 900px; }
```

Then we add the following JavaScript at the end of the <body> to add that class to the header, which triggers the transition:

cssssheen/index.html
```
<script>
  setTimeout(function() {
    document.getElementById('banner').className = 'loaded';
  }, 50);
</script>
```

In the preceding image, it might appear that all we're doing is moving a blurry bar across the screen. But now that we're done styling the sheen, we can clean up the overall look by tweaking the style once more. We add a style of overflow: hidden; to the header, which hides the part of the sheen that hangs over the edges:

cssssheen/style.css
```
#banner {
  overflow: hidden;
}
```

With all of our styles in place, we can trigger the entire animation with the change of a CSS class. We no longer have to rely on a whole JavaScript animation suite or Flash for adding smooth animations to our websites.

This approach has the added advantage of saving our users' bandwidth. Although this doesn't affect most users, we don't always know when a user might visit our site from an iPad or other mobile device using cellular coverage.

This approach requires fewer files to download, so our users enjoy faster load times with less stress on their data plans. We should always keep site optimization in mind when developing websites.

In browsers that don't support these new style rules, our site simply displays the logo image. By separating style from content, we get the benefit of backward compatibility and better accessibility for users with screen readers, thanks to the alternative text on the <img> tag.

Further Exploration

We covered only a few of the transformations and transitions that are available to us. Other transformation options include scaling and skewing. We can also get more fine-grained control over how long each transformation takes, or even which transformations we actually want to transition. Some browsers also enable us to define our own transitions. The built-in control that web developers finally have over animation is exciting and long overdue.

Also See

- Recipe 1, *Styling Buttons and Links* on page 2
- Recipe 2, *Styling Stand-Alone Quotes with CSS* on page 6
- Recipe 30, *Building Modular Style Sheets with Sass* on page 213

Recipe 4

Creating Interactive Slideshows with jQuery

Problem

A few years ago, if you wanted to have an animated slideshow on your website, you'd probably create a Flash movie. Simple tools make this an easy process, but maintaining the photographs in the slideshow often means rebuilding the Flash movie. Additionally, many mobile devices don't support Flash Player, so those users can't see the slideshows at all. We need an alternative solution that works on multiple platforms and is easy to maintain.

Ingredients

- jQuery
- The Cycle2 jQuery plug-in[4]

Solution

We can build a simple and elegant image slideshow using jQuery and the jQuery Cycle plug-in. This open-source tool will give our users a nice slideshow and only requires a browser with JavaScript support.

Many JavaScript-based image-cycling plug-ins are available, but what sets the Cycle2 plug-in apart is its ease of use. It has many built-in transition effects and provides controls for the user to navigate through images. It's well maintained and has an active developer community. It's the perfect choice for our slideshow.

Our current home page is somewhat static and boring, so our boss wants us to build a slideshow showcasing the best of our company's photographs. We'll take some sample photographs and build a simple prototype that uses the Cycle2 plug-in.

We start by creating a simple home-page template containing the usual boilerplate code, named index.html, that will hold our image slideshow:

---

4. http://jquery.malsup.com/cycle2/

```
image_cycling/index.html
<!DOCTYPE html>
<html lang="en-US">
  <head>
    <meta charset="utf-8">
    <title>AwesomeCo</title>
  </head>
  <body>
    <h1>AwesomeCo</h1>
  </body>
</html>
```

Next, we download the Cycle2 plug-in and place it in the same folder as our HTML page. We also create an images folder and place a few sample images our boss gave us to use for the slideshow. You can find these images in the book's source-code folder in the image_cycling folder.

Next, we add jQuery and the jQuery Cycle2 plug-in to our page, right above the closing <body> tag. We pull jQuery from Google, and we reference our local version of the Cycle2 plug-in. We also need to add a link to a file called rotate.js, which will contain all of the JavaScript we need to configure our image rotator:

```
image_cycling/index.html
<script src="http://ajax.googleapis.com/ajax/libs/jquery/2.1.4/jquery.min.js">
</script>
<script src="jquery.cycle2.min.js"></script>
<script src="rotate.js"></script>
```

Then, we add a <div> with an ID of slideshow and add the images inside:

```
image_cycling/index.html
<div id="slideshow">
  <img src="images/house-light-slide.jpg">
  <img src="images/lake-bench-slide.jpg">
  <img src="images/old-building-slide.jpg">
  <img src="images/oldbarn-slide.jpg">
  <img src="images/streetsign-with-highlights-slide.jpg">
  <img src="images/water-stairs-slide.jpg">
</div>
```

When we look at our page in the browser, we see something like the figure on page 20.

We haven't added the functionality to trigger the Cycle2 plug-in yet, so we see the images listed in order. This also shows us what our page looks like for a user who doesn't have JavaScript support. We see that all of the content is available to users so they don't miss out on anything.

At this point we have a choice to make. Suppose we add the cycle-slideshow auto class to our <div> like this:

```
<div class="cycle-slideshow auto" id="slideshow">
```

Then the plug-in would immediately convert the set of images into a slideshow for us with a nice crossfade transition. And we'd be done. But instead, let's explore how to interact with the slideshow programmatically using its Java-Script API.

We start by adding the JavaScript to initialize the plug-in and start the slideshow. We create the rotate.js file and add this code, which configures the jQuery Cycle plug-in:

```
image_cycling/rotate.js
(function($){
  $('#slideshow').cycle({fx: 'fade'});
})(jQuery);
```

The jQuery Cycle2 plug-in has many options that control how the slideshow's transitions work. We can make the images fade, fade with zooming, wipe, or even toss as they transition. You can find the full list of options on Cycle2's website.[5] Let's stick with the fade function, because it's simple and elegant. That's what the fx: 'fade' in the cycle() call does.

Now that we have all the pieces in place, let's look at our page again. This time we see only one image, and after a few seconds, we begin to see the images rotate.

When we show our boss the working slideshow, she says, "That's great, but I'd like to have a Pause button to let customers pause the slideshow on an image they like." Lucky for us, the plug-in we've used makes this easy.

We'll add a pause button to the page with JavaScript, since it's needed only when the slideshow is active. This way, we don't present useless controls to users who don't have JavaScript support. We'll do this with function called setupButtons(). It adds our button to the page and attaches a click event that tells the slideshow to either pause or resume, based on the current state. We also toggle the text of the button so it's apparent whether the slideshow can be paused or resumed.

We place this code *above* our code that initializes the slideshow:

image_cycling/rotate.js

```
function setupButton() {
  var $pauseButton, $slideShow;

  $slideShow = $('#slideshow');
  $pauseButton = $('<button>Pause</button>');

  $pauseButton.on('click', function() {
    if (isPaused($slideShow)) {
      playSlideShow($slideShow, $(this));
    } else {
      pauseSlideShow($slideShow, $(this));
    }
  });

  function isPaused($player) {
    return $player.is('.cycle-paused');
  }

  function playSlideShow($player, $button) {
    $player.cycle('resume');
    $button.html('Pause');
  }
```

---

5. http://jquery.malsup.com/cycle2/api/#options

```
  function pauseSlideShow($player, $button) {
    $player.cycle('pause');
    $button.html('Resume');
  }

  $pauseButton.insertAfter($slideShow);
}
```

First, we define the setupButton() function and declare variables for the Pause button and our slideshow. Then we use jQuery to locate the slideshow by its ID. As a reminder, we're using dollar signs in front of variables that reference jQuery objects.

Then we use jQuery to create the Pause button by using an HTML fragment. We're using a button element here, but you could use any element that responds to a click event.

Next, we add a click() event to the button. If the slideshow is currently running, then we pause the slideshow and change the button text to Resume. Otherwise, we resume the slideshow and change the button text back to Pause.

When the slideshow is paused, the plug-in applies the .cycle-paused class to the <div> containing our slideshow. We use that to see if the slideshow is paused. It's a cleaner technique than looking at the current name of the button.

We add the Pause button by inserting the new button into the DOM, right after the slideShow using insertAfter().

Finally, we need to invoke the setupButton() to place the button on the page. We place that right below our cycle() call that fires off the slideshow:

image_cycling/rotate.js
```
$('#slideshow').cycle({fx: 'fade'});
setupButton();
```

Let's check out the page in the browser again. We can see the Pause button show up on the page, as in the figure on page 23.

After our slideshow starts, we can click the Pause button, and we'll see the Resume button replace the Pause button as the transitions stop. When we click the Resume button, the images will begin to change again.

AwesomeCo

Pause

Further Exploration

This slideshow was easy to implement, and with all of the options that are provided at the plug-in's website,[6] we can extend the slideshow to include even more functionality.

To enhance the visual experience, the Cycle2 plug-in has many transition settings, such as shuffle, a toss, and uncover transitions. We can change our slideshow to use any of these by changing the value of the fx: option in our cycle() call. We can also cycle other elements besides images, including more complex HTML regions and even videos.

In addition to implementing the animation features, we can improve the way pages load by taking advantage of the plug-in's ability to preload the images. Instead of loading all the images in the HTML, we can load one image:

image_cycling/index_preload.html

```
<!DOCTYPE html>
<html lang="en-US">
  <head>
    <meta charset="utf-8">
    <title>AwesomeCo</title>
  </head>
  <body>
```

---

6.   http://jquery.malsup.com/cycle2/api/#options

```
  <h1>AwesomeCo</h1>
  <div id="slideshow">
    <img src="images/house-light-slide.jpg">
  </div>
  <script
    src="http://ajax.googleapis.com/ajax/libs/jquery/2.1.4/jquery.min.js">
  </script>
  <script src="jquery.cycle2.min.js"></script>
  <script src="preload.js"></script>
  </body>
</html>
```

Then, we specify the rest in our JavaScript code:

image_cycling/preload.js

```
(function($){
  var images = [
    '<img src="images/lake-bench-slide.jpg">',
    '<img src="images/old-building-slide.jpg">',
    '<img src="images/oldbarn-slide.jpg">',
    '<img src="images/streetsign-with-highlights-slide.jpg">',
    '<img src="images/water-stairs-slide.jpg">'
  ];

  $('#slideshow').cycle(
    {
      fx: 'fade',
      load: true,
      progressive: images
    }
  );
})(jQuery);
```

We pass the array of HTML elements for the slideshow when we create the slideshow. This can drastically improve load time, because the images can load in the background while the first image is displayed to the visitor.

In this example we're loading images, but this can actually be any HTML you want. You could even use jQuery to fetch other off-the-page elements.

These are some of the possibilities baked into the Cycle2 plug-in, so go explore and try them.

Also See

- Recipe 3, *Creating Animations with CSS3 Transformations* on page 13
- Recipe 37, *Testing JavaScript with Jasmine* on page 267

Recipe 5

Creating and Styling Accessible Tooltips

Problem

We have a page with lots of jargon, and we've been asked to build in functionality that lets visitors hover over terms to see their definitions. However, we
have to ensure that the functionality can be used with assistive devices such
as screen readers, since the page we're building will be accessed by people
with disabilities.

Ingredient

- jQuery

Solution

With a small amount of CSS, some jQuery, the HTML5 ARIA specification,[7]
and only a tiny amount of effort, we can create tooltips that work for everyone.
When we're done we'll have something that looks like this:

> It's a perfectly cromulent word.
>
> Another paragr   **adjective** Appearing legitimate but actually being spurious.

We'll construct a library that'll work for widespread use throughout our site,
but let's develop it by making a prototype page with a basic HTML skeleton:

accessible_tooltips/index.html

```
<!DOCTYPE html>
<html>
  <head>
    <meta charset="utf-8">
    <title>Definitions</title>
    <link rel="stylesheet" href="tooltips.css">
  </head>
  <body>

  </body>
</html>
```

---

7.   http://www.w3.org/TR/html5-author/wai-aria.html

The skeleton includes link to a style sheet file, tooltips.css, which will control the visibility of elements and the way our tooltips look. It'll also contain code that styles the word so it's apparent to users that they can interact with it.

Next, let's add some dummy text. We need a paragraph, and in that paragraph we want to have a specific keyword. When we hover over that word we want the definition to appear, so let's mark up the paragraph like this:

```
accessible_tooltips/index.html
<p>It's a perfectly
  <span class="definition" aria-describedby="def-test" tabindex="0">
    cromulent
    <span class="tooltip" id="def-test" role="tooltip">
      <b>adjective</b>
      Appearing legitimate but actually being spurious.
    </span>
  </span>
  word.
</p>

<p>Another paragraph of text.</p>
```

We place the keyword in a <span> tag, and we place the definition of that word inside its own <span>. We apply a tabindex to the outer <span> so that visitors can interact with the keyword via the keyboard by pressing the Tab key.

We also associate the keyword to its definition in our markup, using the aria-describedby tag, and we apply role="tooltip" to the element that makes up the tooltip. These small touches are what make interfaces more friendly to technologies like screen readers, which are used by blind and low-vision visitors who need the text on the screen read to them by the computer.

Now let's link up jQuery and our own custom tooltips.js file:

```
accessible_tooltips/index.html
<script
  src="http://ajax.googleapis.com/ajax/libs/jquery/2.1.4/jquery.min.js">
</script>
<script src="tooltips.js"></script>
```

We'll look through our document for any elements that have the definition class. For each one we find, we'll find its associated tooltip and hide it. But we won't use jQuery's show() or hide() methods. Instead, we modify the aria-hidden attribute of the tooltip, setting its value to true to ensure that screen-reading software is aware of the tooltip's visible state:

```
accessible_tooltips/tooltips.js
(function($){
  var $definitions = $('.definition');
```

```
$definitions.find('.tooltip').attr('aria-hidden','true');
})(jQuery);
```

Then in tooltips.css we locate the elements with the aria-hidden attributes and style them appropriately:

accessible_tooltips/tooltips.css

```
.definition .tooltip[aria-hidden='true'] {
  display: none;
}

.definition .tooltip[aria-hidden='false'] {
  display:block ;
}
```

As soon as our JavaScript code sets the aria-hidden attribute to true, these CSS rules hide the element. And when we set the value to false, the elements show up again.

While we're here, let's add the styling for the definition. We add an underline to the word so we let users know it's something they can interact with. And we set the display property of the word we're defining to inline-block, which helps the definition appear closer to the word and ensures that any trailing spaces aren't underlined. We also add a slight drop shadow and a background to the tooltip:

accessible_tooltips/tooltips.css

```
.definition {
  display: inline-block;
  text-decoration: underline;
}

.definition .tooltip {
  background-color: #ffe;
  box-shadow: 5px 5px 5px #ddd;
  padding: 1em;
  position: absolute;
}
```

All that's left to do is apply the actual behavior. When the user hovers or tabs to a keyword, we want to show the definition. And when the user moves focus away, we want to hide it. That means we need to handle mouse events as well as focus events for keyboard navigation. That turns out to be pretty easy with jQuery:

accessible_tooltips/tooltips.js

```
function showTip(){
  $(this).find('.tooltip').attr('aria-hidden', 'false');
}
```

```
function hideTip(){
  $(this).find('.tooltip').attr('aria-hidden', 'true');
}

$definitions.on('mouseover focusin', showTip);
$definitions.on('mouseout focusout', hideTip);
```

And if you want to support other events, such as the touch events we work with in Recipe 25, *Mobile Drag and Drop* on page 173, you can add those to the event handlers, too.

That's all there is to it. When we open the page, we can hover over our word and see the definition. Best of all, because we applied a tabindex, we can activate it when we hit the Tab key also. And because the tooltip is associated with its parent, it should work well for screen-reading software.

Further Exploration

In our implementation, the tooltip is a child element of the element we hover on, and we used a <span> element, so we can't place <div> elements or other block-level elements in the tooltip. But it doesn't have to work that way. We could move the tooltip contents elsewhere in the markup and then use the aria-describedby role to locate the element and display its contents in our Java-Script code. Then we could place video content, images, or pretty much anything we want in that tooltip. And it would be accessible to everyone.

In this recipe we used our tooltips for definitions, but we can place any content we want, whether it's more information about a hyperlink or an inline help documentation for user interface items. Don't get carried away; the information you place should supplement the main content. After all, it does require interaction from the user to read the content you've hidden. Also, be sure you don't attach it to an element in such a way that it's triggered accidentally, obscuring the text on the screen. Some people track the words they read with the mouse, and surprise pop-ups won't keep you in their good graces.

Also See

- Recipe 31, *Cleaner JavaScript with CoffeeScript* on page 221
- Recipe 30, *Building Modular Style Sheets with Sass* on page 213
- Recipe 37, *Testing JavaScript with Jasmine* on page 267
- Recipe 25, *Mobile Drag and Drop* on page 173

Recipe 6

Using Font Icons

Problem

Adding icons to a website can help illustrate what a button does or where a link goes, highlight a message, or otherwise clarify a page's components and functions. But creating those icons can be a lot of work, especially if you're not a graphic designer. Whether we're creating a site concept, redesigning an existing page, or working on a project without access to a designer, it'd be great to have access to icons that are easy to use and modify, that add visual interest, and that have a uniform look—without having to go dig around the web for icons.

Ingredients

- CSS3
- Font Awesome[8]

Solution

Font icons are vector images that can be manipulated with CSS, enabling us to have lightweight icons that are easily adaptable to our needs and style without having to create new graphics. We can also use drop shadows and easy scaling to adjust the way they look, and even use CSS animations such as the ones in Recipe 3, *Creating Animations with CSS3 Transformations* on page 13.

We'll use the Font Awesome font icon library in our solution. Font Awesome is one of the most popular font icon sets. It includes hundreds of icons we can use for many common user interface elements as well as many other situations, such as media-player controls and brand logos.

We start with a simple HTML page containing some basic elements on the page, like a header and some navigation:

---

8. http://fontawesome.io

fonticons/original.html
```html
<!DOCTYPE html>
<html>
  <head>
    <meta charset="utf-8">
    <title>Font Icons</title>
    <link rel="stylesheet" href="original-style.css">
  </head>
  <body>
    <div id="header">
      <div id="header_navigation">
        <a href="#"><i class="fa fa-user"></i> My Account</a>
      </div>
      <span id="logo">
        <strong>AwesomeCo</strong>
      </span>
    </div>
    <div id="navigation">
      <ul>
        <li>Home</li>
        <li>Team</li>
        <li>Store</li>
        <li>Puppies</li>
      </ul>
    </div>
    <div id="content">
    </div>
  </body>
</html>
```

Next, we create a style sheet that sets up a simple two-column layout with a header and left-side navigation:

fonticons/original-style.css
```css
body {
  height: 100%;
  width: 580px;
}

a {
  text-decoration: none;
  color: black;
}

#header {
  background-color: #ccc;
  height: 100px;
  padding: 5px;
  text-align: center;
  width: 100%;
}
```

```
#header #logo { font-size: 3em; }

#header #header_navigation {
  text-align: right;
  width: 100%;
}

#navigation {
  background-color: #888;
  float: left;
  min-height: 600px;
  width: 150px;
}

#navigation li i { margin-right: 5px; }

#content{
  float: left;
  margin: 5px;
  width: 600px;
}
```

We include the Font Awesome style sheet. This gives us access to all of the icons in the library, and it needs to be loaded only once no matter how many icons we use on the page:

fonticons/original.html

```
➤    <link rel="stylesheet" href="http://maxcdn.bootstrapcdn.com/font-awesome/
➤  4.3.0/css/font-awesome.min.css">
    <link rel="stylesheet" href="original-style.css">
```

This single style sheet link loads the Font Awesome style sheet from the Bootstrap CDN and makes the icons available to use on our site with some easy CSS classes. Right now the page looks like the following figure:

The page doesn't have much on it now, but it includes some elements that would benefit from having icons on them. Let's start by adding an icon next to the My Account link in the upper-right corner, so that it stands out a bit more and gives some clues as to what it's about.

The My Account section of the site is where our users manage their information, so let's use an icon that represents a person. The <user> icon looks like a good one:

```
fonticons/index.html
<a href="#"><i class="fa fa-user"></i> My Account</a>
```

The <i> tag is a short tag that creates an inline element. A <span> tag could also be used, but generally the <i> tag is used for brevity. The Font Awesome style sheet gives us access to all of its classes, so we can load the font icon associated with the class into the <i> tag. We use two classes: <fa> to indicate that we want to use a Font Awesome icon, and <fa-user> to load the actual Font Awesome <user> icon. Then we can refresh the page, and we see the icon alongside the My Account link, as in the following figure:

That was simple, wasn't it? Now that we've added one icon to the header, let's replace the bullets on the left-hand navigation list with icons that communicate more about what each list item is for.

Font Awesome includes a shortcut to replace bullets with icons, so we don't have to go through the work of removing the bullets ourselves with CSS:

```
fonticons/index.html
<div id="navigation">
  <ul class="fa-ul">
    <li><i class="fa fa-li fa-home"></i> Home</li>
    <li><i class="fa fa-li fa-users"></i> Team</li>
    <li><i class="fa fa-li fa-shopping-cart"></i> Store</li>
    <li><i class="fa fa-li fa-paw"></i> Puppies</li>
  </ul>
</div>
```

We add a <fa-ul> class to the <ul> tag and a <fa-li> class to each of the <li> tags, along with the <fa> and <fa-ICON> classes we would normally add to the <i> elements. Now when we reload the page we see the bullet icons, as in the following figure:

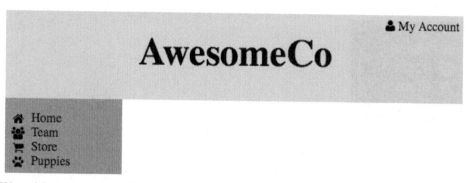

We added icons for all of the navigation items, and we're pretty happy with how things look, but the client wants to change the color scheme of the sidebar to black. We're using black text in the original design, which means our icons are also black and disappear on the black background, so we need to change that. We've also been asked to increase the size of the icons and text on the page. Fortunately, font icons are treated no differently than any text on the page, so it's easy to change the color and size:

fonticons/style.css
```
#navigation {
  background-color: black;
  color: white;
  float: left;
  font-size: 1.3em;
  min-height: 600px;
  width: 150px;
}
```

We want the icon color to match the font color in the navigation, so all we need to do is change the <color> style and the <background-color>. Now, when we reload the page, our icons' colors change along with the color changes we make, and everything continues to match the style guide. And we didn't have to make a single new icon to do it.

We also increased the font size slightly, and the icons adjusted accordingly, as shown in the following image:

If we had made the icons as regular image files, we would have had to redraw them for the new navigation-item size. But because they're vector images, they automatically adjust to the new line size, and we do no extra work!

Font icons give us many great options for adding graphical elements to our sites in a flexible and easily adaptable way. With them we can avoid a lot of trouble having to re-create images if other elements of the design change. Plus, they're fast to load, so our users don't have to wait for multiple images to load.

Further Exploration

Font Awesome includes a lot of ways to manipulate the icons. We can flip them, stack them on top of one another, make them rotate, and more. Beyond the built-in effects, we can use CSS3 animation to change the way the icons render so that we get the exact look that we want.

Also See

- Recipe 3, *Creating Animations with CSS3 Transformations* on page 13
- Recipe 1, *Styling Buttons and Links* on page 2
- Recipe 2, *Styling Stand-Alone Quotes with CSS* on page 6
- Recipe 30, *Building Modular Style Sheets with Sass* on page 213

## CHAPTER 2

User Interface Recipes

Whether you're delivering static content or presenting an interactive application, you have to create a usable interface. This collection of recipes explores the presentation of information as well as some new ways to build more maintainable and responsive client-side interfaces.

Recipe 7

Creating an HTML Email Template

Problem

Building HTML emails is a bit like traveling back in time—a time before CSS, when everyone used tables for layout and <font> tags reigned supreme. A lot of the best practices we've come to know and love aren't usable in HTML emails, because the email readers don't handle them. Testing a web page on multiple browsers is easy compared to the amount of testing we have to do when we create an email that will be read in Outlook, Hotmail, Gmail, or Thunderbird, not to mention the various mail applications on mobile devices.

But our job isn't to complain about how difficult things are going to be; our job is to deliver results. And we have a lot of work to do. Not only do we need to produce readable HTML emails; we also need to ensure that our messages don't get flagged as spam. We need to build something that is usable, readable, and effective on multiple platforms.

Ingredients

* A free trial account on Litmus.com for testing emails

Solution

Designing HTML emails means discarding many current web development techniques because of the constraints of email clients. While staying aware of these limitations, we also need to avoid techniques that might get our messages marked as junk, and we need to easily test our email on multiple devices. The best approach will be to use good old trusty HTML with table-based layouts.

HTML Email Basics

Conceptually, HTML emails aren't difficult. After all, creating a simple HTML page is something we can do without much effort. But as with web pages, we can't guarantee that all users will see the same thing when they look at what we create. Each email client does something a little different when presenting messages to its users.

For starters, many web-based clients like Gmail, Hotmail, and Yahoo often strip out or ignore style sheet definitions from the markup. Google Mail actually removes styles declared in the <style> tag, in an attempt to prevent styles in emails from colliding with the styles it uses to display its interface. We also can't rely on an external style sheet, because many email clients won't automatically fetch remote files without first prompting the user. So, we can't really use CSS for layout in an HTML email.

Google Mail and Yahoo either remove or rename the <body> tag in the email, so it's best to wrap the email in another tag that can stand in for the <body>.

Some clients choke on CSS shorthand declarations, so any definitions we do use need to be spelled out. For example, older clients might ignore this definition:

```
#header{padding: 20px;}
```

So instead, we need to expand it:

```
#header{
  padding-top: 20px;
  padding-right: 20px;
  padding-bottom: 20px;
  padding-left: 20px;
}
```

Desktop clients such as Outlook can't handle background images, and some older ones can't display PNG images. That might not seem like a big deal at first, but millions of enterprise users use these as their primary client.

These aren't the only issues we'll run into, but they are the most prevalent. The Email Standards Project[1] has comprehensive lists of issues for the various email clients.

Partying Like It's 1999

When it comes down to it, the most effective HTML emails are designed using the most basic HTML features:

- They're built with simple HTML markup with minimal CSS styling.
- They're laid out with HTML tables instead of more modern techniques.
- They don't use intricate typography.
- The CSS styles are extremely simple.

In short, we need to develop emails as if the last ten years of web development didn't happen. With that in mind, let's code up a simple invoice email template

---

1. http://www.email-standards.org/

using tables for layout. The application developers will take this template and handle all of the real content, but we need to figure out how to code up the template so that it's readable in all of the popular email clients.

Our invoice will have the typical items: a header and footer, as well as sections for our address and the customer's billing address. It'll have a list of the items the customer purchased, and each line will have the price, quantity, and subtotal. We'll need to provide the grand total for the invoice, and we'll have an area to display some notes to the customer.

Since some web-based email clients strip out or rename the <body> element, we'll need to use our own top-level element to act as the container for our email. To keep it as bulletproof as possible, we'll create an outer table for the container and place additional tables inside of that container for the header, footer, and content. The following figure gives a rough example of how we'll mark this up:

Let's start by writing the wrapper for the email template, using an HTML 4.0 doctype:

```
htmlemail/template.html
<!DOCTYPE html PUBLIC "-//W3C//DTD HTML 4.01//EN"
        "http://www.w3.org/TR/html4/strict.dtd">
<html>
<head>
  <meta content="text/html; charset=ISO-8859-1" http-equiv="content-type">
  <title>Invoice</title>
</head>
<body>
  <center>
    <table id="inv_container"
      width="95%" border="0" cellpadding="0" cellspacing="0">
      <tr>
        <td align="center" valign="top">
        </td>
      </tr>
    </table>
  </center>
</body>
</html>
```

To ensure that our invoice shows up centered in the email client, we must resort to the old, deprecated <center> tag. It's the only approach that comes close to working across all of the various clients. (Don't worry, though; we won't be using <blink>.)

Next, we need to create the header. We use one table for our company name and a second table with two columns for the invoice number and the date:

```
htmlemail/template.html
<table border="0" cellpadding="0" cellspacing="0" width="100%">
  <tr>
    <td align="center" bgcolor="#5d8eb6" valign="top">
    <h1><font color="white">AwesomeCo</font></h1>
    </td>
  </tr>
</table>

<table border="0" cellpadding="0" cellspacing="0" width="98%">
  <tr>
    <td align="left"  width="70%"><h2>Invoice for Order #533102 </h2></td>
    <td align="right" width="30%"><h3>December 31, 2099</h3></td>
  </tr>
</table>
```

Some of the web-based clients strip out CSS, so we have to use HTML attributes to specify the background and text color. The first table has a width of 100 percent, but the second table has a width of 98 percent. Since our tables are centered on the page, this gives us space on the left and right edges so that the text isn't touching the edge of the outer table.

Next, let's add another table that contains the From and To addresses:

```
htmlemail/template.html
<table id="inv_addresses" border="0"
       cellpadding="2" cellspacing="0" width="98%">
  <tr>
    <td align="left" valign="top" width="50%">
      <h3>From</h3>
      AwesomeCo Inc. <br>
      123 Fake Street <br>
      Chicago, IL 55555
    </td>
    <td align="left" valign="top" width="50%">
      <h3>To</h3>
      GNB <br>
      456 Industry Way <br>
      New York, NY 55555
    </td>
  </tr>
</table>
```

Next, we add a table for the invoice itself:

```
htmlemail/template.html
<table border="0" cellpadding="2" cellspacing="0" width="98%">
  <caption>Order Summary</caption>
  <tr>
    <th bgcolor="#cccccc" align="left" valign="top">SKU</th>
    <th bgcolor="#cccccc" align="left" valign="top">Item</th>
    <th bgcolor="#cccccc" valign="top">Price</th>
    <th bgcolor="#cccccc" valign="top" width="10%">QTY</th>
    <th bgcolor="#cccccc" valign="top" width="10%">Total</th>
  </tr>
  <tr>
    <td valign="top">10042</td>
    <td valign="top">15-inch MacBook Pro</td>
    <td align="right" valign="top">$1799.00</td>
    <td align="center" valign="top">1</td>
    <td align="right" valign="top">$1799.00</td>
  </tr>
  <tr>
    <td valign="top">20005</td>
    <td valign="top">Mini-Display Port to DVI Adapter</td>
    <td align="right" valign="top">$19.99</td>
    <td align="center" valign="top">1</td>
    <td align="right" valign="top">$19.99</td>
  </tr>
</table>
```

This is an actual data table, so we'll make sure it has all of the right attributes, such as column headers and a caption.

Then we add a table for the total. We need to use a separate table for this because, believe it or not, some email clients still have trouble displaying tables with rows that span multiple columns.

```
htmlemail/template.html
<hr>
<table border="0" cellpadding="2" cellspacing="0" width="98%">
  <tr>
    <td align="right" valign="top">Subtotal: </td>
    <td align="right" valign="top" width="10%">$1818.99</td>
  </tr>
  <tr>
    <td align="right" valign="top">Total Due: </td>
    <td align="right" valign="top"><b>$1818.99</b> </td>
  </tr>
</table>
```

We place another simple table to display the invoice notes next:

```
htmlemail/template.html
<table border="0" cellpadding="0" cellspacing="0" width="98%">
  <tr><td align="left">
    <h2>Notes</h2>
    <p>Thank you for your business!</p>
  </td></tr>
</table>
```

And finally, we add the footer, which we define as a single-celled table with full width, like the header:

```
htmlemail/template.html
<table id="inv_footer" border="0"
      cellpadding="0" cellspacing="0" width="100%">
  <tr>
    <td align="center" valign="top">
    <h4>Copyright &copy; 2099 AwesomeCo</h4>
    <h4>
      You are receiving this email because you purchased
      products from us.
    </h4>
    </td>
  </tr>
</table>
```

The footer is a good place to explain to recipients why they got the email in the first place. For an invoice the reason is obvious, but for a newsletter we'd use this area to give readers some links to manage their subscriptions or opt out of future mailings.

With that, we've created a simple but readable HTML invoice. But what about those clients that can't handle HTML emails?

 Joe asks:

Couldn't We Use Semantic Markup Instead of Tables?

Many standards-focused developers choose to avoid using tables in favor of semantic markup that relies on CSS to manage the layout. They're not concerned with the mail clients stripping out the CSS, because the email will still be readable and accessible.

Unfortunately, if your stakeholders insist that the design of the email must be consistent across clients, standards-based web development techniques won't cut it. That's why we use a table-based approach in this recipe.

Supporting the Unsupportable

Not every HTML email client supports HTML email, and, as we've learned, even those that do are inconsistent. We should provide a way for people to read the content under those situations, and the most common solution is to provide a link at the top of the message that links to a copy of the email that we host on our servers. When users click the link, they can read the message in their web browser of choice.

In our case, we can place a link to a copy of the invoice that's within the user's account. We want to place the link at the top of the email, above the content table, so that it's easily visible. As a bonus, some mail programs provide a preview that lets the reader jump into the invoice without opening the email.

`htmlemail/template.html`

```
<p>
  Unable to view this invoice?
  <a href="#">View it in your browser instead</a>.
</p>
```

Third-party systems like MailChimp and Campaign Monitor provide this functionality by hosting the HTML email on their servers as static pages.

We could also construct a multipart email, sending both a plain-text version of the invoice and the HTML version. When we do this, we're inserting two bodies into the email and using a special set of headers in the email that tell the email client that the email contains both text and HTML versions. To do that effectively, we'd need to develop and maintain a text version of the invoice in addition to our HTML version. Alternatively, we could place a link to the web-page version of the invoice that we're hosting.

Sending multipart emails is beyond the scope of this recipe, but most web-based frameworks and email clients have options for sending out multipart messages. Wikipedia's entry on MIME[2] has a good overview of how multipart messages work.

Styling with CSS

We're using tables for layout because we can't rely on floating or absolute positioning with CSS, since many web-based email clients strip out CSS styles. Those clients aren't stripping things out because their developers are mean-spirited standards haters. They're doing it because if they allowed CSS, the email's contents could potentially conflict with styles in the web-based application.

For two reasons, however, we may still want to try to use CSS. First, we want things to look nicer for people who have email clients that support CSS. Second, we can reuse this invoice template for the static page we talked about in *Supporting the Unsupportable*, on page 42.

Since many email clients strip off the <head> section of our document, we'll place our style information in a <style> tag right above our container table.

Let's remove the margins around our heading tags to reduce the wasted space. Let's also apply a background color and a border to our table and add some space between each of the inner tables—except for the footer—so things aren't so crowded:

htmlemail/template.html
```
<style>
  table#inv_addresses h3,
  table#inv_footer h4{
    margin: 0;
  }

  table{ margin-bottom: 20px; }

  table#inv_footer{ margin-bottom: 0; }

  body{ background-color: #eeeeee; }
```

---

2.   http://en.wikipedia.org/wiki/MIME

```
table#inv_container{
  background-color: #ffffff;
  border: 1px solid #000000;
}
</style>
```

With the styles in place, the invoice looks like the following figure:

We're not done, though; we need to test things out.

Testing Our Emails

Before we can show it off to our client, we need to see how this email works in some email readers. We can send it around to our colleagues, or we could create accounts at Gmail, Yahoo Mail, Hotmail, and others to see how things look. But manual testing is time-consuming.

Litmus[3] provides a suite of tools that help people test web pages and emails. It supports a wide range of email clients and browsers, including mobile devices. Although the service isn't free, it does provide a trial account that we can use to ensure that our invoices work as expected.

Within a Litmus account, we can create a test that lets us choose the target clients. We can then email our invoice to some addresses that Litmus provides, or we can upload our HTML file through the web interface. Using the HTML upload doesn't provide a text fallback, so some of the test results will show

---

3.   http://litmus.com/

only the HTML source, not a text fallback—but that's good enough for our test.

Litmus renders our email on the target email clients and provides us with a detailed report, like the one in the following figure:

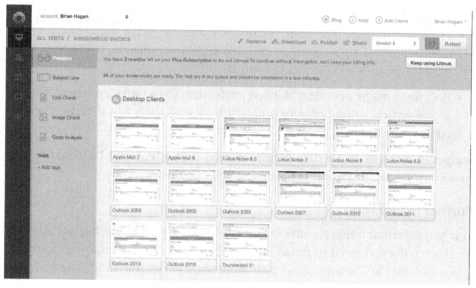

Each thumbnail is clickable so you can get a more detailed view of how things work on an individual device. You'll want to check all of the devices and browsers that matter to you and make any adjustments necessary.

With the code we've written, it looks like we have an email invoice that looks fairly consistent across the major platforms and is readable on most of the others. In your own projects, you may have to do a little more tweaking to get the results you want.

Images and Emails

We haven't talked about images yet in this recipe for two reasons. First, we'd need to host our images on a server and include absolute links into the email. The second reason is that many email clients turn images off, since many companies that send emails use images to track whether the email was opened. The email message contains a link to an image on their server, and when you open the email, the images load, and the sender now knows it's been opened.

If you do decide to use images in your emails, follow a few simple rules:

- Be sure to host the images on a server that will be available, and don't change the URLs to the images. You never know when someone will open the email you sent.

- Since images are often disabled by default, make sure you specify useful and descriptive alt attributes on your images.

- Place the images into your email with regular <img> tags. Many email clients don't support images as table-cell backgrounds, and even fewer support images as CSS backgrounds.

- Because images are often blocked by default, it's a bad idea to use images as the entire content of your email. It may look nice, but it causes accessibility problems.

Images in emails can be effective when used properly. Don't be afraid to use them, but be mindful of the issues you will encounter.

Further Exploration

Our simple email template presents a readable invoice to our recipients, but an invoice doesn't need to be as engaging as a marketing announcement or a newsletter. For that, we'd need to do more styling, use more images, and do more exception handling for various email clients.

MailChimp[4] knows a thing or two about sending emails. After all, that's its business. If you're looking to learn more about email templates, you can dig into the email templates MailChimp has open sourced.[5] They're tested on all of the major clients, too, and have some well-commented source code that gives more insight into some of the hacks we have to employ to make things work well across all of the major email clients.

Also See

- Recipe 38, *Using Dropbox to Collaborate and Host a Static Site* on page 278
- Recipe 28, *Rapid, Responsive Design with Skeleton* on page 194
- Recipe 11, *Rendering HTML with Handlebars Templates* on page 69
- Recipe 30, *Building Modular Style Sheets with Sass* on page 213
- Recipe 44, *Automating Static Site Deployment with Grunt* on page 304

---

4. http://www.mailchimp.com
5. https://github.com/mailchimp/Email-Blueprints

Recipe 8

Swapping Between Content with Tabbed Interfaces

Problem

We sometimes have multiple, similar pieces of information that we want to display together, such as a phrase in multiple languages or code examples in several programming languages. We could display them one after another, but that can take up a lot of space, especially with longer content. We need to give our users an easier way to compare content, without taking up an unnecessary amount of screen space.

Ingredients

- jQuery

Solution

We can use CSS and JavaScript to display the content on our page in a slick tabbed interface. Each section of content will have a tab generated for it based on a data attribute, and only one tab's content will be displayed at a time. We'll also make sure that we can have as many tabs as we want so that our design is flexible. In the end, we'll have something that looks like this:

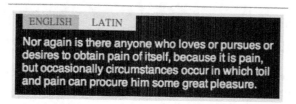

We've been asked to display product descriptions in multiple languages in an attempt to reach a wider audience. We'll build a simple proof-of-concept page so we can determine the best approach.

Building the HTML

Let's start by building out the HTML for the elements we want to show our users. As a proof of concept, let's use two pieces of text, one in English and one in its Latin translation. To start, we create this index.html file to set up the basic structure of our elements:

swapping/index.html

```
<!DOCTYPE html>
<html>

  <head>
    <title>Swapping Examples</title>

    <link rel="stylesheet" href="swapping.css" type="text/css" media="all" />
  </head>
  <body>
    <div class="languages">
      <div class="language" data-tab-title="English">
        Nor again is there anyone who loves or pursues or desires
        to obtain pain of itself, because it is pain, but occasionally
        circumstances occur in which toil and pain can procure him some
        great pleasure.
      </div>

      <div class="language" data-tab-title="Latin">
        Lorem ipsum dolor sit amet, consectetur adipisicing elit, sed
        do eiusmod tempor incididunt ut labore et dolore magna aliqua.
        Ut enim ad minim veniam, quis nostrud exercitation ullamco
        laboris nisi ut aliquip ex ea commodo consequat.
      </div>
    </div>
  </body>
</html>
```

This index.html contains a languages <div> that holds each of the sections we want to display. Inside that are our individual language <div>s, which contain the content we want users to switch between.

> \\// **Joe asks:**
> ~ʃ   # Couldn't We Use jQuery UI Tabs to Do This?
>
> Yes, we definitely could, but there's a lot in UI tabs that we won't be using, such as event hooks. Creating our own tabs lets us focus on keeping things light and gives us more insight into how things work.

Now, let's pull together some JavaScript to create a tabbed interface so our users can toggle between the two examples.

Creating the Tabbed Interface

We'll use the jQuery library to get some helper methods and shortcuts, and we'll put our code in a custom file called swapping.js. We need to link both of those files right above the closing <body> tag in our HTML page:

swapping/index.html

```
➤    <script
➤      src="http://ajax.googleapis.com/ajax/libs/jquery/2.1.3/jquery.min.js">
➤    </script>
➤    <script src="swapping.js"></script>
   </body>
 </html>
```

Then we need to write the code to make the tabs swap. First, we create a function that adds the markup for the tabs to the DOM. We call it createTabs(), and we place it in swapping.js:

swapping/swapping.js

```
function createTabs($container, childSelector) {
  var $list = $('<ul>').addClass('tabs');
  $container.find(childSelector).each(function() {
    var $newTab = createTab($container, $(this), childSelector);
    $list.append($newTab);
  });
  $container.prepend($list);
}
```

This function takes in two arguments. The first argument is a jQuery object that represents the element on the page that should contain the tabs. The second argument is the CSS selector that the function should use to find each element that will be a tab. For our example, we might invoke this function like this:

```
createTabs($('.languages'), '.language');
```

But don't do that yet.

The createTabs() function starts by creating a new unordered list that will hold each of the tabs to be created. We then find each of the child elements that matches the childSelector and pass each child element to a function called createTab() that returns a newly created list item, which we add to the unordered list. That means we need to define a createTab() function next, and that code looks like this:

swapping/swapping.js

```
function createTab($container, $content, childSelector) {
  var tabTitle, $newTab;
  tabTitle = $content.data('tab-title');
  $newTab = $('<li>').addClass('tab').html(tabTitle);
  $newTab.on('click', function() {
    switchTab($container, $(this), $content, childSelector);
  });
  return $newTab;
}
```

In the createTab() function, we read the data-tab-title attribute of the element that's passed in to determine what the tab's title should be. Then we add a class for styling purposes, and finally we add a click observer for this new tab element that will be responsible for changing which tab content is visible to the user.

At this point, if we were to call createTabs($('.languages'), '.language');, we would at least have an idea of what our tabs will look like. But clicking on the tabs will only cause an exception, because we haven't defined the switchTab() function yet. So let's do that now.

Switching Between Tabs

When we switch tabs, we have to hide all of the examples that we don't want to show, and we also have to remove the selected class from those tabs. Rather than finding the current active tab and content, it's easier to get everything to an unselected state and then activate the tab we want. This also increases the code's readability. So we first write the code to hide everything:

swapping/swapping.js
```
$container.find(childSelector).hide();
$container.find('ul.tabs > li').removeClass('selected');
```

With all of the tabs hidden, we can now find and activate the selected tab. To do that we add a selected class to the tab, and we make the tab's content visible by calling the jQuery slideDown() function, or any other jQuery function that makes a <div> element visible:

swapping/swapping.js
```
$content.slideDown('fast');
$tab.addClass('selected');
```

In the end, we have a function that looks like this:

swapping/swapping.js
```
function switchTab($container, $tab, $content, childSelector) {
  $container.find(childSelector).hide();
  $container.find('ul.tabs > li').removeClass('selected');

  $content.slideDown('fast');
  $tab.addClass('selected');
}
```

Tying It All Together

We're almost done, but our solution lacks a few finishing touches. For one thing, when we bring up the page, we see all of the content still, instead of only the first tab. Also, if we had multiple groups of tabs on a single page—

for example, multiple <div>s with the languages class—the same tabs would appear in all of the containers. To fix this we create one more function, initTabs(), that iterates over each of the containers and adds the tabs separately. And for each of the containers, we show only the first tab. We'll invoke this function when we load the page, and it will invoke our createTabs() for each group of tabs on the page.

swapping/swapping.js
```
function initTabs($containers, childSelector){
  $containers.each(function() {
    var $div, $firstTab;
    $div = $(this);
    createTabs($div, childSelector);
    $firstTab = $div.find('ul.tabs > li').first();
    switchTab($div, $firstTab, $div.find(childSelector).first(), childSelector);
  });
}
```

To fire this off, we add a call to initTabs() at the bottom of the script:

swapping/swapping.js
```
initTabs($('div.languages'), 'div.language');
```

All that's left to do now is to make the tabs look a little nicer.

Styling the Tabs

Now that we have all of the behavior wired up, let's apply a little CSS to make it look more like the interface we want:

swapping/swapping.css
```
li.tab {
  background-color: #DDD;
  color: #333;
  cursor: pointer;
  float: left;
  font-size: 120%;
  list-style: none outside none;
  line-height: 1.5;
  margin: 0;
  padding: 0;
  text-align: center;
  text-transform: uppercase;
  width: 80px;
}

li.tab.selected { background-color: #AAA; }

ul.tabs {
  font-size: 12px;
```

```
    line-height: 1;
    list-style: none outside none;
    margin: 0;
    padding: 0;
    position: absolute;
    right: 20;
    top: 0;
}

div.language {
    font-family: "Helvetica", "san-serif";
    font-size: 16px;
}

div.languages {
    background-color: #000;
    border: 5px solid #DDD;
    color: #DDD;
    font-size: 14px;
    margin-bottom: 20px;
    padding: 10px;
    padding-top: 30px;
    position: relative;
}
```

That's it. We now have some generic code that we can use to build out our real site so we can easily switch the product descriptions between different languages.

This solution saves quite a bit of space; we often see it used on sites where space is limited. Some sites use this technique to show product information, reviews, and related items as tabs, while still making that information viewable in a linear format when JavaScript is unavailable.

Further Exploration

What if we wanted to always load a specific tab on the page? For example, if we display code examples in Ruby, Python, and Java, and pythonistas are interested only in the Python examples, it'd be nice if they didn't have to click the Python tab on every new page they visit. We'll leave it up to you to explore that solution on your own.

Also See

- Recipe 9, *Accessible Expand and Collapse* on page 53

Recipe 9

Accessible Expand and Collapse

Problem

When we need to present long, categorized lists on a website, the best way to do it is with nested, unordered lists. However, with this kind of layout, it can be hard for users to quickly navigate, or even comprehend, such a large list. Anything we can do to assist our users will be appreciated. Plus, we want to make sure that our list is accessible in case JavaScript is disabled or a user is visiting our site through a screen reader.

Ingredient

- jQuery

Solution

A relatively easy way to organize a nested list, without separating the categories into different pages, is to make the list collapsible. This means that entire sections of the list can be hidden or displayed to better convey selective information. At the same time, the user can easily manipulate which content to make visible.

For our example, we'll start with an unordered list that displays products grouped by subcategories:

collapsiblelist/index.html
```
<!DOCTYPE html>
<html>
  <head>
    <meta charset="utf-8">
    <title>Our example collapsible list</title>
    <link rel="stylesheet" href="style.css">
  </head>
  <body>
    <h1>Categorized Products</h1>

    <ul class='collapsible'>
      <li>
        Music Players
        <ul>
```

```
        <li>16 Gb MP3 player</li>
        <li>32 Gb MP3 player</li>
        <li>64 Gb MP3 player</li>
      </ul>
    </li>
    <li class='expanded'>
      Cameras &amp; Camcorders

      <ul>
        <li>
          SLR
          <ul>
            <li>D2000</li>
            <li>D2100</li>
          </ul>
        </li>
        <li class='expanded'>
          Point and Shoot
          <ul>
            <li>G6</li>
            <li>G12</li>
            <li>CS240</li>
            <li>L120</li>
          </ul>
        </li>
        <li>
          Camcorders
          <ul>
            <li>HD Cam</li>
            <li>HDR-150</li>
            <li>Standard Def Cam</li>
          </ul>
        </li>
      </ul>
    </li>
  </ul>
  <script
    src="http://ajax.googleapis.com/ajax/libs/jquery/2.1.3/jquery.min.js">
  </script>
  <script src='collapsible.js'></script>
```

We want to be able to indicate that some of the nodes should be collapsed or expanded from the start. It would be tempting to simply mark the collapsed nodes by setting the style to display: none. But that would break accessibility, since screen readers ignore content hidden in this way. Instead, we'll rely on CSS to toggle each node's visibility at runtime. We'll do this by adding a CSS class of expanded to set the initial state of the list.

For example, suppose we know that a user wants to look at point-and-shoot cameras when first reaching this page. This markup doesn't show the limited list yet:

```
collapsiblelist/style.css
ul.collapsible li.collapsed > ul {
  visibility: hidden;
  height: 0;
}
```

Right now it displays the full categorized product list:

Categorized Products

- Music Players
  - 16 Gb MP3 player
  - 32 Gb MP3 player
  - 64 Gb MP3 player
- Cameras & Camcorders
  - SLR
    - D2000
    - D2100
  - Point and Shoot
    - G6
    - G12
    - CS240
    - L120
  - Camcorders
    - HD Cam
    - HDR-150
    - Standard Def Cam

But once the list is made collapsible, and the expanded class is added to that category, users see only the names of the types of products they were looking for, as shown in the figure on page 56.

```
<li class='expanded'>
  Point and Shoot
```

Next we need to write the JavaScript for adding our collapsible functionality, as well as some expand-all and collapse-all helper links at the top of the list. We'll add the links via the JavaScript code as well. As with the collapsible functionality itself, we don't want to change the markup unless we know this code is going to be used. This also gives us the advantage of being able to easily apply this behavior to any list on our site without having to change any markup beyond adding a .collapsible class to a <ul> element.

Categorized Products

Expand all | Collapse all
+Music Players
+Tablets
+Computers
- Cameras & Camcorders
    +SLR
    - Point and Shoot
        G6
        G12
        CS240
        L120
    +Camcorders

`collapsiblelist/collapsible.js`

```
(function($) {
  $.fn.prependToggleAllLinks = function() {
    var $container = $('<div>').attr('class', 'expand_or_collapse_all');
    $container.append(
        $('<a>')
          .attr('href', '#')
          .html('Expand all')
          .click(handleExpandAll.bind(this))
      ).append(' | ')
      .append(
        $('<a>')
          .attr('href', '#')
          .html('Collapse all')
          .click(handleCollapseAll.bind(this))
      );
    this.prepend($container);
    return this;
  };

  function handleExpandAll(event) {
    this.find('li.collapsed').toggleExpandCollapse(event);
  }

  function handleCollapseAll(event) {
    this.find('li.expanded').toggleExpandCollapse(event);
  }
})(jQuery);
```

For this recipe, we wrap all of the code in a self-executing function where we
pass in jQuery as an argument and assign it to the $ variable. This is to avoid
a conflict with any other frameworks or code that also use the dollar sign.

We can quickly create a virtual DOM object by wrapping a string representing the element type we want, in this case an <a> tag, in a jQuery element. Then we set the attributes and HTML through jQuery's API. For simplicity, we'll create two links (Expand all and Collapse all) separated by a pipe symbol. The two links will trigger their corresponding helper functions when they're clicked.

For the click events, notice the use of the bind() function. This keeps the this keyword the same when in the handleExpandAll() and handleCollapseAll() functions. That way we'll continue to interact with the jQuery element that was used to initialize this plug-in in the first place. Which leads us to the next function.

The prependToggleAllLinks() function adds the expand-all/collapse-all links, but these links won't work yet, since we're calling a function that doesn't exist yet: toggleExpandCollapse(). Next we write that function, which toggles whether a node is expanded or collapsed. Since this is a function that will act on a DOM object, we write it as a jQuery plug-in. That means we'll assign the function definition to the jQuery.fn prototype. We can then trigger the function within the scope of the element that it's called against. Finally, to ensure that our jQuery function is chainable and a responsible jQuery citizen, we return this. This is a good practice to follow when writing jQuery plug-ins; *our* plug-in functions will work the same way that we expect other jQuery plug-ins to work.

collapsiblelist/collapsible.js
```
(function($) {
  $.fn.toggleExpandCollapse = function(event) {
    event.stopPropagation();
    if (this.find('ul').length > 0) {
      event.preventDefault();

      this.toggleClass('collapsed').toggleClass('expanded');
    }

    return this;
  };
})(jQuery);
```

We'll bind the toggleExpandCollapse() to the click event for all <li> elements, including the elements with nothing underneath them, which are also known as *leaf nodes*. That's because we want the leaf nodes to do something cru-cial—absolutely nothing. Unhandled click events bubble up the DOM, so if we only attach a click observer to the <li> elements with .expanded or .collapsed classes, the click event for a leaf node would bubble up to the parent <li> element, which *is* one of our collapsible nodes. That means the code would trigger that node's click event, which would make the leaf node's parent collapse suddenly and unexpectedly, and we'd be liable for causing undue harm to our users' fragile psyches. To prevent this Rube Goldberg–styled catastrophe from happening, we call event.stopPropagation(). Adding an event handler to all <li> elements ensures that the click event will never bubble up and nothing will happen, as we expect. For more details on event propagation, read *Why Not Return False?*, on page 58.

⸛⸛ Joe asks:

Why Not Return False?

In a jQuery function, return false works double duty by telling the event not to bubble up the DOM tree and not to do whatever the element's default action is. This works for most events, but sometimes we want to make the distinction between stopping event propagation and preventing a default action from triggering. Or we may be in a situation where we always want to prevent the default action, even if the code in our function somehow breaks. That's why at times it may make more sense to call event.stopPropagation() or event.preventDefault() explicitly rather than waiting until the end of the function to return false.[a]

---

a.   http://api.jquery.com/category/events/event-object/

Now we write the makeCollapsible() function that gets called when we select the list element we want to turn into a collapsible list. This function also hides any nodes that weren't marked as .expanded and adds the .collapsed class to the rest of the <li> elements:

collapsiblelist/collapsible.js
```
$.fn.makeCollapsible = function() {
  this.prependToggleAllLinks();
  this.find('li').click(function(event) {
    $(this).toggleExpandCollapse(event);
  });
  this.find('li ul')
    .parent(':not(.expanded)')
    .addClass('collapsed');

  return this;
};
```

We bind the click event to all of the <li> elements that are in a .collapsible list. We also add the expand/collapse classes to all of the <li> elements, except the products themselves. These classes will help us when it comes time to style our list.

When the DOM is ready, we tie it all together by initializing the list and adding the Expand all | Collapse all links to the page:

```
collapsiblelist/index.html
<script>
  $('ul.collapsible').makeCollapsible();
</script>
```

Since this is a jQuery plug-in, we can easily add this functionality to any list on our site by adding a .collapsible class to an unordered list. This makes the code easily reusable so that any long and cluttered list can be made easy to navigate and understand.

Finally, we add some style to this list and attach it to the same .collapsible class that our code depends on:

```
collapsiblelist/style.css
ul.collapsible li.collapsed > ul {
  visibility: hidden;
  height: 0;
}
ul.collapsible li {
  cursor: default;
  list-style: none;
}

ul.collapsible li.expanded, ul.collapsible li.collapsed {
  cursor: pointer;
}

ul.collapsible li:before {
  display: block;
  float: left;
  text-align: center;
  width: 10px;
}

ul.collapsible li.expanded:before { content: '-'; }

ul.collapsible li.collapsed:before { content: '+'; }
```

Further Exploration

If we start out by building solid, working markup without JavaScript, we can build on that foundation to add in extra behavior. And if we write the Java-Script and connect the behavior into the page by using CSS classes rather than adding the JavaScript directly to the HTML, everything is completely decoupled. This also keeps our sites from becoming too JavaScript-dependent, which means more people can use our sites when JavaScript isn't available.

We call this *progressive enhancement,* and it's an approach we strongly recommend.

This same approach could be used for building photo galleries. We'd make each thumbnail link to a larger version of the image that opens on its own page. Then we'd use JavaScript to intercept the click event on the image and display the full-sized image in a lightbox, along with any additional controls that are useful only when JavaScript is enabled, as we did in this recipe.

When submitting data to a server, rather than retrieving it as in the previous example, it would make sense to create a form with a regular HTTP POST request first, and then intercept the form's submit event with JavaScript and do the post via Ajax. This sounds like more work, but you end up saving a lot of time; you get to leverage the form's semantic markup and use things like jQuery's serialize() method to prepare the form data, rather than reading each input field and constructing your own POST request.

Techniques like this are well supported by jQuery and other modern libraries because they make it easy to build simple, accessible solutions for your audience.

Also See

- Recipe 10, *Interacting with Web Pages Using Keyboard Shortcuts* on page 61
- Recipe 12, *Displaying Information with Endless Pagination* on page 76

Recipe 10

Interacting with Web Pages Using Keyboard Shortcuts

Problem

Website visitors expect to use the mouse to interact with the site, but using the mouse isn't always the most efficient way. Keyboard shortcuts are common; Gmail, Tumblr, and Facebook use them as a way to improve accessibility and allow users to quickly and comfortably perform common tasks. Facebook even supports some of the Vim commands discussed in Recipe 40, *Changing Web Server Configuration Files with Vim* on page 287. We want to bring this functionality to our site, but we need to make sure we don't interfere with our application's normal, expected behavior, such as our search box.

Ingredients

- jQuery

Solution

Keyboard shortcuts use JavaScript to monitor the page for certain keys being pressed. We accomplish this by binding a function to the document's keydown event. Each key press is identified by a unique code. When a key is pressed, we check whether a code matches one we are using for a shortcut and invoke the specified function for that key.

We have a site with a large number of blog entries about a variety of topics. After some usability testing, we saw that users decide whether they want to read the entry by scanning the title and part of the first sentence. If they're not interested, they scroll on to the next article. Because some entries are long, users end up doing a lot of scrolling before they get to the next article. We'll create some basic shortcuts to let users quickly jump among the entries on the page, navigate between pages, and easily access the search box. We'll work with an interface that looks like the one in the following figure:

Getting Set Up

First we'll add the ability to scroll between entries on the current page. We'll start by creating a page containing several items that all share a class of entry and use the j key to go to the next entry and k to go to the previous one. These letters are used for navigating to previous and next records in many applications, including Vim, which we cover in Recipe 40, *Changing Web Server Configuration Files with Vim* on page 287, so it's a good idea to stick with the convention. Once we have these shortcuts set up, we'll handle navigating between pages using the right and left arrows, followed by creating a shortcut to the search box.

Let's start by creating a prototype that has a search box and a few search results so we have something we can test our keyboard navigation on:

keyboardnavigation/index.html
```html
<!DOCTYPE html>
<html lang="en-US">
  <head>
    <meta charset="utf-8">
    <title>Keyboard Navigation</title>
  </head>
  <body>
    <p>Make this page longer so you can tell that we're scrolling!</p>
    <form>
      <input id="search" type="text" size="28" value="search">
    </form>
    <div id="entry_1" class="entry">
      <h2>This is the title</h2>
      <p>Lorem ipsum dolor sit amet...</p>
    </div>
```

```
<div id="entry_2" class="entry">
  <h2>This is the title of the second one</h2>
  <p>In hac habitasse platea dictumst...</p>
</div>
<script
  src="http://ajax.googleapis.com/ajax/libs/jquery/2.1.4/jquery.min.js">
</script>
<script
  src='keyboard_navigation.js'></script>
</body>
</html>
```

Because of size constraints, this example page is short. To see the full effect as we scroll between elements, add a few more of the <div id="entry_x" class="entry"> sections. Make sure the content is longer than your browser can display at once so that you can see the effect of scrolling between entries, and make sure that each entry's ID is unique.

Catching Key Presses

We'll use jQuery to set up a few event handlers when the page loads. When someone presses one of our navigation keys, we'll call the functions that navigate through the page. The $(document).keydown() function allows us to specify exactly what to call for different keys by using a case statement. Each case we define represents a different key by its key code:[6]

```
keyboardnavigation/keyboard_navigation.js
$(document).keydown(function(e) {
  if($(document.activeElement)[0] === $(document.body)[0]){
    switch(e.keyCode){
    // In Page Navigation
    case 74: // j
      scrollToNext();
      break;
    case 75: // k
      scrollToPrevious();
      break;
    // Between Page Navigation
    case 39: // right arrow
      loadNextPage();
      break;
    case 37: // left arrow
      loadPreviousPage();
      break;
    // Search
    case 191: // / (and ? with shift)
```

---

6. To find other key codes, check out the list at http://www.cambiaresearch.com/c4/702b8cd1-e5b0-42e6-83ac-25f0306e3e25/javascript-char-codes-key-codes.aspx.

```
      if(e.shiftKey){
        $('#search').focus().val('');
        return false;
      }
      break;
    }
  }
});
```

Before we check whether one of our keys is pressed, it's important to make sure we're not interrupting normal user activity. The first line of our keydown function is if($(document.activeElement)[0] == $(document.body)[0]), which makes sure that the active element on the page is the body of the page itself. By doing this, we avoid catching key presses when a user is typing in a search box or a text area.

Scrolling

Scrolling between entries on our page involves getting a list of the current entries and knowing which one we last used the keyboard to scroll to. First we want to set everything so that when we first scroll on the page we go to the first entry on the page:

keyboardnavigation/keyboard_navigation.js
```
var currentEntry = -1;
```

When the page loads, we set a variable called currentEntry to -1, meaning that we haven't scrolled anywhere yet. We use -1 because we are going to figure out which entry to display by loading all objects on the page with a class of .entry and picking the correct one based on its index in the resulting array. JavaScript arrays are zero-based, so the first entry will be at the 0 position.

In *Catching Key Presses*, on page 63, we defined the functions to call when certain keys were pressed. When the j key is pressed, we want to scroll to the next entry on the page, so we call the scrollToNext() function:

keyboardnavigation/keyboard_navigation.js
```
function scrollToNext(){
  if($('.entry').size() > currentEntry + 1){
    currentEntry++;
    scrollToEntry(currentEntry);
  }
}
```

In scrollToNext(), we first check that we're not trying to scroll to an entry that doesn't exist by ensuring that incrementing the currentEntry counter won't exceed the number of entries on the page. If there's an entry to scroll to, we increase the currentEntry by 1 and call scrollToEntry():

keyboardnavigation/keyboard_navigation.js
```
function scrollToEntry(entryIndex){
  var top = $("#" + $('.entry')[entryIndex].id).offset().top;
  $('html,body').animate({ scrollTop: top }, 'slow');
}
```

scrollToEntry() uses the jQuery animation libraries to scroll our view to the ID of the specified entry. Since the currentEntry represents the index of the entry we want to display, we grab the ID of that entry and tell jQuery to scroll there.

When the user presses the k key, we call a similar function called scrollToPrevious():

keyboardnavigation/keyboard_navigation.js
```
function scrollToPrevious(){
  if(currentEntry > 0){
    currentEntry--;
    scrollToEntry(currentEntry);
  }
}
```

scrollToPrevious() makes sure we aren't trying to load a smaller entry than 0, since that will always be the first entry on the page. If we're not on the first entry, we reduce the currentEntry by 1 and once again call scrollToEntry().

Now that our users can scroll between entries on the page, it's easy for them to quickly review the page content. But when they get to the end of the page, they need to be able to move to the next page of records. Let's work on that next.

Pagination

Navigation between pages can happen in a variety of ways. For this example, we'll assume that the desired page is indicated by the page=5 querystring in the URL; however, this could easily be changed to work with p=5, entries/5, or any other page indicator you might encounter.

To keep our code nice and clean, let's write a function called getQueryString() that pulls the page number out of the URL:

keyboardnavigation/keyboard_navigation.js
```
function getQueryString(name){
  var reg = new RegExp("(^|&)"+ name +"=([^&]*)(&|$)");
  var r = window.location.search.substr(1).match(reg);
  var val = null;
  if (r !== null) val = unescape(r[2]);
  return val;
}
```

Now we'll build a getCurrentPageNumber() function that uses the getQueryString() function to check whether page even exists. If it does, we get it and turn it from a string to an integer and then return it. If it doesn't exist, that means that no page is currently set. If this is the case, we'll assume we're on the first page and return 1. It's important that we return an integer and not a string, because we're going to need to do math with the page number.

```
keyboardnavigation/keyboard_navigation.js
function getCurrentPageNumber(){
  return parseInt(getQueryString('page') || 1);
}
```

Our keycode watcher listens for the left and right arrows to be pressed. When the user presses the right arrow, we call the loadNextPage() function, which figures out what page number we're on and directs the browser to the next one:

```
keyboardnavigation/keyboard_navigation.js
function loadNextPage(){
  var pageNumber = getCurrentPageNumber() + 1;
  var url = window.location.href;
  if (url.indexOf('page=') !== -1){
    window.location.href = replacePageNumber(pageNumber);
  else {
    var joinChar = (url.indexOf('?') > -1) ? '&' : '?';
    window.location.href += joinChar + pageNumber;
  }
}
```

We first determine our current page number, and then increase pageNumber by 1 because we're going to the next page. Then we grab the current URL so we can update it and load the next page. This is the most involved part of the process, because the URL can be structured in several ways.

First we check whether the URL contains page= in the querystring. If it does, as in http://example.com?page=4, then we need to replace the current number using a regular expression and the replace() function:

```
keyboardnavigation/keyboard_navigation.js
if (url.indexOf('page=') !== -1){
  window.location.href = replacePageNumber(pageNumber);
```

We also need to replace the page number when going to the previous page, so we have a replacePageNumber() function. If our URL structure changes, we only have to update our code in one place:

```
keyboardnavigation/keyboard_navigation.js
function replacePageNumber(pageNumber){
  return window.location.href.replace(/page=(\d+)/,'page='+pageNumber);
}
```

If the URL doesn't contain page=, then we need to add the entire parameter to the querystring. Before we do that we should check whether the URL contains other parameters. If it does, they'll be listed after the ? in the URL, so we check for ?. If it exists, as in http://example.com?foo=bar, then we add an ampersand (&) before the parameter name. Otherwise, we need to add the ? before appending the page parameter to the URL:

keyboardnavigation/keyboard_navigation.js
```
else {
  var joinChar = (url.indexOf('?') > -1) ? '&' : '?';
  window.location.href += joinChar + pageNumber;
}
```

We can use a similar, but simpler, technique to load the previous page. After figuring out the current page number and reducing it by 1, we need to make sure we're not trying to load a page number that's less than 1. So first we make sure the new pageNumber is greater than 0. If it is, we update page= with the new number, and we're on our way:

keyboardnavigation/keyboard_navigation.js
```
function loadPreviousPage(){
  pageNumber = getCurrentPageNumber() - 1;
  if (pageNumber > 0){
    window.location.href = replacePageNumber(pageNumber);
  }
}
```

Now that we can move between pages and among entries, let's create a way for users to quickly get access to the search box.

Navigating to the Search Box

The keyboard shortcut that makes the most sense for navigating to the search box is the ? key, but that's done by pressing two keys together, so we need to do things a little bit differently from our other shortcuts. First, we watch for the keycode of 191, which represents the / key. When this key is pressed, we query the shiftKey property on the event, which returns true if the Shift key is down:

keyboardnavigation/keyboard_navigation.js
```
case 191: // / (and ? with shift)
  if(e.shiftKey){
    $('#search').focus().val('');
    return false;
  }
  break;
}
```

If the `Shift` key was pressed, we retrieve the search box by using its DOM ID and call the `focus()` method to place the cursor inside the search box. We then erase any content currently in it by calling `val('')` with an empty string. Finally, we call `return false;`, which prevents the `?` that was typed from being returned by the function and placed in the search box.

Further Exploration

We've added some quick keyboard shortcuts that let our users navigate throughout our site without having to take their hands off of their keyboards. Once the framework is in place, adding new keyboard shortcuts is a breeze. You could use keyboard shortcuts to display a lightbox with the full article that opens when the user presses the spacebar. You could use keyboard shortcuts to pop up a console with information about ongoing tasks or use them to reveal further content in a blog post.

Many of the other JavaScript-based chapters in this book could have keyboard shortcuts added to them, such as browsing through the images in Recipe 4, *Creating Interactive Slideshows with jQuery* on page 18, or using the keyboard or scanning and expanding items in Recipe 9, *Accessible Expand and Collapse* on page 53.

Also See

- Recipe 4, *Creating Interactive Slideshows with jQuery* on page 18
- Recipe 9, *Accessible Expand and Collapse* on page 53
- Recipe 31, *Cleaner JavaScript with CoffeeScript* on page 221
- Recipe 40, *Changing Web Server Configuration Files with Vim* on page 287

Recipe 11

Rendering HTML with Handlebars Templates

Problem

Amazing interfaces require lots of dynamic and asynchronous HTML. Thanks to Ajax and JavaScript libraries like jQuery, we can change the user interface without reloading the page by generating HTML with JavaScript. We typically use methods such as string concatenation to add new elements to our interfaces, but these are hard to manage and are prone to error. We have to dance around mixing single and double quotes and often are left to use jQuery's append() method endlessly.

Ingredients

- jQuery
- Handlebars.js[7]
- QEDServer (for our test server)[8]

Solution

Thankfully, client-side templating tools such as Handlebars allow us to write *real* HTML, render data with it, and insert it into the document. With Handlebars, we can create client-side views with clean HTML that are abstracted away from the JavaScript code. It allows for conditional logic as well as iteration.

With Handlebars, we can simplify HTML creation when generating new content. Let's explore the Handlebars templating syntax by working with a JavaScript-driven product-management application.

The existing application lets us manage products by adding new ones to a list. The example uses our standard development server, since the requests are all handled by JavaScript and Ajax. When the user fills in the form to add a new product and submits the form, the associated code tells the server to save the product and then renders a new product in the list. To build the list

---

7. http://handlebarsjs.com/
8. A version for this book is available at http://webdevelopmentrecipes.com/.

of products, we have to use string concatenation, which becomes awkward and hard to read:

```
handlebars/old_index.html
var newProduct = $('<div class="product"></div>');
newProduct.append('<span class="product-name">' +
                    products[index].name + '</span>');
newProduct.append('<em class="product-price">' +
                    products[index].price + '</em>');
newProduct.append('<div class="product-description">' +
                    products[index].description + '</div>');

$("body").append(newProduct);
```

What a mess! We want something more readable and easier to maintain.

Rendering a Template

Using Handlebars is as easy as loading the script on the page. For this exercise, we'll use QEDServer as our back end so we can use its products API. So, first, we create a basic HTML page called index.html in the QEDServer public folder. We create a basic HTML5 template and load jQuery and Handlebars right above the closing <body> tag:

```
handlebars/index.html
<!DOCTYPE html>
<html lang="en">
  <head>
    <meta charset="utf-8">
    <title>List Products</title>
  </head>
  <body>
    <script src="http://ajax.googleapis.com/ajax/libs/jquery/2.1.4/jquery.min.js">
    </script>
    <script src="http://cdnjs.cloudflare.com/ajax/libs/handlebars.js/3.0.3/
              handlebars.min.js"></script>
  </body>
</html>
```

Note that we load Handlebars from a CDN as we do with jQuery. However, you can always download your own local copy and keep it with your code.

To refactor our existing application, we first need to know how to render a template using Handlebars. This involves two steps. First, we compile a Handlebars template. Second, we convert the template to HTML. The process looks like this:

```
template = Handlebars.compile(templateString);
html = template(data);
```

The first line compiles the template, which we pass in as a string. The second line converts the compiled template to HTML. We pass the data to be injected into the HTML. The data variable is an object whose keys become the local variables in the template. Examine the following code:

```
var artist = {name: "John Coltrane"};
var template =
    Handlebars.compile('<span class="artist name">{{ name }}</span>');
var html = template(artist);
$('body').append(rendered);
```

The html variable contains our final HTML that was spit back out of the conversion. To place the name property in our HTML, Handlebars uses a style of tags with double curly braces. Inside the curly braces, we place the name of a property. The data from our object gets injected into those curly braces when we render the template, converting it to HTML. We can then append the rendered HTML to the <body>, as if we'd built up our own string.

This is the simplest method for rendering a template with Handlebars. Our application will also contain code that's related to sending a request to a server to retrieve the data, but the process for creating the template will be the same.

Displaying Products from the Server

Now that you understand how to render a template, we can remove the old method of string concatenation from the existing application. Let's examine the existing app's code again to see what we can change:

handlebars/old_index.html
```
<script>
  $.getJSON('/products.json', function(products) {
    for(var index = 0, length = products.length; index < length; index++){
      var newProduct = $('<div class="product"></div>');
      newProduct.append('<span class="product-name">' +
                        products[index].name + '</span>');
      newProduct.append('<em class="product-price">' +
                        products[index].price + '</em>');
      newProduct.append('<div class="product-description">' +
                        products[index].description + '</div>');

      $("body").append(newProduct);
    }
  });
</script>
```

In this version we use jQuery to get the products from the API, and then we iterate over the products, constructing new elements and appending them to the list of products. This messy code is a headache to read and even worse to maintain. Instead of using jQuery's append() method to build up the HTML incrementally, let's use Handlebars to render the HTML by passing the data we get from the server to a Handlebars template. Our first step toward reducing the JavaScript madness is to build that template.

If we create a <script> element with a content type of text/x-handlebars-template, then we can place Handlebars HTML inside of that element and pull it out for our template. The browser will ignore the contents of the <script> tag when the page renders, thanks to the content type we chose. We'll give the <script> tag an ID so that we can reference it with jQuery and grab its content so we can send it to the Handlebars renderer. Above the calls to the jQuery libraries, add this code:

handlebars/index.html
```
<script type="text/x-handlebars-template" id="products_template">
</script>
```

When we get our data from the server, it'll come back in object form:

```
{
  name: "iPad",
  description: "Ooooh shiny!"
  price: "$499"
}
```

So we can use the object's properties as the variable names in our template, like this:

handlebars/index.html
```
<div class="product">
  <h2>
    <span class="product-name">{{name}}</span>
    <em class="product-price">{{price}}</em>
  </h2>
</div>
```

We access the object's name and price properties right in between the HTML tags, using the curly-brace syntax Handlebars understands. The actual values will get placed in those placeholders when we render the template.

Now let's tackle the description of the product. We don't need to show the description if no description is coming back from the server. We don't want to render the corresponding <div> if the description isn't present. Thankfully, Handlebars allows for conditional statements. We can check whether the description is there and conditionally render the <div>:

handlebars/index.html

```
{{#if description}}
  <div class="product-description">{{description}}</div>
{{/if}}
```

The template we've made renders a single product. In our original code, we used a JavaScript for loop to iterate over the products and render a chunk of HTML. But with Handlebars, we can render all of our products by altering the template to tell the templating engine that it should render multiple products:

handlebars/index.html

```
{{#products}}
  <div class="product">
    <h2>
      <span class="product-name">{{name}}</span>
      <em class="product-price">{{price}}</em>
    </h2>
    {{#if description}}
      <div class="product-description">{{description}}</div>
    {{/if}}
  </div>
{{/products}}
```

With our template in place, we can change how we insert the HTML. We grab a reference to the template with jQuery and use the html() function to grab the inner content. Then all we need to do is pass the HTML and the data to Handlebars:

handlebars/index.html

```
<script>
  (function(){
    $.getJSON('/products.json', function(products) {
      var data = {products: products};
      var template = Handlebars.compile($("#products_template").html());
      var html = template(data);
      $("body").append(html);
    });
  })();
</script>
```

And now our list of products is built using client-side templates instead of HTML. It's so much simpler now, and if we decide we want to change the HTML, it's easy to do—much easier than modifying strings of HTML embedded in JavaScript strings. Handlebars templates give us a simple way to remove string concatenation and build our interfaces in a semantic and readable way.

> \\//   **Joe asks:**
>
> ⎨ ⎬   ## Can We Use External Templates?
>
> Inline templates are handy, but we want to remove the template logic from the server views. On our server, we create a folder to hold all of our view files. Then, when we want to render one of the templates, we make a GET request with jQuery and fetch the template:
>
> ```
> $.get("http://mysite.com/js_views/external_template.html",
>   function(template) {
>     var template, html;
>     template = Handlebars.compile(template);
>     html = template(data)
>     $("body").append(html);
>   }
> );
> ```
>
> This allows us to serve views separate from our client views.

Further Exploration

One downside to the way we used Handlebars is that the templates must be compiled to HTML in the browser, and that can significantly slow down some sites, especially on mobile devices. Handlebars offers a solution to this, though. By installing a command-line tool, you can precompile your templates before you deploy your site. Check out the Handlebars documentation for more details on how that works.[9]

Client-side templating tools let you keep your client-side code clean, but you can also use Handlebars to create server-side templates in Node.js applications.

This means you can use Handlebars templates as the templating engine on both the back end and front end of a project. For example, if you have a Handlebars template that represents a row of an HTML table and you use that template inside a loop to construct the initial table when you initially render the page, you can reuse that same template to append a row to the table after a successful Ajax request.

And if you don't use Node as your server-side language, you've got another option. Handlebars is mostly compatible with another templating library called Mustache, and implementations of Mustache are available in Node, Ruby,

---

9.   http://handlebarsjs.com/precompilation.html

Java, Python, ColdFusion, and many more. You can find more on these implementations at the official site.[10]

Also See

- Recipe 12, *Displaying Information with Endless Pagination* on page 76
- Recipe 14, *Snappier Client-Side Interfaces with Knockout.js* on page 87
- Recipe 22, *Building a Status Site with JavaScript and CouchDB* on page 154

---

10. http://mustache.github.com/

Recipe 12

Displaying Information with Endless Pagination

Problem

To prevent information overload for our users and to keep our servers from grinding to a halt, it's important to limit how much data is shown at once on our list pages. This is traditionally handled by adding pagination to these pages. That is, we show only a small subset of data to start with while allowing the users to jump among the pages of information at their own discretion. What they see is a small part of all of the information that is potentially available to them.

As websites have evolved, web developers have learned that most of the time users go through these pages sequentially. They would actually be happy to scroll through an entire list of data until they find what they're looking for or reach the end of the dataset. We need to provide that type of experience for our users without taxing our servers.

Ingredients

- jQuery
- Handlebars[11]
- QEDServer (for our test server)[12]

Solution

By implementing endless pagination, we can provide an efficient way of managing our resources while improving the end-user experience. Instead of forcing users to choose the next page of results and then reloading the entire interface, we load the next page of results in the background and add those results to the current page as the user scrolls toward the end of the page.

We want to add a list of our products to our site, but our inventory is much too big to reasonably load all at once. We'll have to add pagination for this list and limit the user to loading ten products at a time. To make our users'

---

11. http://handlebarsjs.com
12. A version for this book is available at http://webdevelopmentrecipes.com/.

lives even easier, we're going to ditch the Next Page button and automatically load the following page when we think they're ready for it. It will seem to the users as if the entire product list was available to them since they first loaded the page.

We'll use QEDServer and its product catalog to build a working prototype. We'll place all of our code in the public folder in QEDServer's workspace, start up QEDServer, and then create a new file called products.html in the public folder that QEDServer creates. You can look at *QEDServer*, on page xii, for details on how QEDServer works.

To keep our code clean, we'll use the Handlebars template library to separate our pagination functionality from the presentation of the actual products. For more details about Handlebars, check out Recipe 11, *Rendering HTML with Handlebars Templates* on page 69.

We start out by creating a simple HTML5 skeleton in products.html that includes jQuery, the Handlebars template library, and endless_pagination.js, which we'll create to hold our pagination code:

endlesspagination/products.html

```html
<!DOCTYPE html>
<html>
  <head>
    <meta charset='utf-8'>
    <title>AwesomeCo Products</title>
    <link rel='stylesheet' href='endless_pagination.css'>
  </head>
  <body>
    <div id="wrap">
      <header>
        <h1>Products</h1>
      </header>
    </div>
    <script
      src="http://ajax.googleapis.com/ajax/libs/jquery/2.1.4/jquery.min.js">
    </script>
    <script src="http://cdnjs.cloudflare.com/ajax/libs/handlebars.js/3.0.3/
handlebars.min.js">
    </script>
    <script src="endless_pagination.js"></script>
  </body>
</html>
```

For the body of this initial page, we add a content placeholder and a spinner image. The spinner is there so that if the user ever *does* reach the end of the current page, it will indicate that the next page is already loading, as shown in the following figure:

Here's how we code that up:

endlesspagination/products.html

```
<div id='content'>
</div>
<img src='spinner.gif' id='next_page_spinner' />
```

And here's the basic CSS we need for our page, which goes in endless_pagination.css:

endlesspagination/endless_pagination.css

```
.product {
  margin: 40px auto;
}

.product a {
  /* Make the text big enough that the products run off the page */
  font-size: 300%;
}

#current_page {
  display: none;
}
```

QEDServer's API is set up to return paginated results and responds to JSON requests. We can see this by navigating to http://localhost:8080/products.json?page=2. Notice that the page number is part of the URL.

Now that we know what information we're getting from the server, we can start building the code that'll update the interface. We'll write a function that takes in a JSON array, marks it up using a Handlebars template, and appends it to the end of the page. We'll put this code into a file named endless_pagination.js. We start by writing the functions that'll do the heavy lifting. First we need a function that renders the JSON response into HTML:

```
endlesspagination/endless_pagination.js
(function($) {
  function loadData(data) {
    $('#content').append(Handlebars.compile("{{#products}} |
      <div class='product'> |
        <a href='/products/{{id}}'>{{name}}</a> |
        <br> |
        <span class='description'>{{description}}</span> |
      </div>{{/products}}")({ products: data }));
  }
})(jQuery);
```

All of our code will be in this same self-executing function, where we're defining loadData().

As we loop through each product, our template will create a <div> where the content is the name of the product as a link. Then the new items are appended to the end of the product list so they appear on the page.

Next, since we're going to request the next page when we reach the end of the current page, we need a way to determine what the next page is. We can do this by storing the current page as a global variable. Then when we're ready, we can build the URL for the next page:

```
endlesspagination/endless_pagination.js
var currentPage = 0;
function nextPageWithJSON() {
  currentPage += 1;
  var newURL = '/products.json?page=' + currentPage;

  var splitHref = document.URL.split('?');
  var parameters = splitHref[1];
  if (parameters) {
    parameters = parameters.replace(/[?&]page=[^&]*/, '');
    newURL += '&' + parameters;
  }
  return newURL;
}
```

The nextPageWithJSON() function increments the currentPage variable and appends it to the current URL as a page= parameter. We also want to remember any other parameters that were in the current URL. At the same time, we want to make sure that the old page parameter, if it exists, gets overridden. This way we'll get the desired response from the server.

Now that we have functions in place to show new content and determine what the URL is for the next page, let's add the function that requests that content from our server. At its core, this function is an Ajax call to the server. However, we do need to implement a rudimentary way to prevent extra, unwanted calls to the server. We add a global variable called loadingPage that we initialize to 0. We increment it before we make the Ajax call and set it back when we're done. This creates a *mutex*, or locking mechanism. Without this lock in place, we could potentially make dozens of calls to the server for the next page, which the server would obligingly deliver, even if it's not really what we want.

```
endlesspagination/endless_pagination.js
var loadingPage = 0;
function getNextPage() {
    if (loadingPage === 0) {
        loadingPage++;
        $.getJSON(nextPageWithJSON(), {}, updateContent)
            .complete(function() { loadingPage--; });
    }
}

function updateContent(response) {
  loadData(response);
}
```

After the Ajax call finishes, we pass the response to the loadData() function we defined earlier. After loadData() adds the new content, we update the URL stored in the nextPage variable. This way, we're all set up to make the *next* Ajax call.

Now we need a way to determine whether the user is ready to load the next page. Normally this is where the user would click the Next Page link, but instead we want a function that returns true when the bottom of the browser's screen is within a given distance of the bottom of the page:

```
function readyForNextPage() {
  if (!$('#next_page_spinner').is(':visible')) return;

  var threshold = 200;
  var bottomPosition = $(window).scrollTop() + $(window).height();
  var distanceFromBottom = $(document).height() - bottomPosition;
  return distanceFromBottom <= threshold;
}
```

Finally, we apply a scroll event handler that calls the observeScroll() function. That way, every time the user scrolls through the page, we call the newly created readyForNextPage() helper function. When the helper function returns true, we call getNextPage() to make our Ajax request:

```
function observeScroll(event) {
  if (readyForNextPage()) getNextPage();
}
$(document).scroll(observeScroll);
```

The first time we load the page, we call getNextPage() directly. This is because readyForNextPage() returns false until the user scrolls, but there's no *need* to scroll when the only thing visible on the page is a spinner. This first call is how the user sees the first page of products.

We've taken care of the endless part of endless pagination, but in reality there *will* be an end to our content. We want to hide the spinner after the user sees the last product, since it would make the user think that either the Internet connection has slowed or our site is broken. To remove the spinner, we add a final check to hide it when the server returns an empty list:

```
function loadData(data) {
  $('#content').append(Handlebars.compile("{{#products}} \
    <div class='product'> \
      <a href='/products/{{id}}'>{{name}}</a> \
      <br> \
      <span class='description'>{{description}}</span> \
    </div>{{/products}}")({ products: data }));
  if (data.length === 0) $('#next_page_spinner').hide();
}
```

And that's it. When we reach the bottom of our list, the spinner disappears.

Further Exploration

This technique is excellent for displaying long lists of information and is a behavior users have come to expect. Since we've separated our functionality into separate functions, it'll be easy to adapt this solution to other scenarios. We can change the code to load the content earlier or later by changing the threshold variable or to render an HTML or XML response instead of one from JSON by modifying the loadData() function. And best of all, we can rest easy knowing that our site will still be accessible even if jQuery somehow goes missing, which we can test by disabling JavaScript.

In Recipe 13, *Extending Endless Pagination with pushState()* on page 82, we'll explore how we can make this code more user-friendly by adding support for URL changes and the back button.

Also See

- Recipe 13, *Extending Endless Pagination with pushState()* on page 82
- Recipe 11, *Rendering HTML with Handlebars Templates* on page 69

Recipe 13

Extending Endless Pagination with pushState()

Problem

One of the things that makes the Internet great is that, from news articles to cat GIFs, everyone can easily share links with one another. But with more applications using Ajax, this is no longer the case by default; clicking an Ajax link no longer guarantees that the browser's URL is updated to reflect what the user is seeing. For many Ajax requests this is fine, but when large parts of the site change after a request, not keeping the URL up to date can cause issues. Not only does this prevent the sharing of links, but it breaks the back and refresh buttons.

Unfortunately, the endless-pagination code we wrote in Recipe 12, *Displaying Information with Endless Pagination* on page 76, has the same issue. As we scroll through the page and request new pages via Ajax, the browser's URL never updates to reflect the new content on the screen.

So, for example, if a user is on page 5 of a catalog and wants to share it with some friends via email, he'd likely copy and paste the browser's URL and say, "Check out this great deal!" Unfortunately, when the friends open the link they'll see page 1 and have no idea what he was talking about.

A user's own experience is also affected. When she clicks the back button on an all-Ajax site, she often ends up at whatever page led her to the site instead of the last Ajax page loaded. Then, frustrated, she clicks the forward button and ends up somewhere completely different. Thankfully, we have a solution for these common problems.

Ingredients

- jQuery
- Handlebars.js[13]
- QEDServer (for our test server)[14]

---

13. http://handlebarsjs.com/
14. A version for this book is available at http://webdevelopmentrecipes.com/.

Solution

We'll start with the code that we wrote in Recipe 12, *Displaying Information with Endless Pagination* on page 76, and finish implementing it. The old code works, but users can't easily share links with anyone. To keep our web karma in alignment and prevent user frustration, the right thing to do is to make this list page stateless. When we change the page that the user is looking at, we'll change the current URL to reflect these changes.

The HTML5 specification introduced a JavaScript function called pushState(), which lets us alter the URL without leaving the page. This is great news for web developers! We can make an entire Ajax web application that never goes through the traditional request/reload life cycle while behaving like a multi-page site. This means there's no need to re-request resources like images, style sheets, or JavaScript files every time we move to a new screen. And users can quickly share the current URL with others or use the refresh and back buttons as usual.

Using the pushState() Function

Although pushState() is widely implemented, some older browser versions don't support it. The available fallback solution relies on modifying the hash portion of a URL, but it's ugly—and it's not only an issue of having URLs that are displeasing to the eye. The Internet has a good long-term memory. Web pages may exist that include links that were added years ago, but the content has moved to a new server. If we use the URL hash as a stopgap for important information, we could be stuck supporting those deprecated links until the end of time. Since URL hashes are never sent to the server, our application would have to continue to read the URLs with JavaScript and redirect to the requested page.

With that said, let's see what it takes to make our endless products page stateless.

Parameters to Track

Because we don't know which page a user will load on the first request, we'll keep track of the starting page as well as the current page. If users go directly to page three, we want them to be able to get back to page three on subsequent visits. If they start scrolling down from page three and load multiple pages, for instance to page seven, we want to know that, too. We need a way to keep track of the start and end pages so that a hard refresh won't require the user to scroll through the site again.

Next we need a way to send the start and end pages from the client. The most direct way is to set these parameters in the URL during a GET request. When a page is first loaded, we'll set the page parameter of the URL to be the current page and assume the user wants to see only that page. If the client also passes in a start_page parameter, we'll know that the user wants to see a range of pages, from start_page through page. So following our earlier example, if the user is on page seven but started browsing from page three, our URL would look like this: http://localhost:8080/products?start_page=3&page=7.

This set of parameters should be enough information for us to re-create a list of products from the server and subsequently show users the same page they saw when they last visited this page:

```
statefulpagination/stateful_pagination.js
function getParameterByName(name) {
  var match = RegExp('[?&]' + name + '=([^&]*)')
    .exec(window.location.search);

  return match && decodeURIComponent(match[1].replace(/\+/g, ' '));
}


var currentPage = 0;
var startPage = 0;

function readParameters() {
  startPage = parseInt(getParameterByName('start_page'));
  if (isNaN(startPage)) {
    startPage = parseInt(getParameterByName('page'));
  }
  if (isNaN(startPage)) {
    startPage = 1;
  }
  currentPage = startPage - 1;

  if (getParameterByName('page')) {
    endPage = parseInt(getParameterByName('page'));
    for (i = currentPage; i < endPage; i++) {
      getNextPage(true);
    }
  }

  observeScroll();
}
```

All we're doing here is figuring out the start_page and current_page and then requesting those pages from the server. We use mostly the same function from the previous chapter, getNextPage(), but it's been slightly modified to allow multiple requests at a time:

```
var loadingPage = 0;
function getNextPage(ignoreMutexBlocking) {
  if (!ignoreMutexBlocking && loadingPage != 0) return;

  loadingPage++;
  $.getJSON(nextPageWithJSON(), {}, updateContent).
    complete(function() { loadingPage-- });
}
```

Normally when the user is scrolling we want to prevent multiple, overlapping requests. But right now it's all right, since we know exactly which pages should be requested, so we'll pass in true to ignore the mutex block. Then we want to call the readParameters() function when the page loads to set the initial state of the page:

```
readParameters();
```

Just as we tracked the currentPage in the code on page 79, we want to track the startPage. We'll grab this parameter from the URL so we can make the requests for the pages that haven't been loaded yet. This number will never change, but we do want to make sure that it gets added to the URL and stays there every time a new page is requested.

Updating the Browser's URL

To update the URL, let's write a function called updateBrowserUrl() that'll call pushState() and set the parameters for the start_page and page. It's important to remember that not every browser supports pushState(), so we need to check that it's defined before we can call it:

```
function updateBrowserUrl() {
  if (window.history.pushState == undefined) return;

  var newURL = '?start_page=' + startPage + '&page=' + currentPage;
  window.history.pushState({}, '', newURL);
}
```

The pushState() function takes three parameters. The first allows us to track any state we want with a JSON object. This argument could potentially be a storage point for information we want the browser to remember that doesn't make sense to have in the parameters, such as the JSON we've already received from the server when we scrolled. But since our data is relatively lightweight and easy to get from the server, we skip this. For now we'll pass in an empty hash. The second argument is the title of the page. This feature isn't widely implemented yet, and for our purposes, even if it were, we don't have a reason to update this page's title. We pass in a filler argument again; this time an empty string.

Now we get to the meat, or the tofu if you're vegetarian, of the pushState() function. The third parameter is how we want the URL to change. This method is flexible and can be either an absolute path or only the parameters to be updated at the end of the URL. For security reasons, we can't change the domain of the URL, but we can change everything after the top-level domain with relative ease. Since we're worried only about updating the parameters of the URL, we prepend the pushState()'s third parameter with a question mark (?). Finally, we set the start_page and page parameters, and if they already exist, pushState() is smart enough to update these parameters for us.

Lastly, we add a call to updateBrowserUrl() from the updateContent() function to make our endless pagination code state-aware:

statefulpagination/stateful_pagination.js

```
function updateContent(response) {
  loadData(response);
  updateBrowserUrl();
}
```

Now our users can use the back button to leave our page and return with the forward button without losing their spot. They can also hit the refresh button with impunity and get the same results. Most important, our links are now sharable across the web. We've been able to make the URL for our index page behave like a traditional non-Ajax site with minimal effort, thanks to the hard work of modern browser developers.

Further Exploration

As we add more JavaScript and Ajax to our pages, we have to be aware of how the interfaces behave. HTML5's pushState() method and the History API give us the tools we need to provide support for the regular controls in the browser that people already know how to use. Abstraction layers like History.js[15] make it even easier to use and provide graceful fallbacks for browsers that don't support the History API.

The approaches we discussed in this recipe are regularly being used by frameworks like Backbone.js, which means even easier back button support for the most complex single-page applications.

Also See

- Recipe 11, *Rendering HTML with Handlebars Templates* on page 69
- Recipe 13, *Extending Endless Pagination with pushState()* on page 82

---

15. https://github.com/browserstate/history.js

Recipe 14

Snappier Client-Side Interfaces with Knockout.js

Problem

When developing modern web applications, we often try to update only part of the interface in response to user interaction instead of refreshing the entire page. Calls to the server are often expensive, and refreshing the entire page can cause users to lose their place.

Unfortunately, the JavaScript code for this can quickly become difficult to manage. We start out watching only a couple of events, but eventually we have several callbacks updating several regions of the page, which becomes a maintenance nightmare. We need an easy-to-use tool that keeps track of all of this for us.

Ingredients

- Knockout.js[16]

Solution

Knockout.js is a simple yet powerful framework that lets us bind objects to our interface and can automatically update one part of the interface when another part changes, without lots of nested event handlers. Knockout.js uses *view models*, which encapsulate much of the view logic associated with interface changes. We can then bind properties of these models to elements in our interface.

We want our customers to be able to modify the quantity of items in their shopping carts and see the updated total in real time. We can use Knockout's view models and data bindings to build the update screen for our shopping cart. We'll have a line for each item, a field for the customer to update the quantity, and a button to remove the item from the cart. We'll update the subtotal for each line when the quantity changes, and we'll update the grand total whenever anything on the line changes. When we're done, we'll have an interface that looks like the following figure:

---

16. http://knockoutjs.com

Product	Price	Quantity	Total	
Macbook Pro 15 inch	1699	1	1699	Remove
Mini Display Port to VGA Adapter	29	1	29	Remove
Magic Trackpad	69	1	69	Remove
Apple Wireless Keyboard	69	1	69	Remove
Total			1866	

Knockout Basics

Knockout's view models are regular JavaScript objects with properties, methods, and a few special keywords. Here's a simple Person object with methods for first name, last name, and full name:

knockout/binding.html

```
(function(){
  var Person = function(){
    this.firstname = ko.observable("John");
    this.lastname = ko.observable("Smith");
    this.fullname = ko.computed(function(){
      return(
        this.firstname() + " " + this.lastname()
      );
    }, this);
  };

  ko.applyBindings( new Person );
})();
```

We use HTML5's data- attributes to bind this object's methods and logic to elements on our interface:

knockout/binding.html

```
<p>First name: <input type="text" data-bind="value: firstname"></p>
<p>Last name: <input type="text" data-bind="value: lastname"></p>
<p>Full name:
    <span aria-live="polite" data-bind="text: fullname"></span>
</p>
```

When we update either the first-name or the last-name text box, the full name shows up on the page. Since the update happens dynamically, this can cause troubles for blind users with screen readers. To solve that issue, we use the aria-live attribute to give the screen readers a hint that this part changes dynamically.

That's a relatively trivial example, so let's dig into Knockout a little more by building a single line of our cart, getting the total to change when we update the quantity. Then we'll refactor it so we can build the entire shopping cart. We'll start with the data model.

We'll represent the line item by using a simple JavaScript object called LineItem with properties for name and price. Create a new HTML page and include the Knockout.js library right above the page's closing <body> tag:

knockout/item.html

```html
<!DOCTYPE html>
<html>
  <head>
    <meta charset="utf-8">
    <title>Update Quantities</title>
  </head>

  <body>
    <script src="http://ajax.aspnetcdn.com/ajax/knockout/knockout-3.3.0.js">
    </script>
  </body>

</html>
```

Add a new <script> block at the bottom of the page, above the closing <body> tag and below the <script> tag we just added. Add the following code between the <script> tags:

knockout/item.html

```javascript
(function(){
  var LineItem = function(product_name, product_price){
    this.name = product_name;
    this.price = product_price;
  };
})();
```

In JavaScript, functions are object constructors, so we can use a function to mimic a class. In this case, the class's constructor accepts the name and the price when we create a new LineItem instance.

Now we need to tell Knockout that we want to use this lineItem class as our view model, so that its properties are visible to our HTML markup. We do that by adding the following call to our script block:

knockout/item.html

```javascript
var item = new LineItem("Macbook Pro 15", 1699.00);
ko.applyBindings(item);
```

We're creating a new instance of our LineItem to Knockout's applyBindings() method, and we're setting the product name and price. We'll make this more dynamic later; for now we'll hard-code these values.

With the object in place, we can build our interface and pull data from the object. We use an HTML table to mark up our cart, and we use <thead> and <tbody> tags to give it a little more structure:

```
knockout/item.html
<div role="application">
  <table>
    <thead>
      <tr>
        <th>Product</th>
        <th>Price</th>
        <th>Quantity</th>
        <th>Total</th>
      </tr>
    </thead>
    <tbody>
      <tr aria-live="polite">
        <td data-bind="text: name"></td>
        <td data-bind="text: price"></td>
      </tr>
    </tbody>
  </table>
</div>
```

Since our table row updates based on user input, we use the aria-live attribute on the table row so screen readers know to watch that row for changes. We also wrap the whole cart within a <div> with the HTML5 ARIA role of application, which tells screen readers that this is an interactive application. You can learn about these in the HTML5 specification.[17]

Pay special attention to these two lines:

```
knockout/item.html
<td data-bind="text: name"></td>
<td data-bind="text: price"></td>
```

Our LineItem instance is now a global, visible object on our page, and its name and price properties are visible as well. So with these two lines we're saying that we want the text of each element to get its value from the property we specify.

When we load the page in our browser, we see the row of our table start to take shape, and the name and price are filled in!

Let's add a text field to the table so that the user can update the quantity:

---

17. http://www.w3.org/TR/html5-author/wai-aria.html

knockout/item.html
```
<td><input type="text" name="quantity"
    data-bind='value: quantity, valueUpdate: "keyup"'>
</td>
```

In Knockout, we reference data fields within regular HTML elements with text, but HTML form elements like <input> have value attributes. This time we bind the value attribute to a quantity property in our view model, which we need to define next.

The quantity property isn't only for displaying data; it'll set data as well. And when we set data, we need events to fire. We do that by using Knockout's ko.observable() function as the value of our quantity property in our class:

knockout/item.html
```
this.quantity = ko.observable(1);
```

We're passing a default value to ko.observable() so the text field has a value when we bring the page up for the first time.

Now we can enter the quantity, but we need to show the row's subtotal. Let's add a table column to print out the subtotal:

knockout/item.html
```
<td data-bind="text: subtotal "></td>
```

As with our name and price columns, we set the text of the table cell to the value of our view model's subtotal property.

This brings us to one of the more powerful features of Knockout.js: the computed() method. We defined our quantity property as *observable*, which means that other elements notice when that field changes. We declare a computed() method, which executes code whenever our observed field changes, and we assign computed() to a property on our object so it can be bound to our user interface:

knockout/item.html
```
this.subtotal = ko.computed(function() {
  return(
    this.price * parseInt("0"+this.quantity(), 10)
  ); //<label id="code.subtotal" />
}, this);
```

But how does the computed() method know which fields to watch? It looks at the observable properties we access in the function we define! Since we're adding the price and quantity together, Knockout tracks them both and runs the preceding code when either one changes.

The computed() method takes a second parameter that specifies the context for the properties. This is necessary because of how JavaScript's functions and objects work; you can read more about this in the Knockout.js documentation.

And that's it for a single row. When we change the quantity, our price updates in real time. Now let's take what we learned here and turn this into a multiple-line shopping cart with line totals and a grand total.

Joe asks:
What About Knockout and Accessibility?

Interfaces that rely heavily on JavaScript often raise a red flag when it comes to accessibility, but the use of JavaScript alone doesn't make a site inaccessible to the disabled.

In this recipe, we made use of the HTML5 ARIA roles and attributes to help screen readers understand the application we're developing. But accessibility is about much more than screen readers; it's about making our applications usable by the widest audience possible.

Knockout is a JavaScript solution and will work only when JavaScript is enabled or available, so you need to take that under consideration. We recommend that you build applications to work without JavaScript and then use Knockout to *enhance* your application. Our example uses Knockout to render the cart's contents, but if we were using a server-side framework we could render the HTML for the cart and use Knockout's binding features on top of the rendered HTML. The accessibility of a site depends much more on the implementation than on the library or technology used.

Using Control Flow Bindings

Binding objects to HTML is handy, but users will likely have more than one item in their carts, and duplicating all that code will get tedious—not to mention more difficult—since we'll have more than one LineItem object to bind. We need to rethink the interface a bit.

Instead of working with a LineItem as the view model, let's create another object that represents the shopping cart. This Cart object will hold all of the LineItem objects. Using what we know about Knockout's computed() method, we can give this new Cart object a property that computes the total when any item in the cart changes.

But what about the HTML for the line item? Well, we can reduce duplication by using a *control-flow binding* and tell Knockout to render our line-item HTML once for each item in our cart. Let's get started.

First, let's define an array of items we'll use to populate the cart:

knockout/update_cart.html
```
var products = [
  {name: "Macbook Pro 15 inch", price: 1699.00},
  {name: "Mini Display Port to VGA Adapter", price: 29.00},
  {name: "Magic Trackpad", price: 69.00},
  {name: "Apple Wireless Keyboard", price: 69.00}
];
```

In a real-world situation, we would get this data from a web service or Ajax call or by generating this array on the server side when we serve up the page.

Now, let's create a Cart object that holds the items. We define it the same way we defined our LineItem:

knockout/update_cart.html
```
var Cart = function(items){
  this.items = ko.observableArray();

  for(var i in items){
    var item = new LineItem(items[i].name, items[i].price);
    this.items.push(item);
  }
}
```

We also need to change the binding in our templates from using the LineItem class to using the Cart class:

knockout/update_cart.html
```
var cartViewModel = new Cart(products);
ko.applyBindings(cartViewModel);
```

The items are stored in the cart using an observableArray(), which works like observable() but has the properties of an array. When we created a new instance of our cart, we passed in the array of data. Our object iterates over the items of data and creates new LineItem instances that get stored in the items array. Since this array is observable, our user interface will change whenever the array's contents change. Of course, now that we're dealing with more than one item, we need to modify the user interface.

Next we modify our HTML page and tell Knockout to repeat the table rows by using a Knockout data-bind call on the <tbody> tag:

knockout/update_cart.html
```
<tbody data-bind="foreach: items">
  <tr aria=live="polite">
    <td data-bind="text: name"></td>
    <td data-bind="text: price"></td>
    <td><input type="text" name="quantity" data-bind='value: quantity'></td>
```

```
  <td data-bind="text: subtotal "></td>
</tr>
</tbody>
```

We tell Knockout to render the contents of the <tbody> for each entry in the items array. We don't have to change anything else in that row.

At this point, we have multiple lines displaying on the page, each subtotaling correctly. Now let's handle computing the grand total and removal of items.

The Grand Total

We saw how Knockout's computed() method works when we used it to calculate the subtotal for each item. We can use the same approach to calculate the total for the entire cart by adding a computed() to the Cart itself:

knockout/update_cart.html
```
this.total = ko.computed(function(){
  var total = 0;
  for (item in this.items()){
    total += this.items()[item].subtotal();
  }
  return total;
}, this);
```

Any time any of the items in our array changes, this code will fire. To display the grand total on the form, we simply need to add the appropriate table row. Since it's the total for the cart and not for a line item, it doesn't go in the <tbody>. Instead, we'll put it in a <tfoot> tag, which we place right above the closing <thead> tag. Placing the footer *above* the table body can help some browsers and assistive devices more quickly identify the table structure.

knockout/update_cart.html
```
<tfoot>
  <tr>
    <td colspan="4">Total</td>
    <td aria-live="polite" data-bind="text: total()"></td>
  </tr>
</tfoot>
```

When we refresh our page, we can change any quantity and update both the line total and the cart total simultaneously. Now, about that Remove button...

Be Sure to Reconcile with the Server!

Building a shopping cart update screen entirely on the client side is becoming more popular. In some cases, it may not be possible to send Ajax requests back and forth every time a user makes a change to the interface, due to bandwidth issues or back-end limitations.

When you use an approach like this, you'll want to synchronize the data in the cart on the client side with data on the server. After all, you wouldn't want someone changing prices on you!

When the user checks out, submit the updated quantities to the server and recompute the totals on the server side before checking out.

Removing Items

To wrap up this project, we need to add a Remove button to the end of each row that removes the item from the row. Thanks to all the work we've done, this is a simple task. First, we add the ability to remove an item from the cart by adding a remove() method to our Cart:

knockout/update_cart.html
```
this.remove = function(item){
  this.items.remove(item);
}.bind(this);
```

Notice the use of bind(this)() after the declaration of the function. We need that so the function can reference the scope of the Cart. If we omit it, the remove() function can't figure out where this.items is.

With the remove() method in place, we modify the table to add the Remove button:

knockout/update_cart.html
```
<td>
  <button
    data-bind="click: $parent.remove">Remove
  </button>
</td>
```

This time, instead of binding data to the interface, we bind an event and a function we want to call—in this case, the remove() method of our cartViewModel instance. But at this point in our code, we're within the context of a specific item. Knockout lets us use the $parent property to reference the parent view model. And best of all, it automatically passes a reference to the current item to the function.

That's it! Since the items array is an observableArray, our entire interface gets updated. Even our grand total changes!

Further Exploration

Knockout is great for situations where we need to build a dynamic single-page interface. And because it's not tied to a specific web framework, we can use it anywhere.

More important, the view models Knockout uses are ordinary JavaScript, so we can use Knockout to implement many commonly requested user interface features. For example, we could very easily implement an Ajax-based live search, build in-place editing controls that save the data back to the server, or even update the contents of one drop-down field based on the selected value of another field.

Also See

- Recipe 11, *Rendering HTML with Handlebars Templates* on page 69
- Recipe 15, *Creating a Search Interface with React* on page 97
- Recipe 16, *Creating Client-Side Apps with Angular.js* on page 107

Creating a Search Interface with React

Problem

Thanks to Gmail and Facebook, people are accustomed to seeing real-time search results, instead of the "traditional" approach in which they type in a value, hit a submit button, and wait for the entire results page to redraw. So we've been asked to build a simple product-search interface, with the explicit requirement that the search must be quick and must be done without refreshing the page.

Ingredients

- jQuery
- React[18]
- QEDServer (for our test server)[19]

Solution

React is a JavaScript library designed for creating user interfaces that need to efficiently respond to a flow of data. Manipulating the DOM is one of the most expensive things we can do in a web browser. React solves this by using a *virtual DOM* for its components. We don't ever manipulate elements on our page. Instead, we create them as React components that get rendered to the page. When we update our data, these components get refreshed—but only the components that changed, rather than the whole page. It's incredibly fast, but it'll require us to think differently about how we construct our page.

To test this out, we'll create a simple search interface using QEDServer and its product database as the back end for our Ajax requests. We'll place all of our files in the public folder that QEDServer creates in our workspace so our development server will serve them properly and allow us to make Ajax requests. So, start up QEDServer and ensure that it's running at http://local-host:8080/.

---

18. http://facebook.github.io/react/index.html
19. A version for this book is available at http://webdevelopmentrecipes.com/.

We'll place a new index.html file inside the public folder that QEDServer created for us when we started it up. In this file, we place our usual HTML skeleton and a <div> element that will hold our application. We'll tell React to render its contents into this area of the page. We also import a few libraries in the header section of the page:

```
react/index.html
<!DOCTYPE html>
<html>
  <head>
    <meta charset="utf-8">
    <title>Product Search</title>
  </head>
  <body>
    <div aria-live="polite" id="content">Waiting...</div>
    <script src="https://code.jquery.com/jquery-2.1.4.min.js"></script>
    <script src="https://fb.me/react-0.13.3.js"></script>
    <script src="https://fb.me/JSXTransformer-0.13.3.js"></script>
    <script type="text/jsx" src="search.js"></script>
  </body>
</html>
```

We're including React, but we're going to use jQuery for making our Ajax requests. React is purely a UI library; it doesn't have its own way of fetching data from servers. The third library we're loading is React's JSX Transformer. React has its own dialect of JavaScript, called JSX, that makes creating templates easier. In production applications, you'd set up a development workflow that converts JSX files into regular JavaScript files—much as we do when we use CoffeeScript in Recipe 31, *Cleaner JavaScript with CoffeeScript* on page 221. But since we're only exploring, we can skip that step for now and do the transformations in the browser in exchange for a hit on performance. The last file we're including is the file that will contain the JavaScript code that builds our search interface. We have to specify that we're using JSX for this file so that the JSX Transformer can convert it.

Our Component Architecture

We'll create a component called ProductSearch, which will be made up of two smaller components—a ProductSearchForm and a ProductList—as illustrated in the diagram on page 99.

The top-level component will communicate with our back end and will render the two child components. When a visitor submits the search form, we'll pass the data up from the inner component to the outer component. The outer component will fetch the search results from the back end and then rerender the list of products using the new data.

Let's start by creating the outer component. In search.js, we create the initial version of our ProductSearch component:

```
react/search.js
var ProductSearch = React.createClass({
  render: function() {
    return (
      <div>
        <h1>Product Search</h1>
      </div>
    );
  }
});
```

The preceding code doesn't do too much other than render a <div> with an <h1> inside. But it won't actually render the component until we tell React to render it, like this:

```
React.render(<ProductSearch />, document.getElementById('content'));
```

We pass in the component we want to render, and the element on the HTML page that'll contain the component. In our case, we're rendering our Product-Search component into the element on our page that has the ID of content. When we reload the page in our browser, we see the component rendered to the screen, as in the figure on page 100.

Now let's get a little more interesting content on the page.

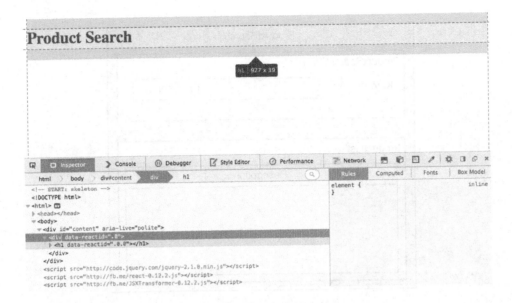

Rendering Server-Side Data

Let's fetch the most recent results from the server and use that data to render the list of products so there's something there when the page loads.

To do this, we'll declare the ProductList component, which can display data. The ProductSearch component will do the fetching of data and then render the ProductList component, passing it the data to display. This way we can reuse the ProductList component elsewhere in our app if we want to.

But first we need some data we can render. We'll fetch the data from our back end and store it in the ProductSearch component's *state*. You can think of the component's state as its own internal data collection. It can't be accessed outside of the component.

To use the state, we need to set up its initial value by declaring a method called getInitialState(). This method needs to return a data structure making up the initial value of the component's state. We have it return an empty data object:

react/search.js
```
var ProductSearch = React.createClass({
    getInitialState: function() {
        return {data: []};
    },
```

If we declare a method called componentDidMount(), it'll run automatically when the component is attached to the page. This is a great place for us to hit our back end and grab the initial data we want to display. We do that with a little bit of jQuery:

react/search.js

```
var ProductSearch = React.createClass({
  componentDidMount: function() {
    $.ajax({
      url: '/products.json',
      dataType: 'json',
      success: function(data) {
        this.setState({data: data});
      }.bind(this),
      error: function(xhr, status, err) {
        console.error(this.props.url, status, err.toString());
      }.bind(this)
    });
  },
```

When we successfully get data back from our server, we call this.setState, which updates the data in the state by merging what we pass in with what's in the current state. Any time we update the component's state, the component's render() method will be called.

Now we can render the list of products. We alter the ProductSearch component's render() method by adding in our ProductList component, passing the data as an attribute:

react/search.js

```
render: function() {
  return (
    <div>
      <h1>Product Search</h1>
      { /* START_HIGHLIGHT */ }
      <ProductList data={this.state.data} />
    </div>
  );
}
```

Finally, we define the ProductList component, which renders the data. The data was passed in as an attribute called data, so to access it inside the ProductList component we use this.props.data. Any attributes passed to a component become its properties. We use properties to pass data around our components, and we use this.state to manage the component's internal data that should trigger rendering.

Our list of products will be an HTML table, with the results displayed as the table rows. So our ProductList component ends up looking like this:

```
react/search.js
var ProductList = React.createClass({
  render: function() {
    var products = this.props.data.map(function (product) {
      return (
        <tr>
          <td>{product.name}</td>
          <td>{product.description}</td>
          <td>{product.price}</td>
        </tr>
      );
    });
    return (
      <table>
        <thead>
          <tr>
            <th>Name</th><th>Description</th><th>Price</th>
          </tr>
        </thead>
        <tbody>
          {products}
        </tbody>
      </table>
    );
  }
});
```

We first take the data stored in the component's props and transform it into an array of table rows by using JavaScript's map() function. Then we return an HTML table that contains those rows. This pattern is common in rendering collections of data in React. You construct the inner part first and then wrap it with the outer parts of the component.

When we refresh the page in the browser, we see our list of products, as in the figure on page 103.

The outer component is rendering the inner component, passing it data. The inner component doesn't need to know where it got its data from; it's completely decoupled. That means we can send it data we get from a search query, rather than the most recent data. So let's build the search feature.

Adding the Form

Our ProductSearchForm will contain the HTML form that visitors will use to perform the search. The outer component, ProductSearch, is responsible for talking to our back end, but we have to put the code that handles the form submission inside the ProductSearchForm component. So we'll make the submit handler in

Product Search

Keywords [ ] [search]

Name	Description	Price
AirPort Express	Description of AirPort Express	99.0
DVI to VGA Adapter	Description of DVI to VGA Adapter	29.0
Mini DVI to VGA Adapter	Description of Mini DVI to VGA Adapter	29.0
Mini DisplayPort to DVI Adapter	Description of Mini DisplayPort to DVI Adapter	29.0
Mini DisplayPort to VGA Adapter	Description of Mini DisplayPort to VGA Adapter	29.0
Apple Wireless Keyboard	Description of Apple Wireless Keyboard	69.0
Airport Extreme Base Station	Description of Airport Extreme Base Station	179.0
Apple Magic Trackpad	Description of Apple Magic Trackpad	69.0
Apple Keyboard with Numeric Keypad	Description of Apple Keyboard with Numeric Keypad	49.0
Apple Magic Mouse	Description of Apple Magic Mouse	69.0

ProductSearchForm delegate to a function that we declare in the ProductSearch component. The following diagram explains how this will work:

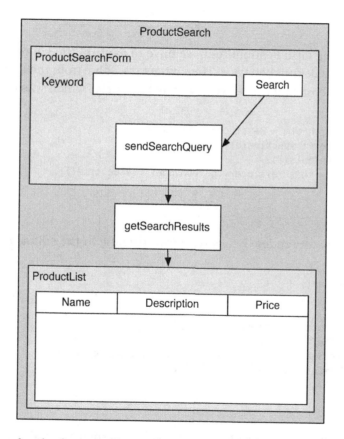

When we render the form, we'll pass a reference to the getSearchResults() function into the ProductForm component. So, let's build the ProductForm component first and get it rendering. We'll wire it up later.

The form itself ends up being another component with a render() function that returns an HTML form. However, we can add a few important pieces to the markup. We use the ref attribute to name a form field so we can easily locate it later. And we attach the function that will handle the form directly to the form by using the onSubmit attribute:

```
react/search.js
var ProductSearchForm = React.createClass({
  render: function(){
    return (
      <form onSubmit={this.sendSearchQuery}>
        <label forInput="query">Keywords</label>
        <input id="query" type="search" ref="query" />
        <input type="submit" value="search" />
      </form>
    );
  }
});
```

Then, when the form is submitted, we have to capture the submission event and prevent its default behavior. Then we get the value from the form by using this.refs and referencing the ref we gave our form field, which was query:

```
react/search.js
var ProductSearchForm = React.createClass({
➤   sendSearchQuery: function(e){
➤     e.preventDefault();
➤     var query = this.refs.query.getDOMNode().value.trim();
➤
➤
➤   },
```

In ProductSearch, we render the search form, passing in the callback function:

```
react/search.js
  render: function() {
    return (
      <div>
        <h1>Product Search</h1>
        { /* START_HIGHLIGHT */ }
        <ProductSearchForm onSearchRequest={this.getResults} />
➤        <ProductList data={this.state.data} />
      </div>
    );
  }
```

And then in ProductSearchForm's sendSearchQuery() method we add a line of code that invokes the callback, passing it the query. Since we pass it in to the

component, we access it via this.props, as we did when we accessed the data
we wanted to display:

```
react/search.js
sendSearchQuery: function(e){
  e.preventDefault();
  var query = this.refs.query.getDOMNode().value.trim();

➤  this.props.onSearchRequest(query);

},
```

All that remains is to declare the getResults() method in the ProductSearch component. This method looks almost identical to the method that we used to display
our initial data from the server, but it sends the request to /products.json?q=
followed by the search query:

```
react/search.js
getResults: function(query){
  $.ajax({
    url: '/products.json?q=' + query,
    dataType: 'json',
    success: function(data) {
      this.setState({data: data});
    }.bind(this),
    error: function(xhr, status, err) {
      console.error(this.props.url, status, err.toString());
    }.bind(this)
  });
},
```

And with that, we have a complete search page, driven by React, as shown
in the following figure:

Product Search

Keywords [Keyboard|] [search]

Name	Description	Price
Apple Keyboard with Numeric Keypad	Description of Apple Keyboard with Numeric Keypad	49.0
Apple Wireless Keyboard	Description of Apple Wireless Keyboard	69.0

Of course we can do lots more. The price should be formatted in dollars and
cents, and we should probably add in support for pagination so we can see
more results. But this is a great start and solves our immediate problem. We
can show off this interface and get the feedback we need.

Further Exploration

We built the entire application using the client-side JSX Transformer, but if you're going to do more with React you'll want to look into precompiling your JSX code. You can use npm to install the compiler:

```
$ npm install -g react-tools
```

Then create a src folder and a build folder:

```
$ mkdir src/
$ mkdir build/
```

Place your JSX code in the src folder. Then run the jsx command-line tool, tell it to watch the src folder for any changes, and place the resulting JavaScript code in the build folder:

```
$ jsx --watch src/ build/
```

Finally, ensure that your HTML file references the JavaScript code from the build folder. When it comes time to deploy files to production, you only need to transfer your HTML pages and the build folder.

The application we built was small. If you plan to build a more robust application with React, you might want to look at the Flux architecture,[20] a design pattern for developing more complex apps with React.

Also See

- Recipe 16, *Creating Client-Side Apps with Angular.js* on page 107
- Recipe 14, *Snappier Client-Side Interfaces with Knockout.js* on page 87
- Recipe 31, *Cleaner JavaScript with CoffeeScript* on page 221

---

20. http://facebook.github.io/flux/docs/overview.html

Recipe 16

Creating Client-Side Apps with Angular.js

Problem

As users demand more robust and responsive client-side applications, developers respond with amazing JavaScript libraries. But as applications get more complex, the client-side code starts to look like a kitchen junk drawer, with libraries crammed together in a disorganized pile of event bindings, jQuery Ajax calls, and JSON parsing functions.

We need to develop our client-side applications with the same approach we've used for years for our server-side code. We need a framework. With a robust JavaScript framework, we can keep our code organized, reduce duplication, and use a coding standard that other developers can understand.

Our boss has asked us to build a proof-of-concept (PoC) application to make our product-management interface much more responsive. The current interface is slow and requires a full page refresh every time a user adds or modifies product information. The boss wants us to build a single-page interface, and we must do it all without changing our back-end application. We need a framework that will let us develop the application quickly while keeping things organized so we can maintain them over the long term.

Ingredients

- Angular[21]
- QEDServer (for our test server)[22]

Solution

We have our pick of JavaScript frameworks that will help us solve this issue. For this case we choose Angular because its Model-View-Controller (MVC) style architecture draws parallels to some common web frameworks such as Ruby on Rails, ASP.NET MVC, and Spring MVC for Java. The MVC pattern allows us to organize our code in a common way that keeps things like display logic from getting mixed up with domain objects. In addition to the MVC

---

21. http://angularjs.org/
22. A version for this book is available at http://webdevelopmentrecipes.com/.

architecture pattern, Angular's support for two-way data binding, HTML templates, deep linking, and dependency injection makes it a great fit for our PoC.

Before we get into building our interface, let's take a 30,000-foot overview of what Angular is and how we can use it to solve our problem.

Angular Basics

Angular uses a different philosophy from other JavaScript frameworks. Others work around the issue that HTML isn't designed for dynamic views, whereas Angular solves that problem head-on by extending HTML.

Frameworks like jQuery focus on manipulating the DOM and targeting elements with CSS selectors. Angular uses properties added to HTML elements for controlling and manipulating the view. Let's look at a few concepts and terms to get our feet wet:

- *Representational state transfer* (REST) is a software architecture style that is commonly used on the web as a means of communication among multiple systems.

- *Resource* is Angular's built-in way of communicating with RESTful web services.

- *Router* is an Angular module that allows us to specify routes and how our application will respond to them.

- *Views* complement the route service. They allow us to create snippets of HTML—often referred to as *templates*—that we can substitute in our page.

- *Directives* are markers on HTML elements that tell Angular to attach behavior to those elements and their children, if any. Angular comes with a set of built-in directives such as ng-view and ng-app. We can create our own directives if the built-in ones do not meet our needs.

- *Scopes* are objects on the application model that mimic the application's DOM structure. Scopes are arranged hierarchically, and every application has a single root scope. The root scope can be used as a mechanism to provide a publish-and-subscribe message-bus pattern.

Building Our Interface

We'll build a simple, single-page interface to manage products in our store. One version of the interface will end up like the one in the following figure:

We'll have a form at the top of the page for adding or editing products, and below that we'll always display a list of the products. We'll use Angular to talk to our back end to retrieve or modify our product inventory, using its REST-like interface:

- A GET request to http://example.com/products.json retrieves the list of products.

- A GET request to /products/1.json retrieves a JSON representation of the product with the ID of 1.

- A POST request to /products.json with a JSON representation of a product in the request body creates a new product.

- A PUT request to http://example.com/products/1.json with a JSON representation of a product in the request body updates the product with the ID of 1.

- A DELETE request to /products/1.json deletes the product with the ID of 1.

To build our interface we'll organize our code into templates and controllers. To keep things separate and easier to organize we start by creating a couple of folders inside of the QEDServer public directory: a folder for controllers (named controllers) and another for templates (named templates).

All Products

Let's create index.html alongside the folders we just created and add some boilerplate code to it:

angular/index.html

```
<!DOCTYPE html>
<html lang="en-US">
  <head>
    <meta charset="utf-8">
    <title>Products</title>
    <link rel="stylesheet" href="/style.css">
  </head>
</html>
```

Next, let's add the elements that make this an Angular application. We add a <body> tag and its content, as well as the Angular libraries:

angular/index.html

```
  <body ng-app="products">
    <div id="wrap">
      <ng-view> </ng-view>
    </div>
    <script src="//ajax.googleapis.com/ajax/libs/angularjs/
1.3.16/angular.min.js"></script>
    <script src="//ajax.googleapis.com/ajax/libs/angularjs/
1.3.16/angular-resource.min.js"></script>
    <script src="//ajax.googleapis.com/ajax/libs/angularjs/
1.3.16/angular-route.min.js"></script>
  </body>
```

Angular directives let us attach Angular functionality to the DOM. In our <body> tag we have an ng-app directive that tells Angular that this is the root element for our application. It also gives our application a name.

The next directive we add is the <ng-view> tag. This directive is used to mark where we'll add different sections of the page.

Directives can be attributes, like the ng-app attribute, or tags, like <ng-view>. Angular has many built-in directives, and their use is based entirely on how the directive was defined by the developer of the directive.

In our mock-up we have a list of products at the bottom of the page. As we work forward we'll swap out the top of the page with elements needed for actions such as creating, editing, and viewing our products. Those elements will be rendered into the <ng-view> area. The one thing that will stay consistent is the list of products, so we add some markup for that right below our closing <ng-view> tag:

```
angular/index.html
<div ng-controller="ProductsCtrl as productsCtrl"
    ng-init="productsCtrl.get()">
  <h2>Other Products</h2>
  <div>
    <ul>
      <li ng-repeat="product in productsCtrl.products">
      <a href="#/products/{{product.id}}">
        {{ product.name }} $ {{ product.price }}
      </a>
      </li>
    </ul>
  </div>
  <a href="#/products/new">Add a new product</a>
</div>
```

We're adding a few more ng directives here. First we specify a directive on the outside <div> called ng-controller. In Angular apps, *controllers* are where we set up the data to be sent to our view. In this case we're setting that value to ProductsCtrl as productsList, which specifies the name of the controller, followed by the variable we use to reference that controller in this block of HTML.

Joe asks:
What Is $scope and Why Should I Avoid It?

If you've looked into Angular at all, you've undoubtedly seen $scope in many code examples. $scope is a common way to get data from the controller to the view, and from the view to the controller.

Angular version 1.2.0 introduced the controller as syntax, which lets us name our objects in our controllers and views. This keeps our Angular code more consistent with standard JavaScript, and some developers consider it easier to read.

The $scope approach to building applications is valid, and it's fine for simple examples. But in our experience, the controller as syntax is clearer to read and understand, and it offers more flexibility down the road.

The last directive in the outside <div> takes advantage of this controller definition. The ng-init directive specifies a method call of productsList.get(), which translates to calling a method called .get() on the ProductsCtrl. To make that work, we need to define a .get() function in our controller that will fetch the products from the back end and store them in a variable inside of the controller.

The ng-repeat directive, which is added to the <li> tag, starts to show some of the power of Angular. This directive iterates everything inside of the <li> block for all of the objects in a collection. In our case we loop over all of the products and add a new <li> for each. The last bit of syntax should look familiar from our work in Recipe 11, *Rendering HTML with Handlebars Templates* on page 69. The {{ is followed by some code we want evaluated, then closed with }}.

Now that we have our first block of HTML ready, let's get it connected to our controller.

Let's start by adding a couple of files and then including them just before our HTML file's closing <body> tag. We'll need a routes.js file in the same directory as our HTML file. We also need to create the ProductsCtrl.js file inside the controllers folder we created earlier. And we must include them in our index.html page right above the closing <body> tag, below our other scripts:

angular/index.html
```
<script src="./routes.js"></script>
<script src="./controllers/ProductsCtrl.js"></script>
```

Now we can start defining our routes, where we specify which controllers and views are needed for each URL pattern:

angular/routes.js
```
var ProductsApp = angular.module("products", ["ngResource", "ngRoute"]);
```

We start out by declaring ProductsApp, which we define as an Angular module. All of our other Angular components will be built from this module. We assign angular.module() to the ProductsApp variable, which is Angular's way of specifying a main() method for our application.

We pass in two arguments to angular.module(). The first argument is our application, which matches what we defined in our ng-app directive. The second argument is an array of modules that our application depends on. In this case we're requiring the use of ngResource, which lets us talk to web services, and ngRoute, which lets us define routes for our application. Since not every Angular application needs these features, we must specifically load them in *and* make sure we've included those libraries in our HTML page.

Next, we configure our application by loading our ngRoute module's dependencies via Angular's dependency-injection mechanism and specify our main controller and route:

angular/routes.js
```
ProductsApp.config(['$routeProvider', function($routeProvider) {
  $routeProvider.
    when("/", { controller: "ProductsCtrl" }).
    otherwise({ redirectTo: "/" });
}]);
```

Let's look closer at the lines inside of the callback function where we're defining our routes:

```
angular/routes.js
$routeProvider.
  when("/", { controller: "ProductsCtrl" }).
  otherwise({ redirectTo: "/" });
```

We start off with the $routeProvider we passed into the function and are calling the when() with two parameters: the path and a route hash. The path is the URL that this route will respond to. The route hash tells Angular which controller is used to respond to the route. In this case it should use ProductsCtrl. This means we need to create a controller called ProductsCtrl. The second method in the chain is otherwise(), which is used when our app doesn't have a route that matches. We'll send the user to the root of our app.

Now let's create the ProductsCtrl that we referenced in the route. We create a file called controllers/ProductsCtrl.js and add the following code:

```
angular/controllers/ProductsCtrl.js
ProductsApp.controller("ProductsCtrl", function($resource, $rootScope) {
  var Products = $resource('/products.json');
  this.get = function() {
    this.products = Products.query();
  };
  $rootScope.$on("products.updated", this.get.bind(this));
});
```

In ProductsCtrl.js, we start by calling the controller() function against our ProductsApp to register a controller with our app. The controller() function takes two parameters: the name of our controller and a callback function that handles our controller's logic. The code we've added in this controller requires Angular's $resource and $rootScope modules, so we include these modules via Angular's dependency-injection mechanism. The first line in the controller defines our product's resource, which will allow us to communicate with the QEDServer's products endpoint.

Next we define a get() function, which we use for assigning the products sent back to us from the server to the view. Lastly, we create a listener on $rootScope called products.updated, which triggers a call to the QEDServer to get all the products. Note that we bind it to this so the scope of the function doesn't change on us during the callback. This call to the QEDServer will happen any time we choose to broadcast an products.updated event. With this all set up, we're ready to give our app a test.

Displaying a Single Product

We make sure our QEDServer is running by using the specific executable for our system. Then, if we access http://localhost:8080/index.html, we should see something similar to the following figure:

Other Products

- Time Capsule - 3TB $ 499.0
- Time Capsule - 2TB $ 299.0
- AirPort Express $ 99.0
- Canon Rebel XS Kit (Black) $ 549.95
- DVI to VGA Adapter $ 29.0
- Mini DVI to VGA Adapter $ 29.0
- Mini DisplayPort to DVI Adapter $ 29.0
- Mini DisplayPort to VGA Adapter $ 29.0
- Apple Wireless Keyboard $ 69.0
- Airport Extreme Base Station $ 179.0

Add a new product

When we click the links, notice that the URL is changing but nothing is happening on the screen. That's because we haven't yet defined our /products/product_id route. Let's add a route to handle this in routes.js:

angular/routes.js
```
when("/products/:id", {
  controller:  "ProductCtrl as productCtrl",
  templateUrl: "/templates/show.html"
}).
```

The show route looks similar to the index route with a couple of slight modifications. We are now passing in a templateUrl option to this route's option hash to specify a template to display in place of the ng-view directive. We're also specifying the controller by using the controller as syntax, as we did in our main index.html file. This lets us create an alias for our controller so we can easily and clearly reference it in our template.

Now let's build our show template. Add the following code in a file in the templates directory called show.html:

angular/templates/show.html
```
<div>
  <div>
    <h2>{{ productCtrl.product.name }}</h2>
    <p> {{ productCtrl.product.description }} </p>
    <p> {{ productCtrl.product.price }} </p>
  </div>
  <a href="#/products/{{productCtrl.product.id}}/edit">Edit</a>
</div>
```

Here we set up some HTML and then insert some placeholders that our controller will populate with data. Our template items here give us an idea of how we should structure our controller.

Let's add a definition for our ProductCtrl to the ProductsCtrl.js file. You could create a new file for this controller, but you'd need to go back and link that new file to the index.html file. To keep things simple, we'll add this code right below our existing ProductsCtrl:

angular/controllers/ProductsCtrl.js
```
ProductsApp.controller("ProductCtrl", function($resource, $routeParams) {
  var Product = $resource('/products/:id.json', { id: "@id" });
  this.product = Product.get({ id: $routeParams.id });
});
```

This new controller isn't much different from ProductsCtrl. Again, we have a controller name followed by the controller function. This time, however, the function takes in $routeParams in addition to $resource. $routeParams is an Angular service that allows us to access the current route parameters. In this case we're interested in pulling the id from the query string.

Let's dig deeper and explore the code inside of our ProductCtrl, starting with the first line. Again, we're creating a variable to hold our $resource, which we use to get a specific product from the back end. The Product function does a get() call on our resource and passes the ID from our $routeParams service, assigning the response to this.product. In our show template we are setting our binding to Product.product.some_attribute. So in our code this is our controller, and product is the one product from our back-end system.

Now we're ready to test our show route so we can move on to editing products. To verify the show action, make sure your QEDServer is running and point the browser to http://localhost:8080/index.html. When you click one of the products, you'll see it show up above the list of products, as in the figure on page 116.

Finishing Up

Let's wrap up our PoC by finishing the last two of our create, read, update and delete actions—for editing a product and for creating a new one. We'll add the needed routes and then view and tie them together with the necessary controllers.

Time Capsule - 3TB

Description of Time Capsule - 3TB

499.0

Edit
Other Products

- Time Capsule - 3TB $ 499.0
- Time Capsule - 2TB $ 299.0
- AirPort Express $ 99.0
- Canon Rebel XS Kit (Black) $ 549.95
- DVI to VGA Adapter $ 29.0
- Mini DVI to VGA Adapter $ 29.0
- Mini DisplayPort to DVI Adapter $ 29.0
- Mini DisplayPort to VGA Adapter $ 29.0
- Apple Wireless Keyboard $ 69.0
- Airport Extreme Base Station $ 179.0

Add a new product

We need to add the following code to our routes.js file, between our index route and our show route:

angular/routes.js
```
when("/products/new", {
  controller:  "ProductNewCtrl as productFormCtrl",
  templateUrl: "/templates/form.html"
}).
when("/products/:id/edit", {
  controller:  "ProductEditCtrl as productFormCtrl",
  templateUrl: "/templates/form.html"
}).
```

The makeup of these two routes is consistent with our show route. They use the controller as syntax pattern and specify a template. The controller as syntax names the two controllers we'll end up creating, along with how we should access information in our template. Let's create the template next. We'll want to create a form.html file in our templates folder:

angular/templates/form.html
```
<div>
  <h2>{{ productFormCtrl.product.name }}</h2>
  <p>
    <label for="product_name">Name:</label>
    <input type="text" id="product_name"
           ng-model="productFormCtrl.product.name">
  </p>
  <p>
```

```
    <label for="product_description">Description:</label>
    <textarea id="product_name"
              ng-model="productFormCtrl.product.description"></textarea>
  </p>
  <p>
    <label for="product_price">Price:</label>
    <input type="text" id="product_price"
           ng-model="productFormCtrl.product.price">
  </p>
  <p>
    <button ng-click="productFormCtrl.saveProduct()">Save</button> or
    <a href="#" ng-click="productFormCtrl.cancel()">Cancel</a>
  </p>
</div>
```

Using one template allows us to eliminate code duplication and keep our forms consistent. This works in our case because we can create a save() function in both controllers. Let's create our two controllers and get this PoC completed for our boss.

We'll put the other two controllers in our same ProductsCtrl.js file. We're not doing anything major, so keeping the logic in one file is fine for now:

angular/controllers/ProductsCtrl.js

```
ProductsApp.controller("ProductEditCtrl", function($resource, $routeParams,
  $location, $rootScope) {

  var Product = $resource('/products/:id.json',
    { id: "@id" },
    { update: { method: 'PUT' } }
  );

  var id = $routeParams.id;
  this.product = Product.get({ id: id });

  this.saveProduct = function() {
    var self = this;
    Product.update(self.product, function() {
      alert("Product Updated");
      $location.path("/products/" + self.product.id);
      $rootScope.$broadcast("products.updated");
    });
  };
});

ProductsApp.controller("ProductNewCtrl", function($resource, $location,
  $rootScope) {

  var Product = $resource('/products.json');
  this.product = new Product();
```

```
this.saveProduct = function() {
  var self = this;
  Product.save(self.product, function(product) {
    alert("Product Created");
    self.product = product;
    $location.path("/products/" + self.product.id);
    $rootScope.$broadcast("products.updated");
  });
};
});
```

Again, our new controllers are similar to the ones we've already created. The edit controller is closer to our show controller in that our $resource has some extra parameters. In this case we're specifying an id and an HTTP method for our update service call. The edit controller also has a call to get the details of a product, like the call in our show controller.

Our edit controller uses the Product.get() function to prepopulate the form for our users. The last function of our edit controller is saveProduct(), which sends an HTTP PUT request to our server, triggering a save of the updated information.

The controller for creating new products works in a similar fashion. We start by creating an empty product object. Then—as in our edit controller—we have a saveProduct() function. The function here performs a bit differently in that it sends a POST request to our server, triggering the creation of a new product.

Both the edit controller's and the new controller's saveProduct() functions publish a message on the $rootScope, which we set up a listener for in our ProductsCtrl. By publishing the products.updated event, our list of products will be updated every time we create or save one.

With all of our code in place, we can try out the entire app in our browser and then report back to our boss with our findings:

- Client-side frameworks allow for code organization and consistency with traditional web frameworks.

- Angular allows for easy integration with existing RESTful web services.

- Angular provides snappy user interfaces that provide users with a modern web experience.

Further Exploration

We can take this recipe a bit further and add the delete action to our application, or do some more refactoring to take some of the common elements from the different controllers and combine them into our own modules.

Also See

- Recipe 11, *Rendering HTML with Handlebars Templates* on page 69
- Recipe 14, *Snappier Client-Side Interfaces with Knockout.js* on page 87
- Recipe 15, *Creating a Search Interface with React* on page 97

## CHAPTER 3

Data Recipes

Web developers work with data in many forms. Sometimes we're pulling in a widget from another service, and other times we're taking data from our users. In these recipes, we spend some time consuming, manipulating, and presenting data.

Recipe 17

Adding an Inline Google Map

Problem

People want simple, accessible, and quick ways to locate a geographical destination. Addresses and written directions work, but the simplest method is to glance at a map, memorize the street number and general location, grab your keys, and go. We want to add a map to our site so that visitors can get an immediate a sense of where something is located and how they can get there.

Ingredients

* The Google Maps API

Solution

Using the Google Maps API, we can bring the power and functionality of Google Maps into our own application. We can render maps of two types: static and interactive. The static map is an image that we can insert into our page, whereas the interactive map allows for zooming and panning. The Google Maps API supports any programming language that can make a request to Google's servers. The documentation includes many of JavaScript examples, which is perfect for our needs.[1]

Along with rendering maps, the JavaScript API lets us insert other elements in the maps. We can place markers and bind mouse events to the markers. We can also create pop-out dialog boxes that show information directly within the map. We can show street views, geolocate the user, create routes and directions, and draw custom models on the map. The sky's the limit, at least until Google launches its space program and takes over NASA.[2]

We're working with a local university to develop a map for its web page for new visitors. The admissions office wants to show these visitors where they can find places and where to park. We'll create an interactive map that contains markers and information, using the JavaScript Google Maps API.

---

1. https://developers.google.com/maps/documentation/javascript/reference
2. http://www.google.com/space

We start with our basic HTML5 template:

googlemaps/map_example.html

```html
<!DOCTYPE html>
<html lang="en">
  <head>
    <meta charset="utf-8">
    <title>Freshman Landing Page</title>
    <style>
    </style>
  </head>
  <body>
    <script>
      window.onload = loadMap;
      function loadMap() {
        var latLong = new google.maps.LatLng(44.798609, -91.504912);

        var mapOptions = {
          zoom: 15,
          mapTypeId: google.maps.MapTypeId.ROADMAP,
          center: latLong
        };

        var map = new google.maps.Map(document.getElementById("map_canvas"),
            mapOptions);
        mogiesLatLong = new google.maps.LatLng(44.802293, -91.509376);
        var marker = new google.maps.Marker({
          position: mogiesLatLong,
          map: map,
          title: "Mogie's Pub & Restaurant"
        });
        var mogiesDescription = "<h4>Mogie's Pub & Restaurant</h4>" +
          "<p>Excellent local restaurant with top of the line burgers " +
          "and sandwiches.</p>";
        var infoPopup = new google.maps.InfoWindow({
          content: mogiesDescription
        });
        google.maps.event.addListener(marker, "click", function() {
          infoPopup.open(map,marker);
        });
      }

    </script>
  </body>
</html>
```

Next, we include the Google Maps JavaScript API in our document, right above the closing <body> tag:

```
<script src="https://maps.googleapis.com/maps/api/js?v=3.18"></script>
```

The API requires a <div> to act as a container for the map, so we add that to our page.

```
<body>
    <div id="map_canvas"></div>
```

The map will scale to the size of this container, so let's set dimensions on this <div> with CSS in the <style> section of our page's <head> region:

```
#map_canvas {
    height: 400px;
    width: 600px;
}
```

This container is now ready to hold a map that is 600x400 pixels. Let's go fetch some data.

Loading the Map with JavaScript

At the bottom of our page, right below the <script> tag we added to load the Google Maps API code, we add a <script> block to hold the code that initializes our map. We'll create a function called loadMap() to load the map with the latitude and longitude we want to center on, and we'll run it when the browser window loads. We could put our code in a separate JavaScript file, but keeping it with this file makes development of the map much easier:

```
<script>
    window.onload = loadMap;
</script>
```

Next, we'll create the loadMap() function. Since we're not using a sensor, we'll hard-code our latitude and longitude. These coordinates define the center point of the map. To find these values, we have a few options. We can browse to Google Maps, find what we want to center our map on, right-click a pin, and select What's here? to see the values for latitude and longitude in the search box. Alternatively, we can use the Google Maps / Open Streetmap Latitude, Longitude Popup,[3] a website where you can click a location on a map to find its latitude and longitude.

```
function loadMap() {
    var latLong = new google.maps.LatLng(44.798609, -91.504912);

    var mapOptions = {
        zoom: 15,
```

---

3. http://www.gorissen.info/Pierre/maps/googleMapLocationv3.php

```
    mapTypeId: google.maps.MapTypeId.ROADMAP,
    center: latLong
  };

  var map = new google.maps.Map(document.getElementById("map_canvas"),
      mapOptions);
}
```

Within this function, we create an object to hold options for our map. We can define the type of map we want, a zoom value, and more. The zoom requires some experimentation; the higher the number, the farther in it zooms. A value of 15 works well for street-level maps.

We can change how the map appears by setting a different mapTypeId. Note that zoom values, along with maximum ranges for zoom, change when you change the map type. You can find a reference for map types in the Google Maps API documentation.[4]

Finally, we create the map. The Map constructor requires that we pass the DOM element that will hold the map, along with our object containing the options. When we load this page in our browser, we see a map centered on our desired location that looks like the following figure:

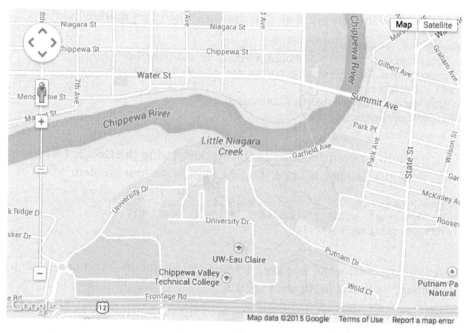

Now let's plot some points of interest on the map that our visitors can click.

---

4. http://code.google.com/apis/maps/documentation/javascript/reference.html#MapTypeId

Creating Marker Points

To show incoming students where they can go to get a bite to eat or otherwise be social, we'll create markers on the map. A marker in Google Maps is one of many overlays that we can add. Overlays respond to a click event, and we will use this to show an info window when the marker is clicked.

Since we already have a map, creating the marker is as simple as invoking the constructor and passing some options:

googlemaps/map_example.html
```
mogiesLatLong = new google.maps.LatLng(44.802293, -91.509376);
var marker = new google.maps.Marker({
  position: mogiesLatLong,
  map: map,
  title: "Mogie's Pub & Restaurant"
});
```

To define a marker, we pass the latitude and longitude coordinates, the map that will hold the marker, and a title that will appear when the user's mouse pointer hovers over the marker. You can get the points of interest for your location by searching through Google Maps, but we're using our favorite burger joint for this example.

Next, we create the info window that appears when this marker is clicked:

googlemaps/map_example.html
```
var mogiesDescription = "<h4>Mogie's Pub & Restaurant</h4>" +
  "<p>Excellent local restaurant with top of the line burgers " +
  "and sandwiches.</p>";
var infoPopup = new google.maps.InfoWindow({
  content: mogiesDescription
});
```

Finally, we add an event handler to the marker. Using the Google Maps event object, we add a listener to open the info window we just created:

googlemaps/map_example.html
```
google.maps.event.addListener(marker, "click", function() {
  infoPopup.open(map,marker);
});
```

When the user clicks the marker, a new window shows information about the location, as in the figure on page 127.

We can add as much HTML content as we want to the window to show more information. From here, we can gather the coordinates of other points of interest and build the rest of the map.

Further Exploration

We've only scratched the surface of what can be accomplished with the Google Maps API. Along with markers, other layers of interaction can make the map more usable for your customers. You can create directions, map routes, use geolocation, and even add street views. Each of these features is well explained in the Google Maps API documentation,[5] with several working examples.

Google Maps is just one component of the Google APIs. To see a full list of Google APIs, take a look at the Google Developers Products Page.[6]

Also See

- Recipe 19, *Building a Simple Contact Form* on page 136
- Recipe 20, *Accessing Cross-Site Data with JSONP* on page 144
- Recipe 21, *Creating a Widget to Embed in Other Sites* on page 148

---

5. https://developers.google.com/maps/documentation/javascript/reference
6. https://developers.google.com/products/

Recipe 18

Creating Charts and Graphs with Highcharts

Problem

Our sales team has developed an affiliate program for our company's shopping site. We've been tasked with developing an interface for our affiliates, and we want to show their data in a visual and attractive way. However, we need to ensure that these charts are viewable on mobile devices as well as desktops.

Ingredients

- jQuery
- Highcharts[7]
- QEDServer (for our test server)[8]

Solution

The Highcharts JavaScript library lets us easily create interactive and readable charts and graphs. It works across platforms, and since it runs on the client's machine, it doesn't require any special configuration on our servers. The interface built into Highcharts is highly interactive and customizable, letting us present data in a number of ways. In this recipe, we'll build and customize a simple chart and then build a more complex one using some remote data.

Building a Simple Chart

Let's create a simple pie chart so you can get acquainted with Highcharts and its various options. First, we build a simple HTML document and include the necessary JavaScript files. We also add a <div> tag, which Highcharts will use to render the chart on our page:

highcharts/example_chart.html
```
<!DOCTYPE html>
<html lang="en">
  <head>
    <meta charset="utf-8">
    <title>Example Pie Chart</title>
```

---

7. http://www.highcharts.com/
8. A version for this book is available at http://webdevelopmentrecipes.com/.

```
</head>
<body>
  <div id="pie_chart"></div>

<script
  src="http://ajax.googleapis.com/ajax/libs/jquery/2.1.4/jquery.min.js">
</script>
<script
  src="http://cdnjs.cloudflare.com/ajax/libs/highcharts/4.1.5/highcharts.js">
</script>
```

All the magic is done by creating a new instance of the Highcharts.Chart class and passing it some options. Highcharts has many options for configuring a chart, and this configuration can quickly get long and unwieldy. To keep it simple, we create a variable called chartOptions and set some values on it that Highcharts expects. For this simple chart we add a new <script> block to the HTML page rather than putting the code in a separate file:

highcharts/example_chart.html
```
<script>
  (function($, Highcharts){
    var chartOptions = {};

    chartOptions.chart = { renderTo: "pie_chart" };
    chartOptions.title = { text: "A sample pie chart" };

    chartOptions.series = [{
      type: "pie",
      name: "Sample chart",
      data: [
        ["Section 1", 30],
        ["Section 2", 50],
        ["Section 3", 20]
      ]
    }];
    var chart = new Highcharts.Chart(chartOptions);

  })(jQuery, Highcharts);
</script>
```

The first value we set is a chart property that contains information about the chart itself. This is where we pass the ID of the <div> we created earlier. Then we set a title for the chart with some sample text. Finally, the series property is an array that contains an object for each type of chart you want to render. Highcharts allows us to pass any number of objects that will be rendered on top of one another. Each object defines a chart type, a name, and a dataset. The format of this data changes depending on the type of chart we're using.

For the pie chart, the data is a two-dimensional array in which the inner arrays are pairs of X and Y data.

With just a few lines of code, we have a chart that looks like the following figure:

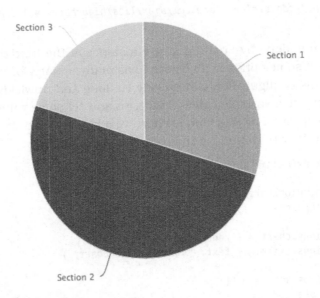

A sample pie chart

Let's go a little further now and explore some additional options to customize our chart.

Customizing Our Chart's Appearance

Highcharts supports pie graphs, line graphs, area graphs, and scatter plots, and the extensibility of the graph types lets us create any number of more interesting graphs.

Consider our chartOptions variable from before. We can define a property on it called plotOptions, which is an object containing a number of settings for modifying how the graph is drawn. Let's define some options on our pie chart from earlier.

We can set options for all charts by defining them in the series property on our chartOptions object, but we can also define options for each chart type. Let's customize our pie chart by changing the appearance of the labels that point to each section of the chart. We add this new code right before we render the chart:

highcharts/example_chart.html

```
var pieChartOptions = {
  dataLabels: {
    style: { fontSize: 20 },
    connectorWidth: 3,
    formatter: function() {
      var label = this.point.name + " : " + this.percentage + "%";
      return label;
    }
  }
};

chartOptions.plotOptions = { pie: pieChartOptions };

var chart = new Highcharts.Chart(chartOptions);
```

We first increase the font size to make it more visible. Then we increase the connector width to match the font size. Lastly, we create a function that returns a newly formatted label with our desired information. The default label shows only the point name, so we change it to show the percentage as well. Our finished chart looks like the following figure:

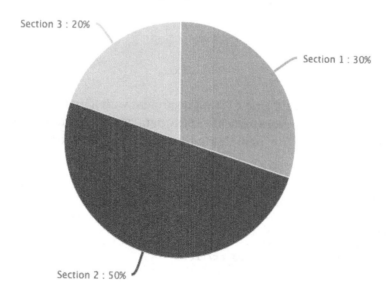

A sample pie chart

The plotOptions property has a ton of options; refer to the Highcharts documentation on the plotOptions property to see them all.[9]

---

9. http://www.highcharts.com/ref/#plotOptions

Now that we know how to create and configure a simple chart, let's use Highcharts to model our affiliate data.

Modeling the Affiliate Datasets

Our affiliate program tracks quite a bit of data, including the customer's name, age, and location. This kind of information is useful for profiling customers and making assumptions about how to market products. It's our job to transform this raw data into a graph that our marketing folks can quickly analyze before they dig into the hard data.

We want our users to be able to glance at the data and understand how old the customers are. Let's use a bar graph so that it's easy to see the mean and the most frequent value. We'll create something that looks like the following figure:

To get started, let's create a new HTML document with jQuery and Highcharts included in it. We'll be working with JSON data and Ajax requests, so fire up QEDServer and place this new HTML file in the public directory of your QED-Server installation:

```
highcharts/affiliates.html
<!DOCTYPE html>
<html lang="en">
  <head>
    <meta charset="utf-8">
    <title>Affiliate Customer Data</title>
  </head>

  <body>
    <div id="customer_data"></div>

    <script
      src="http://ajax.googleapis.com/ajax/libs/jquery/2.1.4/jquery.min.js">
    </script>
```

```
    <script
      src="http://cdnjs.cloudflare.com/ajax/libs/highcharts/4.1.5/highcharts.js">
    </script>
  </body>
</html>
```

Within this file, we create a <script> block and set up our new instance of the Highcharts.Chart class. Let's set a few simple options, including the chart's title and the target element on our page where the chart will go:

highcharts/affiliates.html
```
<script>

(function($, Highcharts) {
  var options = {
    chart: { renderTo: "customer_data" },
    title: { text: "Customer Data" },
    credits: { enabled: false }
  };



})(jQuery, Highcharts);
</script>
```

Now that our document is ready to go, let's do some work with our data.

Showing the Customer Data

Normally, we'd get our customer data from a back-end system, but for the purpose of this recipe, we've created some sample data you can use. You'll find it in the book's source code, which you can download from the book's website.[10] You'll want the highcharts/sample_data/customer_data.json file.

Or you can create the file yourself, using something like this:

```
{
  "customers": [
    { "name": "Adrienne Sargent", "age": 20 },
    { "name": "Stella Albin", "age": 55 },
    { "name": "Dolores Krauss", "age": 28 },
    { "name": "Jerry Ayala", "age": 34 },
    { "name": "Keith Shuman", "age": 35 },
    { "name": "Timothy Navarra", "age": 33 },
    { "name": "Norman Tanaka", "age": 36 }
  ]
}
```

---

10. http://webdevelopmentrecipes.com

Our index.html page and our data file must be hosted on the same web server. Remember that we can't just pull in regular JSON data from a remote server, because of the web browser's security restrictions. So place this sample data file in a folder called sample_data within the public folder that QEDServer uses. This way, QEDServer can serve it from http://localhost:8080/sample_data/customer_data.json, and our page can consume it properly.

To show the ages in a bar graph, we need to pair an age with the number of times it occurs. Right now, we have only a list of ages. Let's write some JavaScript to collect the ages and sum up the frequencies. We make a request to get our customer data and do all our work inside of the success callback, which is invoked when we get data back from our Ajax request:

`highcharts/affiliates.html`
```
$.getJSON('sample_data/customer_data.json', function(data) {
  var ages = [];

  $.each(data.customers, function(index, customer) {
    if (typeof ages[customer.age] === "undefined") {
      ages[customer.age] = 1;
    } else {
      ages[customer.age] += 1;
    }
  });

  var age_data = [];

  $.each(ages, function(index, e) {
    if (typeof e !== "undefined") {
      age_data.push([index, e]);
    }
  });
});
```

Here we use an array to store some intermediate data. The ages array uses ages as indexes and stores the number of occurrences for that age. Then we look through and collect ages that exist in the array to map them to the two-dimensional array that Highcharts needs. Now that we have our data in the correct format, let's render our chart:

`highcharts/affiliates.html`
```
options.series = [{
  type: "column",
  name: "Customer Ages",
  data: age_data
}];

var chart = new Highcharts.Chart(options);
```

Now with our final chart rendered, we can easily see the most frequently occurring ages for our customers.

Further Exploration

Highcharts is a powerful JavaScript library. In this recipe, we built simple to complex charts that only begin to take advantage of the number of available options. The Highcharts reference[11] is a great way to learn what Highcharts is capable of. We recommend taking a look at the documentation and considering what options you would like to use in future projects. Also, the documentation includes a link to an example of most of the available options on JSFiddle.net.[12]

Also See

- Recipe 20, *Accessing Cross-Site Data with JSONP* on page 144
- Recipe 17, *Adding an Inline Google Map* on page 122
- Recipe 10, *Interacting with Web Pages Using Keyboard Shortcuts* on page 61
- Recipe 25, *Mobile Drag and Drop* on page 173

---

11. http://highcharts.com/ref
12. A JavaScript-sharing site: http://jsfiddle.net

Building a Simple Contact Form

Problem

Websites—even mostly static websites—should provide a way for visitors to contact the site's owner. An email address isn't always good enough; it's not inviting or engaging for the user, and it makes it harder for the site owner to sort and organize messages that come from visitors. Sites should have an easy, intuitive way for visitors to get in touch.

Our current website has no way to contact us, and we're concerned that we've missed out on potential business opportunities as a result. Our manager wants us to create a simple form that sends us an email.

Ingredients

- A server running PHP

Solution

A contact form lets visitors email us without having an email client configured, making it more likely that we'll hear from them by email. We can create an HTML form to handle the data entry, write some scripts to handle sending the email, and give users feedback for errors and successful emails.

We can choose among many server-side languages, but the PHP scripting language is perfect for this situation. We needn't do much heavy lifting: the script that processes the data from our contact form will be easy to build, thanks to PHP's simple syntax. PHP is readily available on most shared hosting solutions, and it's easy to install on servers where it's not already present. It's a handy tool for simple back-end functions like this, where heavier frameworks would be overkill.

To create our contact form, we'll create both HTML components and PHP components. We'll use HTML to build the form to ask for the data, and then we'll use PHP to handle the data and send the email. We'll also add a few important interface features, such as error feedback. We'll use our virtual machine to test this form. If you haven't already, refer to either Recipe 39,

Setting Up a Virtual Machine on page 282, or Recipe 45, *Configuring a Virtual Machine with Puppet* on page 317, to create your own PHP development server.

Creating the HTML

Let's start by creating the HTML for the form. The form will ask the user for four things: a name, an email address, a subject, and a message. We'll require that the email address be provided; otherwise, we'll be unable to easily get back to the user. We'll also set a default value for the subject to get them started. Now that we know what we're collecting, let's create the contact.php file and create the form:

```
contact/contact.php
<!DOCTYPE html>
<html lang="en">
  <head>
    <meta charset="utf-8">
    <title>Awesome Web Development - Contact Us</title>
  </head>
  <body>

    <h2>Contact Us</h2>
    <p>
      Please fill out this quick form to send us an email. We are excited
      to hear from you!
    </p>

    <form id="contact-form" action="contact.php" method="post">

      <label for="name">Name</label>
      <input class="full-width" type="text" name="name">

      <label for="email">Your Email</label>
      <input class="full-width" type="text" name="email">

      <label for="subject">Subject</label>
      <input class="full-width" type="text" name="subject"
             value="Web Consulting Inquiry">

      <label for="body">Body</label>
      <textarea class="full-width" name="body"></textarea>

      <input type="submit" name="send" value="Send">

    </form>

  </body>
</html>
```

The form's action points to itself, using the POST method. This lets us do all of the scripting for sending the email on the same page as the contact form. We create a field for each part of the email and include a submit button. At this point, the form is on the page but looks like a jumble of words and boxes. Let's add some styling to arrange the labels and inputs:

```
contact/contact.php
<style type="text/css">
  body {
    font-size: 12px;
    font-family: Verdana;
  }

  #contact-form {
    width: 320px;
  }

  #contact-form label {
    display: block;
    margin: 10px 0px;
  }

  #contact-form input, #contact-form textarea {
    padding: 4px;
  }

  #contact-form .full-width {
    width: 100%;
  }

  #contact-form textarea {
    height: 100px;
  }
</style>
```

We change some font properties, add a good amount of padding and margin, and move form items to read well. The form is much more readable and usable, as shown in the figure on page 139.

Now we're ready to bring the form to life and write some back-end code.

Sending the Email

When the page is processed by PHP, we want to catch any POST requests and send an email. We've already set our page to post to itself, so we just need to add some PHP to the top of the page. When the submit button is clicked, we need to grab data from the $_POST variable, validate the data, and send it through PHP's mail() function. All of our code for the preprocessing is in a PHP block above the <html> tag:

Your Email

Subject

Web Consulting Inquiry

Body

Send

contact/contact.php

```php
<?php
if (isset($_POST["send"])) {
}
?>
```

The preprocessing should run only if the Send button is clicked. Since we gave the button a name attribute in our HTML, we check it in the $_POST array. Now, let's get the data that the user has entered. We can use the same $_POST array to get the data, so let's store the data in variables so that it's easier to work with:

```php
$name = $_POST["name"];
$email = $_POST["email"];
$subject = $_POST["subject"];
$body = $_POST["body"];
```

Now that we have the data in a few variables, we should make sure that the email address the user is giving us is a real address. Let's compare the address against a regular expression to check its validity. Also, we want to let the user know if the email field's content is invalid:

```php
$errors = array();

$email_matcher = "/^[_a-z0-9-]+(\.[_a-z0-9-]+)*" .
"@" .
"[a-z0-9-]+" .
"(\.[a-z0-9-]+)*(\.[a-z]{2,3})$/";

if (preg_match($email_matcher, $email) == 0) {
  array_push($errors, "You did not enter a valid email address");
}
```

We store any form errors in an array that we check later to output a message for each error we find. We define the $errors array here so that it's available for the rest of the HTML page.

Time to send the email! We'll make a call to PHP's mail() function. It accepts a number of arguments: an email address to send to, a subject, a message, and any headers we want to send. Let's set some variables to store these components based on the data we already have and make the call to mail():

```
contact/contact.php
if (count($errors) == 0) {
  $to = "joe@awesomeco.com"; // your email
  $subject = "[Generated from awesomeco.com] " . $subject;

  $from = $name . " <" . $email . ">";
  $headers = "From: " . $from;

  if (!mail($to, $subject, $body, $headers)) {
    array_push($errors, "Mail failed to send.");
  }
}
```

When we call the mail() function, we ensure that no errors in sending the email occurred. The function returns true if the send was successful, so we can use that value as a flag. We save a new string in the $errors array so we can let the user know something went wrong. With the functionality for our email form in place, let's test it and make sure it works.

Testing Our Contact Form

To test our contact form, we need a PHP–enabled folder on our development server. For this recipe, we'll use a virtual machine running on our own network at http://192.168.1.100. If you don't have a virtual machine for development, refer to Recipe 39, *Setting Up a Virtual Machine* on page 282, to set up a server for testing purposes.

With our development server running, let's send it a copy of the file we've been working on. We can use the scp command to send the file (or an SFTP program such as FileZilla for Windows users):

```
$ scp contact.php webdev@192.168.1.100:/var/www/
```

When we navigate to http://192.168.1.100/contact.php, we can enter our data in the fields and click Send. Now check your email. You should receive an email similar to the one shown in the following figure:

[Generated from awesomeco.com] **Web Consulting Inquiry**   Inbox | X

⭐ **John Smith** john@smith.com   show details 11:40 AM (0 minutes ago)

Hello Sir,

I would like a website. Let's talk!

↩ Reply   → Forward

Showing the Form Errors

In our PHP code, we validated that the email address the user entered is real. However, if an invalid address is entered, we're currently not giving the user any feedback. To fix this, we need to head back to our HTML and render the errors:

contact/contact.php
```
<?php if (count($errors) > 0) : ?>
  <h3>There were errors that prevented the email from sending</h3>

  <ul class="errors">
    <?php foreach($errors as $error) : ?>
      <li><?php echo $error; ?></li>
    <?php endforeach; ?>
  </ul>
<?php endif; ?>
```

At the top of our form, we make sure that the $errors array isn't empty. If it contains anything, we know we need to iterate through the array and display the messages. The syntax for the if and foreach blocks is an alternative syntax. It allows us to write normal HTML instead of using the echo() or print() statement and dancing around single and double quotes. Using this code, we'll have a list of errors that we can style. Let's make the header and list items red so they stand out:

contact/contact.php
```
.errors h3, .errors li {
  color: #FF0000;
}

.errors li {
  margin: 5px 0px;
}
```

With the error feedback in place, the user experience is improving. However, the error system in our contact form has one more annoyance. When users make an error in the form, they lose all the data that they previously entered.

Since we have the post data in variables from earlier, we have an easy fix: we add value properties to each <input> field and text into the <textarea>. Our new form fields change to this:

```
<label for="name">Name</label>
<input class="full-width" type="text" name="name"
       value="<?php echo $name; ?>" />

<label for="email">Your Email</label>
<input class="full-width" type="text" name="email"
       value="<?php echo $email; ?>" />

<label for="subject">Subject</label>
<input class="full-width" type="text" name="subject"
  value="<?php echo isset($subject) ?
    $subject : 'Web Consulting Inquiry'; ?>" />

<label for="body">Body</label>
<textarea class="full-width" name="body">&lt;?php echo $body; ?&gt;</textarea>
```

Now, the user experience for the errors section of our contact form is complete. When users enter incorrect data, they see their existing data as expected and feedback regarding the errors. The following figure shows us an example of a user entering an invalid email address:

There were errors that prevented the email from sending

- You did not enter a valid email address

Name

John Smith

Your Email

bademail@website

With our contact form complete, more users will email us, which will improve our business.

Further Exploration

A contact form is only one example of what can be done with a PHP-powered form. Using this concept and focusing on the idea of a web consulting firm, we could also build a form that helps the user find a quote for a service. It's also a good idea to improve the form's usability across platforms. The HTML5 specification defines a number of additional input types, such as the email type. This gives a different touch keyboard on iOS, Android, and other mobile platforms. To learn more about these features available in the HTML5 spec, take a look at *HTML5 and CSS3: Level Up with Today's Web Technologies* [Hog13].

Also See

- Recipe 21, *Creating a Widget to Embed in Other Sites* on page 148
- Recipe 29, *Creating a Simple Blog with Enfield* on page 203
- Recipe 39, *Setting Up a Virtual Machine* on page 282
- Recipe 45, *Configuring a Virtual Machine with Puppet* on page 317
- Recipe 38, *Using Dropbox to Collaborate and Host a Static Site* on page 278
- Recipe 44, *Automating Static Site Deployment with Grunt* on page 304

Recipe 20

Accessing Cross-Site Data with JSONP

Problem

We need to access data from a site in another domain but are unable to do it using a server-side language—either because of restrictions on our web server or because we want to push the load to the user's browser. Regular API calls to external sites are not an option because of the same-origin policy,[13] which prevents client-side programming languages like JavaScript from accessing pages on different domains.

Ingredients

- jQuery
- The Flickr public photos feed[14] or another remote server API that returns JSONP

Solution

We can use JSONP (JSON with Padding) to load remote data from a server that's in another domain. JSONP returns data in the JSON format but wraps it in a call to a function. When the browser loads the script from the remote server, it tries to run the returned function if it exists on the page, with the JSON data passed in as a variable. All we have to do is write the function that will be called and tell it how to process the JSON, and we'll be able to work with data from a remote site.

We'll use the Flickr API to load some recently uploaded public photos. Some APIs let you set the function name that wraps the content when you load the page on its server, but the Flickr API always returns data wrapped in a call to jsonFlickrApi(). This is the function we'll need to write on our page once we have the data loaded from Flickr.

We start with a blank page with no content in the <body>. Everything that ends up being displayed on the page will be loaded dynamically. We include jQuery so that we have access to its ajax() functions:

---

13. https://developer.mozilla.org/en/Same_origin_policy_for_JavaScript
14. https://www.flickr.com/services/feeds/docs/photos_public/

jsonp/index.html

```
<!DOCTYPE html>
<html>
  <head>
    <meta charset="utf-8">
    <title>Photos</title>
  </head>
  <body>
    <h1>Photos</h1>

    <script
      src="https://ajax.googleapis.com/ajax/libs/jquery/2.1.3/jquery.min.js">
    </script>
  </body>
</html>
<!-- end:skeleton -->
```

In another <script> block on our page, we create a function to load photos from Flickr's public feed. In loadPhotos() we make a call to Flickr using jQuery's $.ajax() method:

jsonp/index.html

```
<script>
  function loadPhotos(){
    var callback = "displayPhotos";
    $.ajax({
      url: 'https://api.flickr.com/services/feeds/photos_public.gne' +
           '?format=json' +
           '&jsoncallback=' + callback,
      dataType: "jsonp"
    })
  }
</script>
```

We set the dataType to jsonp so that jQuery knows this request will be across domains and should expect the results to be formatted as JSONP instead of JSON. When the data comes back, it will immediately invoke the function we specify as the jsoncallback, and it will pass all of the data into that function as its argument. We have to define this function and use it to parse out the data to display it on the page.

Notice that we didn't wrap our JavaScript with an Immediately-Invoked Function Expression (IIFE) as we have elsewhere in this book. JSONP works by appending the response to the page as a new <script> block, so the callback we use needs to be in the global scope. To keep things simple, we'll put everything in the global scope for this recipe.

The response we get from Flickr will be similar to the following JSONP, which we'll use to populate our page:

```
jsonp/flickr_response.html
displayPhotos({
    "title":"Uploads from everyone",
    "link":"https://www.flickr.com/photos/",
    "description":"",
    "modified":"2015-04-14T15:04:09Z",
    "generator":"https://www.flickr.com/",
    "items":[
      {
        "title":"some picture",
        "link":"https://www.flickr.com/photos/xxxxx/abc1234"
        "media":{
          "m":"https://farm8.staticflickr.com/nnn/abc_9a18ab9a_m.jpg"
        },
        "date_taken":"2015-04-11T20:03:49-08:00",
        "description":"A picture",
        "published":"2015-04-14T15:04:09Z",
        "author":"nobody@flickr.com (Max Power)",
        "author_id":"xxxxxxxx@N07",
        "tags":""
    },
    ]
})
```

The data we get from Flickr includes the photos and their related information in an array called items, so we want to loop over each entry and build out the image tags to add to the page. So, we declare our displayPhotos() function:

```
jsonp/index.html
function displayPhotos(data){
  $.each(data.items, function(i,item){
    var $imageTag = $('<img>');
    $imageTag.attr('src', item.media.m);
    $('body').append($imageTag);
  });
}
```

Since we're already using jQuery, we use jQuery's $.each()() helper to iterate over the array of photos. Inside our loop we'll work with each photo to build an <img> tag and set its src attribute to the URL of the photo, which we fetch from the item's media.m property. Then we append the newly built <img> to the body of the page.

With all the pieces in place, we only need to call loadPhotos():

```
loadPhotos();
```

And we now have our own gallery of Flickr's recently uploaded photos:

JSONP gives us a way to load dynamic content from external sites without needing to resort to server-side languages. It's an easy way to pull content into our pages.

Further Exploration

To make the interface more interesting, you could refresh the photos at a regular interval, such as every 15 minutes, and update the page with new photos. Of course, users might not want us running scripts in a continuous loop in their machines; they may want to stop and look at the images, or they may not like the idea of the browser constantly making requests to update the page for them. You could add a check box to the page that, when checked, activates the timer and the updater, thereby giving the user control.

JSONP is a great way to communicate with services that are on other servers, but you should also learn about Cross-Origin Resource Sharing (CORS).[15] This standard enables remote servers to allow remote connections directly and is supported in modern browsers. Although CORS isn't in widespread use, you may find it's the perfect solution for your own projects if your front end and back end must be in different domains.

Also See

- Recipe 4, *Creating Interactive Slideshows with jQuery* on page 18
- Recipe 21, *Creating a Widget to Embed in Other Sites* on page 148
- Recipe 15, *Creating a Search Interface with React* on page 97
- Recipe 11, *Rendering HTML with Handlebars Templates* on page 69

---

15. http://enable-cors.org

Recipe 21

Creating a Widget to Embed in Other Sites

Problem

Widgets are small chunks of code—a combination of HTML, JavaScript, and CSS—that web developers can embed in their pages to load content from another site. From general information about our site to tailored content about a user's activities, widgets that we create and share help us expand the reach of our site and allow people to share that they use our site. It's a simple concept, but developing a widget requires some possibly unfamiliar tasks—such as loading data from a remote site and ensuring that your JavaScript doesn't conflict with existing JavaScript on the site where the widget is embedded. We need to encapsulate our code to ensure that the functions we introduce don't inadvertently overwrite existing code or other widgets, which could break a page that worked before our widget was added.

Ingredients

- jQuery
- JSONP

Solution

Using HTML, JavaScript, and a little CSS, we can create widgets to load content from our server so other developers can insert our content into their sites; all those users need to do is load a JavaScript file from our server. (From now on in this recipe, *users* refers to other web developers.) The file they load will construct the HTML element, style the element, and ensure that our code is completely separate from their code so no collisions occur. Best of all, because the widget code is under our control, we can make adjustments and add new features at any time. Visitors will see those changes as we make them available.

We'll create a widget that lets users include the commit logs from the official Ruby on Rails repository[16] on their websites. We'll use JavaScript to create an anonymous function to avoid conflicting with any JavaScript that's already

---

16. https://github.com/rails/rails

on the page. Next we'll check to see whether jQuery is already loaded so that we have access to its shortcuts and helper methods. If it's not, or if it's not the right version, we'll load our own copy. Then we'll execute and create our widget by loading data remotely with JSONP, which lets us access information from a remote server via JavaScript, without issues that could arise from getting that data from a different domain. After loading the content with JavaScript, we'll generate HTML and insert it in the page, as shown in the following figure:

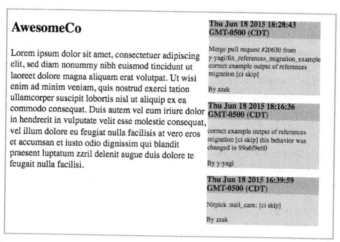

A widget should be simple to add, so we'll design our widget so our users need to add only two lines of code on their sites: a link to the JavaScript and a <div> where the JavaScript will insert the content after it's loaded:

```
widget/index.html
<!DOCTYPE html>
<html>
  <head>
    <title>Widget Examples</title>
  </head>
  <body>
    <div style="width:350px; float:left;">
      <h2>AwesomeCo</h2>
      <p>
        Lorem ipsum dolor sit amet, consectetuer adipiscing elit, sed diam
        nonummy nibh euismod tincidunt ut laoreet dolore magna aliquam erat
        . . . .
      </p>
    </div>
    <script src="widget.js"></script>
    <div id="widget"></div>
  </body>
</html>
```

Since we're using jQuery, the first thing we want to do is make sure it's loaded. Our widget is being loaded on pages we don't control, so we don't know what's available. We also don't want to add any unnecessary extra files to load. To make sure we have what's necessary, we start by checking whether jQuery is available and, if so, which version is running:

```
widget/widget.js
(function() {
  var jQuery;
  if (window.jQuery === undefined || window.jQuery.fn.jquery !== '2.1.3') {
      var jqueryScript = document.createElement('script');
      jqueryScript.setAttribute("src",
        "//ajax.googleapis.com/ajax/libs/jquery/2.1.3/jquery.min.js");
      jqueryScript.setAttribute("type","text/javascript");
      jqueryScript.onload = loadjQuery; // All browser loading, except IE
      jqueryScript.onreadystatechange = function () { // IE loading
      if (this.readyState == 'complete' || this.readyState == 'loaded')
        { loadjQuery(); }
      };
      // Insert jQuery to the head of the page or to the documentElement
      (document.getElementsByTagName("head")[0] ||
        document.documentElement).appendChild(jqueryScript);
  } else {
    // The jQuery version on the window is the one we want to use
    jQuery = window.jQuery;
    widget(jQuery);
  }
```

First we set a jQuery variable to hold the instance of jQuery that we're using. If we find more than one version of jQuery loaded on the page, this will help us ensure that we use the version that we expect.

Next we check whether jQuery is already loaded on the page. If it isn't, window.jQuery returns undefined. If it is loaded, we check to see whether the loaded version is the one our widget requires. If it's not present, or if the loaded version isn't correct, we build a <script> tag for the necessary jQuery version and then insert it into the page. If it is present, we set the jQuery variable to the jQuery that's present on the page.

We load jQuery in noConflict() mode to keep our code from affecting any existing code on the user's page. This gives up jQuery's control of the $ variable, which is commonly used by many JavaScript libraries. Doing this will ensure that when others add our widget to their pages it won't break any JavaScript that they have already written:

```
widget/widget.js
function loadjQuery() {
  // load jQuery in noConflict mode to avoid issues with other libraries
  jQuery = window.jQuery.noConflict(true);
  widget(jQuery);
}
```

When we load jQuery, we use var to assign it to a variable that's scoped to our function. By using var for all of our variables, we ensure that they're scoped to only our function, again ensuring that we don't affect any existing code. If the jQuery version we want is already loaded, we use the existing library; otherwise, we build a <script> tag and insert it into the document. We also specify that we want to use jQuery's noConflict() method, which helps us avoid naming conflicts with other JavaScript libraries or other versions of jQuery that also use $() as a top-level function name.

Additionally, to ensure that any variables and methods we define in our widget can't conflict with existing code, we wrap all of the widget code in an anonymous function:

```
widget/widget.js
(function() {
})();
```

By wrapping all of the widget code like this, we prevent anything other than the code contained in the anonymous function from executing the methods and variables defined within it. Since they can't be accessed, they can't cause conflicts or otherwise impact the code.

Now that we have jQuery in place, we can load our widget's data using JSONP and insert it into the page. We use GitHub's API to load the latest commits to Rails:

```
widget/widget.js
function widget($) {
  // Load Data
  var account = 'rails';
  var project = 'rails';

  jQuery.ajax({
    url: 'http://api.github.com/repos/'+account+'/'+project+'/commits',
    dataType: "jsonp",
    success: function(data){
      jQuery.each(data.data, function(i,commit){
        if(commit.committer !== null){
          var commitDiv = document.createElement('div');
          commitDiv.setAttribute("class", "commit");
          commitDiv.setAttribute("id","commit_"+commit.sha);
```

```
        jQuery('#widget').append(commitDiv);
        jQuery('#commit_'+commit.sha).append("<h3>"+
          new Date(commit.commit.committer.date)+
          "</h3><p>"+commit.commit.message+"</p>"+
          "<p>By "+commit.committer.login+"</p>");
      }
    });
  }
});


var css = jQuery("<link>", {
  rel: "stylesheet",
  type: "text/css",
  href: "widget.css"
});
css.appendTo('head');
}
```

In widget(), we first load our data using JSONP and get ready to display it. We use jQuery's ajax() function to request the data, and then use the success call to create a new <div> for each commit that contains the date of the commit, its author, and its message. As we create each <div>, we append it to the #widget <div> that we had users add to their pages alongside the <script> tag. We also load a style sheet from our server and apply it to the widget.

The style sheet we load sets up some colors, as well as the height and width of the element:

widget/widget.css
```
#widget {
  display:block;
  font-size: 12px;
  height: 370px;
  overflow-y: scroll;
  width:230px;
}

.commit {
  background-color: #C2D5ED;
  margin: 0 0 10px 0;
  width:200px;
}

.commit h3 {
  background-color: #95B4D9;
  display:block;
}
```

It also sets the widget's overflow-y attribute to scroll. This lets us include large amounts of data without worrying about overwhelming the page that our widget is embedded on.

Now we have a simple chunk of code that we can give to those who want to include information from our site on their own. Whether it's information tailored to their specific account or general news about what's happening on our site, widgets make it easy to extend the reach of our content and potentially increase user interaction with our site.

Further Exploration

The widget we created loads content only once, when the page it's embedded on loads, but it doesn't offer any information specific to one visitor or that visitor's account. If we want our widget to include information to identify a visitor so that the remote server can return more relevant data, how might we do that? We could use a variable in the URL of the <script> tag to dynamically generate the JavaScript on the server. Or we could use a different JavaScript file for each user's content.

Widgets can also offer much more interaction, going beyond displaying content from JSON or XML. You could use jQuery to create a widget that visitors can click through to see multiple records, rather than having to scroll as they do in our example. You could load this data when the page loads or make a request to the remote server every time a new record is requested. Or you could have the widget automatically refresh itself every 60 seconds with the latest content.

You could also create an interactive widget that requests data from visitors to our user's site and allows them to submit information to us, whether via email or by submitting to our site.

Widgets have many possibilities. Any time your site has information that users want to share—or when you want to make it easy for users to collect data for your site—giving them a widget is a great option.

Also See

- Recipe 20, *Accessing Cross-Site Data with JSONP* on page 144
- Recipe 31, *Cleaner JavaScript with CoffeeScript* on page 221

Recipe 22

Building a Status Site with JavaScript and CouchDB

Problem

Database-driven applications can be complex. A typical database-driven application usually consists of a mix of HTML, JavaScript, SQL queries, and a server-side programming language, as well as a database server. Developers need to know enough about each of these components to make them work together. We need an alternative that's simple and lets us leverage some of the web development skills we already have, while still giving us the flexibility to get more complex as our needs change.

Ingredients

- CouchDB[17]
- A Cloudant.com account[18]
- Reupholster[19]
- jQuery
- Handlebars[20]

Solution

CouchDB is a document database and web server combined into one small but powerful package. We can build database-driven applications using only HTML and JavaScript and upload them right to the CouchDB server so it can serve them to our end users directly. We'll even use JavaScript to query our data, so we don't need to incorporate yet another language.

As it happens, we have a good excuse for playing with CouchDB. Despite our best efforts, we've been experiencing some network problems with our web servers recently. It's important to communicate this downtime to our end users to keep some of the angry support calls at bay. We'll use CouchDB to develop and host a simple site that will alert our end users to issues with our

---

17. http://couchdb.apache.org/
18. http://cloudant.com
19. https://code.google.com/p/reupholster/downloads/list
20. http://handlebarsjs.com/

network. Since we could be experiencing network trouble, we need to host the status site on a separate network, so we'll use a CouchDB hosting provider called Cloudant instead of setting up our own CouchDB server. Cloudant gives us a small, free CouchDB instance we can use for testing.

To speed up the process, we'll use Reupholster, a tool for building and deploying HTML and JavaScript applications for CouchDB. We'll use Reupholster to create our project and automatically push files up to our CouchDB database. It's nice because it watches our files for changes and then pushes them to the CouchDB server.

Before we start hacking on our status site, let's dig into CouchDB.

Understanding CouchDB

CouchDB is a *document database*. Instead of storing rows in tables, we store *documents* in *collections*. This is different from relational databases like MySQL and Oracle. Relational databases use a *relational model*, in which we divide the data into multiple entities and relate things together to reduce data duplication. We then use queries to pull this data together into something we can use. In a relational model, a person's name and address would be in separate tables. This is a fine, trusted solution, but it's not always a good fit.

In a document database, we're more concerned with storing the data as a document so we can reuse it later, and we're not all that interested in how one document relates to another. While some folks like to pit traditional relational databases and document databases against each other, you'll often find that they serve different needs or can complement each other.

For our status-update system, each status update will be a CouchDB document, and we'll create a simple interface that displays these documents. Let's start by defining our database and our status document.

Creating the Database

We'll use the web interface Cloudant provides to create a new database. When we log into our Cloudant account for the first time, we need to use the Add New Database link in the top-right corner of the Cloudant dashboard. We'll call our database statuses.

We can also use Cloudant to create a few status documents. After we select our database, we'll see a list of documents in the database. The New Document button gives us a simple interface for adding status messages.

Manipulating CouchDB with cURL

Since CouchDB uses a RESTful JSON API, we can create databases, update documents, and run queries from the command line instead of a GUI tool. We can use cURL, a command-line tool for making HTTP requests, to do just that. The cURL program is available for most operating systems and might even be installed for you if you're on OS X or Linux.

For example, instead of creating our statuses database with the GUI, we can use cURL to send a PUT request:

```
curl -X PUT http://awesomeco:****@awesomeco.cloudant.com/statuses
```

And we can push some data:

```
curl -X POST http://awesomeco:****@awesomeco.cloudant.com/statuses \
  -H "Content-Type: application/json" \
  -d '{"title":"Unplanned Downtime","description":"Someone tripped over the cord."}'
```

The -H flag sets the content type, and the -d flag lets us pass a string of data to send.

With cURL, we can set up and seed our database in much less time than we could by using a web console. We could even script it so we can do it over and over again.

Documents are just a collection of keys and values represented as JSON data. Each of our status notifications needs a title and a description, so a JSON representation looks like this:

```
{
  "title": "Unplanned Downtime",
  "description": "Someone tripped over the power cord!"
}
```

We can either add each field to the document using the wizard or click the View Source button and insert the JSON directly. We could also use cURL, as discussed in *Manipulating CouchDB with cURL,* on page 156.

Let's use the GUI to add a couple of documents so we'll have something to display. We first create a new document and set a title and description for a status message. We can leave the _id field alone:

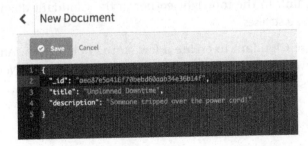

Our database now contains some data. Let's build an interface to display it.

Creating a Simple CouchApp

CouchApps are applications that we can host from CouchDB. The Reupholster application gives us some tools to create and manage these applications. With Reupholster, our work will be automatically synced to our remote database.

With Reupholster downloaded,[21] we can create our first application by double-clicking the downloaded JAR file. It opens a window that we need to fill out. First we need to choose a directory for our code on our local machine, then input the custom template https://github.com/johnsonch/reupholster-sample/zipball/master and follow it up with our specific host and username. After we have everything filled out it should look similar to the following figure:

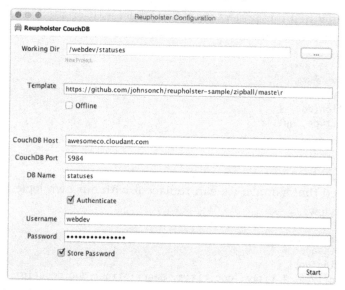

Click Start, which creates a new folder called statuses containing a new CouchApp. The app includes several subfolders, each with a different purpose:

- The docs folder allows us to create documents, and since they are in our project they'll be pushed to the server automatically, rather than via cURL or the Cloudant GUI.

- The tests folder is for placing tests of our applications. Testing CouchApps is a topic too large to adequately cover in this recipe.

- The html folder is where we'll be doing most of our work. This is where we put our HTML, CSS, and JavaScript for our CouchApp.

---

21. https://code.google.com/p/reupholster/downloads/list

Reupholster automatically pushes the statuses folder, which contains our entire app, into the statuses database, where it's stored as a *design document*. We see our app in the browser at http://awesomeco.cloudant.com/statuses/_design/app/_rewrite/, although it will simply show us a boilerplate welcome page.

Now that we know the lay of the land, let's get to work building our status application.

Creating a View to Query Data

We use views in CouchDB to optimize the results we want to return, rather than just querying our documents directly. When we access a view, CouchDB executes a JavaScript function we define to pare down the results and manipulate them into a data structure that works for us.

When we generated our project with Reupholster, it created an app.js file in the root of our project. Inside of that, toward the bottom of the file, we see a sample view:

```
couchapps/statuses/app.js
ddoc.views.byType = {
  map: function(doc) {
    emit(doc.type, null);
  },
  reduce: '_count'
}
```

We don't need that sample; we can replace it with our own logic to generate a messages view:

```
couchapps/statuses/app.js
ddoc.views.messages = {
  map: function(doc) {
    emit( doc.type, { title: doc.title, description: doc.description } )
  }
}
```

We can verify that our view works by pulling up http://awesomeco.cloudant.com/statuses/_design/statuses/_view/messages in our browser. We should see something that looks like the following code:

```
{"total_rows":2,"offset":0,"rows":[
  {"id":"02abeecc98362b3a26f85ea047bfaf5d","key":"messages","value":
    {"title":"Unscheduled Downtime",
    "description":"Someone tripped over the power cord!"}
  }
]}
```

With the view in place, let's whip up some HTML and jQuery code to display the status messages on our site.

Displaying the Messages

To build our simple interface, we can replace all of what's in the default page in html/index.html with this:

```
couchapps/statuses/html/index.html
<!doctype html>
<head>
  <meta charset="utf-8">
  <title>Sample Application</title>
  <meta name="description" content="">
  <meta name="author" content="">
  <script src='js/loader.js'></script>
</head>
<body>
    <div class="container">
      <h1>Awesome Co.</h1>
      <div id="statuses">
        <p>Waiting....</p>
      </div>
    </div>
</body>
</html>
```

We'll then update the contents of the statuses region with the data we pull from our database.

As you learned in Recipe 11, *Rendering HTML with Handlebars Templates* on page 69, we can use templates when we're going to be building up HTML we want to add to the page. Our page includes a JavaScript file called loader.js that loads up several JavaScript libraries we need to make a basic CouchApp run, including jQuery and the jQuery Couch library. We can simply add the CDN URL to the loader script:

```
couchapps/statuses/html/js/loader.js
couchapp_load([
  "http://cdnjs.cloudflare.com/ajax/libs/handlebars.js \
    /3.0.3/handlebars.min.js",
  "http://ajax.googleapis.com/ajax/libs/jquery/2.1.4 \
    /jquery.min.js",
  "https://cdnjs.cloudflare.com/ajax/libs/jquery-browser \
    /0.0.7/jquery.browser.min.js",
  "js/lib/jquery.couch.js"
]);
```

With that in place, we can now add a simple Handlebars template to our index.html page that represents the status message. The jQuery CouchDB plug-in will return a data structure that looks like this:

```
data = {
  rows: [
    {
      id: "9e227166d51569f2713728da59ff9d6b",
      key: "messages",
      value: {
        title: "Unplanned Downtime",
        description: "Someone tripped over the power cord."
      }
    }
  ]
};
```

So, when we want to pull the title and description for each status message into our template, we use Handlebars' iterator to loop over the rows array and then prefix the fields with value, since they're nested under that key in the object. Let's add this template to index.html:

couchapps/statuses/html/index.html
```html
<script type="text/template" id="statuses_template">
{{#status}}
  <div class="status">
    <h2>{{value.title}}</h2>
    <p>{{value.description}}</p>
  </div>
{{/status}}
</script>
```

With the template in place, we need to make a connection to CouchDB and fetch our status messages so we can feed this data into our Handlebars template. We define this as a function inside of a new <script> block on our index.html page:

```html
<script>
$db = $.couch.db("statuses");
var loadStatusMessages = function(){
  $db.view("app/messages",{
    success: function( statuses ) {
        var data = {status: statuses.rows};
        var template = Handlebars.compile($("#statuses_template").html());
        var html = template(data);
        $("#statuses").append(html);
    }
  });
}
</script>
```

When the data is successfully retrieved, our success callback is invoked and we display the data. You can define an error callback yourself, but the CouchDB plug-in throws up an error message for us by default, so we'll skip that part.

Finally, we need to call this function when our page loads:

```
couchapps/statuses/html/index.html
loadStatusMessages();
```

After we save our file, Reupholster again automatically pushes our changed files to the server. Then when we visit our page in the browser again, we see our status messages nicely rendered, as in the following figure:

From here, we can continue to build out this application, making changes to the code, and start up Reupholster to push changes to the server.

Further Exploration

We've built a trivial but functional web application using only HTML and JavaScript, all hosted with a CouchDB database. We could do more and use a JavaScript framework like Angular to organize our code as things get more complex.

The URL for our application is long and ugly, but CouchDB has its own URL-rewriting features, so we can shorten http://awesomeco.cloudant.com/statuses/_design/statuses/index.html to something less clunky, like http://status.awesomeco.com.

CouchDB isn't just a client-side data store, though. We could also integrate CouchDB into server-side applications. It's a good, solid document store that's easy to use and extend. It may not fit every need, but it certainly has its place, especially when we work with data that isn't necessarily relational.

Also See

- Recipe 11, *Rendering HTML with Handlebars Templates* on page 69
- Recipe 14, *Snappier Client-Side Interfaces with Knockout.js* on page 87

## CHAPTER 4

Mobile Recipes

More and more people access websites and applications from mobile devices, and we need to develop with these users in mind. Limited bandwidth, smaller screens, and new user interface interactions create interesting problems for us to solve. With these recipes, you'll learn how to save bandwidth with CSS sprites, work with multitouch interfaces, and build a mobile interface with transitions.

Recipe 23

Targeting Mobile Devices

Problem

As web developers, we're used to accounting for a lot of factors when designing a site. Different browsers and different screen resolutions have always affected how our content looks, and making a site look as good on a 13-inch laptop as on a 30-inch monitor takes work. In the past, we may have considered how our sites looked on PDAs, but with the explosion of smartphones and tablets, we need to be aware of how our sites look on screens that not only are smaller but also can change orientation.

Ingredients

- jQuery
- CSS media queries

Solution

CSS *media queries* let us load specific style sheets based on conditions related to the state of a browser. Media queries have been around since HTML4 and CSS2, but in CSS3 they've been extended, adding attributes like device-width and device-height. Knowing these dimensions, we can target different style sheets for specific widths and heights. This gives us a huge advantage for designing different looks for different screens.

In Recipe 9, *Accessible Expand and Collapse* on page 53, we created a product list that can expand and collapse. Lately, our analytics team has seen a spike in traffic from mobile users, and on an iPhone our site looks like the image. Its small fonts make it hard to navigate on a mobile device, where the primary input device—the user's finger—is much less precise than a mouse pointer.

We'll use the code from Recipe 9, *Accessible Expand and Collapse* on page 53, as a starting point. In the <head> section of our page, we add a few new tags to load CSS styles designed for mobile devices. We'll keep these styles in a file named mobile.css, which we'll put in the same directory as style.css.

targeting_mobile/index.html
```
<link rel="stylesheet" href="mobile.css"
  media="only screen and (max-device-width: 480px)">
<meta name="viewport"
  content="width=device-width;
          height=device-height;
          maximum-scale=1.4;
          initial-scale=1.0;
          user-scalable=yes" />
```

When referencing mobile.css, we use a normal stylesheet link, but we also add the media attribute. By setting the media attribute to only screen and (max-device-width: 480px), we know that it'll get used only by mobile devices with a max screen width of 480 pixels. This way desktop browsers will ignore it, and only mobile devices should use it.

We also add a viewport meta tag to control how the content is viewed in mobile browsers. By default, mobile browsers try to cram the entire page into the viewscreen as if it were a screen many times larger, which makes everything on the page incredibly small and forces the user to zoom in. With the viewport meta tag added, mobile devices automatically begin zoomed in to a comfortable resolution that's easier to read and interact with.

Now let's take a look at some of the design changes we can make to optimize this list for mobile devices. We start by setting the font-weight to be bold on the <body> tag, which makes the text easier to read:

targeting_mobile/mobile.css
```
body { font-weight: bold; }
```

We want to make sure our <ul> uses a significant portion of the width without overflowing. We also want it to hug the left side of the screen more to use all of our screen's real estate:

targeting_mobile/mobile.css
```
ul.collapsible {
  width: 430px;
  margin-left: -10px;
}
```

We declare that the <ul> tag shouldn't be wider than 430 pixels. This way the list will fit comfortably within the 480px breakpoint we declared for this stylesheet. We also add a negative margin-left to move the list closer to the left side of the screen.

Beyond simple appearance, we also have to think about how users will interact with the site on a mobile device. Since phones are manipulated by fingers, rather than a pixel-precise mouse, we want to pad out the <li> elements so users are less likely to tap the wrong link:

targeting_mobile/mobile.css
```
ul li { padding-top: 10px; }
```

Lastly, let's add some extra space to the plus and minus symbols used to show which parts of the list are collapsed; otherwise, they'll crowd the text, making the list harder to read:

targeting_mobile/mobile.css
```
ul.collapsible li:before { width: 20px; }
```

Now when we look at our site on a mobile device, such as on an iPhone, we see that the page appears better suited to its new mobile home. This will work similarly on other mobile devices.

Media queries give us control over how our site looks for multiple devices and orientations. And since mobile users tend to interact with sites differently than desktop users, we can also use media queries to tailor the user experience per device type.

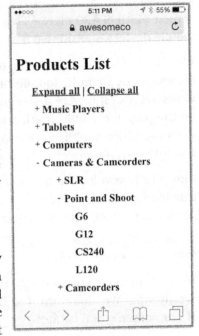

Further Exploration

You can take this recipe further and show specific navigation for mobile users. You can even accentuate things like addresses and phone numbers, which is helpful to mobile users. You can reference styles like Tait Brown's iOS Inspired jQuery Mobile Theme[1] with media queries to give a site an iOS-native feel with relative ease.

---

1.   https://github.com/taitems/iOS-Inspired-jQuery-Mobile-Theme

You can also use frameworks like Skeleton[2] that provide media query support out of the box. We discuss this further in Recipe 28, *Rapid, Responsive Design with Skeleton* on page 194.

Also See

- Recipe 38, *Using Dropbox to Collaborate and Host a Static Site* on page 278
- Recipe 27, *Using Sprites with CSS* on page 190
- Recipe 26, *Creating Interfaces with jQuery Mobile* on page 180
- Recipe 28, *Rapid, Responsive Design with Skeleton* on page 194
- *HTML5 and CSS3: Level Up With Today's Web Technologies* [Hog13]

---

2. http://www.getskeleton.com/

Recipe 24

Touch-Responsive Drop-Down Menus

Problem

Drop-down navigation is a common element in modern websites, and the pattern for implementing it is well established. On desktop browsers these menus work fine and require only some CSS magic. But as in Recipe 25, *Mobile Drag and Drop* on page 173, a user on a mobile device doesn't have a mouse and so can't trigger :hover events, at least not in a consistent way. We need to be aware of this limitation for our mobile users so we can give them the same experience as our desktop users.

Ingredients

- jQuery

Solution

Our first step is to write the markup for our top menu. We'll write the markup so that users can navigate our site without the drop-down links. We can do this by making the top-level links point to pages that include links to all of the appropriate subcategories. This way, any user can reach the subcategories even if the drop-down links are unavailable. Let's mock that up. We start with the markup for our standard HTML template:

```
mobiledropdown/index.html
<!DOCTYPE html>
<html lang="en-US">
  <head>
    <meta charset="utf-8">
    <title>Dropdown navigation</title>
    <link rel="stylesheet" href="mobiledropdown.css">
    <meta name="viewport"
          content="width=device-width, initial-scale=1">
  </head>
  <body>
    <header>
      <h1>Products</h1>
    </header>
    <div class="clear">
      <p>This is where the content for our site goes.</p>
```

```
    </div>
  </body>
</html>
```

Then, inside the <header> section, we add our navigation by using the <nav> tag and unordered lists:

mobiledropdown/index.html

```
<nav class="dropdown">
  <ul>
    <li>
      <a href="categories/1">Electronics</a>
      <ul>
        <li><a href="categories/4">Music Players</a></li>
        <li><a href="categories/5">Tablets</a></li>
        <li><a href="categories/6">Computers</a></li>
        <li><a href="categories/7">Cameras &amp; Camcorders</a></li>
      </ul>
    </li>
    <li>
      <a href="categories/2">Appliances</a>
      <ul>
        <li><a href="categories/8">Washers</a></li>
        <li><a href="categories/9">Dryers</a></li>
        <li><a href="categories/10">Dish Washers</a></li>
      </ul>
    </li>
    <li>
      <a href="categories/3">Entertainment</a>
      <ul>
        <li><a href="categories/11">DVDs</a></li>
        <li><a href="categories/12">Music</a></li>
      </ul>
    </li>
  </ul>
</nav>
```

If you're an experienced web developer, you've seen this popular pattern before: the top-level list items form the navigation bar itself, and the inner lists make up the submenus that drop down.

To pull it together, we use CSS to style the menu:

mobiledropdown/mobiledropdown.css

```
nav.dropdown { position: relative; }

nav.dropdown ul {
  list-style: none;
  padding-left: 0;
}
```

```
nav.dropdown ul li {
  float: left;
  position: relative;
}

nav.dropdown ul li a {
  background: #666;
  color: #FFF;
  display: block;
  padding: 4px 10px;
}

nav.dropdown ul li ul { display: none; }

nav.dropdown ul li:hover ul,
nav.dropdown ul li.hover ul {
  display: block;
  position: absolute;
}

nav.dropdown ul li ul li a {
  background: #444;
  color: #FFF;
  display: block;
  width: 150px;
}

nav.dropdown ul li:hover ul li a:hover {
  background: #888;
  color: #FFF;
  width: 150px;
}

.clear { clear: both; }
```

Our CSS is based on the widely used Son of Suckerfish menu.[3] We hide all the submenus and use :hover to show them. The following figure shows the base menu on the left, and the effect of hovering over the last menu item on the right.

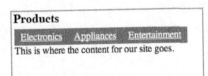 

---

3.   http://www.htmldog.com/articles/suckerfish/dropdowns/

Now, we could say we've handled *mobile* navigation, since users can navigate our site, but the usability isn't where it needs to be yet. Let's fix that.

On the desktop our drop-down lists are controlled by the CSS :hover event. But without a mouse there's no way to hover over a link. On iOS devices, tapping a :hover link activates the hover effect and a second tap follows the link, so this is a good alternative. Unfortunately, in other mobile browsers, tapping a :hover link also activates the hover command—but unless the user slides the finger away from the link before lifting up, the link will be followed. This defeats the purpose of having a drop-down menu, since it only flashes on the screen for a second before the user is taken to another page.

To get around this inconsistent behavior, we'll make the iOS behavior the default for all browsers. We can do this by watching all of the clicks on the page. When a click on the navigation header is detected, we'll prevent the default operation unless the same link is clicked twice in a row. This means we'll need to track a few separate click events: any click on the page, clicks on the top-level categories, and clicks on the subcategories.

We'll place our JavaScript code in the mobiledropdown.js file. We load that file, along with the jQuery library, on our index.html page right above the closing <body> tag:

mobiledropdown/index.html
```
<script
  src="http://ajax.googleapis.com/ajax/libs/jquery/2.1.3/jquery.min.js">
</script>
<script src="mobiledropdown.js"></script>
```

Then, in mobiledropdown.js, we add a global variable that tracks the last element clicked anywhere on the page. Without this variable, we wouldn't know whether the user has tapped on a category or tapped elsewhere on the screen to hide a drop-down list, or even follow a non–drop-down link:

mobiledropdown/mobiledropdown.js
```
var lastTouchedElement;
$('html').on('click', function(event) {
  lastTouchedElement = event.target;
});
```

Next, we want to know when a category-header link was tapped and if it's the same category that was tapped last. On the first tap we'll prevent the default action from occurring; namely, we don't want the user to follow the link just yet. If the user clicks the same link again, *then* the user is allowed to follow the link. The only exception is iOS devices. Since they already work correctly, there's no need to prevent the default action.

```
function doNotTrackClicks() {
  return navigator.userAgent.match(/iPhone|iPad/i);
}

$('nav.dropdown > ul').on('click', '> li', function(event) {
  if (!(doNotTrackClicks() || lastTouchedElement == event.target)) {
    event.preventDefault();
  }
  lastTouchedElement = event.target;
});
```

As long as the link being clicked is different from the last element clicked, and the client isn't an iOS device, we prevent the browser from following the link. We also update lastTouchedElement to the clicked link. Normally this would be handled by the event handler attached to the <html> element, but we need to handle one more click event.

If we were to test the site right now, we'd see that the subcategories have the same behavior as the categories. We have to click on a subcategory twice to follow the link. This is because the subcategory click events bubble up to the category click events and inherit the category link's behavior. To prevent this from happening, we need to call stopPropagation() when a subcategory is clicked. (We talked about event propagation in *Why Not Return False?*, on page 58.)

mobiledropdown/mobiledropdown.js
```
$('nav.dropdown').on('click', 'li', function(event) {
  event.stopPropagation();
});
```

With this code in place, our mobile users now have a consistent experience across platforms. And as long as the individual category pages list links to the subcategories, the site will continue to be accessible for users on devices other than smartphones.

Further Exploration

This recipe's approach also affects desktop browsers, which means that category links have to be double-clicked to be activated. Along with bypassing this code when an iPhone is detected, we could also skip it when the site is not being accessed by a mobile browser. The code for doing this can be found at http://detectmobilebrowsers.com and could easily be applied to our site via jQuery.

Also See

- Recipe 9, *Accessible Expand and Collapse* on page 53

Recipe 25

Mobile Drag and Drop

Problem

We have a pop-up window on our website that we use to display product details. This pop-up is draggable so users can move the detail window to the side of the screen, allowing them to browse the site while the pop-up is visible. Unfortunately, we've received some feedback from users with iPads that they can't move the pop-up windows.

Drag-and-drop functionality has been an easy feature to add to websites for a while now. Various plug-ins are available that can add it with little effort, and it's not even that difficult to write from scratch. The problem with these plug-ins is that most of them don't work on mobile devices, because they respond only to events triggered by the user's mouse. We need to make our interface work for our mobile users by using some new, mobile-specific events.

Ingredients

- jQuery
- QEDServer (for our test server)[4]

Solution

Browsers on mobile devices like the iPad and other touch interfaces have a new set of events they listen for instead of the normal mousedown and mouseup events. Two of these new events, touchstart and touchend, are perfect substitutes.

Layout and Style

We'll use JavaScript to handle these events, but first we need to create our markup. The page is an unordered list of products and a hidden <div> for the draggable window. We put this file in QED's public directory as drag.html:

```
dragndrop/index.html
<header>
  <h1>Products list</h1>
</header>
<div id='content'>
```

---

4. A version for this book is available at http://webdevelopmentrecipes.com/.

```html
<ul>
  <li><a href="product1.html" class="popup">
    AirPort Express Base Station
  </a></li>
  <li><a href="product1.html" class="popup">
    DVI to VGA Adapter
  </a></li>
</ul>
</div>
<div class="popup_window draggable" style="display: none;">
  <div class="header handle">
    <div class="header_text">Product description</div>
    <div class="close">X</div>
    <div class="clear"></div>
  </div>
  <div class="body"></div>
</div>
```

We also need to make sure that the pop-up window is absolutely positioned. Here are some basic styles that we'll need:

```
dragndrop/style.css
.clear {
  clear: both;
  display: block;
  overflow: hidden;
  visibility: hidden;
  height: 0;
  width: 0;
}
.popup_window {
  border: 1px solid #000;
  width: 500px;
  height: 300px;
  box-shadow: 1px 1px 2px #555;
  position: absolute;
  top: 50px;
  left: 50px;
  background: #EEE;
  transition: box-shadow 0.5s ease;
}

ul {
  list-style: none;
  padding-left: 0;
}

.popup_window.dragging {
  box-shadow: 4px 4px 4px #555;
}
.popup_window .header {
```

```
    background: green;
    width: 100%;
    display: block;
}

.draggable .handle { cursor: move; }

.popup_window .header .header_text {
    margin: 5px;
    display: inline;
    color: #FFF;
}

.popup_window .header .close {
    float: right;
    padding: 2px 5px;
    border: 1px solid #999;
    background: red;
    color: #FFF;
    cursor: pointer;
    margin: 0;
}
.popup_window .header:after { clear: both; }
```

Additionally, we need to create an individual product page that the links will point to. Normally this page would be built on the server, but for demonstration purposes we create a single page for all of the product links. This page, which we name product1.html, also goes in QED's public directory:

```
dragndrop/product1.html
<h3>Product Name</h3>
<div class='product_details'>
  <missing>Need a real product page</missing>
  <p>This is a product description. Below is a list of features:</p>
  <ul>
    <li>Durable</li>
    <li>Fireproof</li>
    <li>Impenetrable</li>
    <li>Fuzzy</li>
  </ul>
</div>
```

Basic Drag and Drop

So far our links work fine, but we want them to load the pages that they reference into the pop-up window, rather than redirecting the browser. We add the popup classes to our product links so we know which links should be loaded into the pop-up when clicked:

dragndrop/dragndrop.js

```
$('.popup').on('click', updatePopup);

function updatePopup(event) {
  $.get($(event.target).attr('href'), [], updatePopupContent);
  return false;
}

function updatePopupContent(data) {
  var popupWindow = $('div.popup_window');
  popupWindow.find('.body').html($(data));
  popupWindow.fadeIn();
}

$('.popup_window .close').on('click', hidePopup);
function hidePopup() {
  $(this).parents('.popup_window').fadeOut();
  return false;
}
```

These functions give us a way to hide and show the pop-up window. Everything looks great; we can load it dynamically with new data and still see most of the page. The problem is that it's in the way, as shown in the following figure:

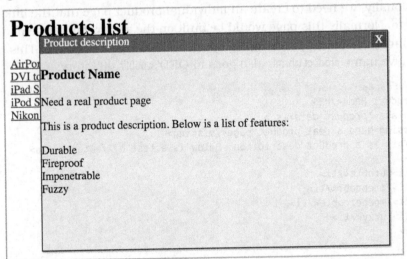

We currently have no way of moving this pop-up, so let's fix that by making it draggable. We'll start by making it work in desktop browsers and then apply the same logic to the touch events.

dragndrop/dragndrop.js

```
$('.draggable .handle').on('mousedown', dragPopup);
function dragPopup(event) {
  event.preventDefault();
```

```
  var handle = $(event.target);
  var draggableWindow = $(handle.parents('.draggable')[0]);
  draggableWindow.addClass('dragging');
  var cursor = event;
  var cursorOffset = {
    pageX: cursor.pageX - parseInt(draggableWindow.css('left')),
    pageY: cursor.pageY - parseInt(draggableWindow.css('top'))
  };
    $(document).mousemove(function(moveEvent) {
      observeMove(moveEvent, cursorOffset,
        moveEvent, draggableWindow);
    });
    $(document).mouseup(function(up_event) {
      unbindMovePopup(up_event, draggableWindow);
    });
}
function observeMove(event, cursorOffset, cursorPosition, draggableWindow) {
  event.preventDefault();
  var left = cursorPosition.pageX - cursorOffset.pageX;
  var top  = cursorPosition.pageY - cursorOffset.pageY;
  draggableWindow.css('left', left).css('top', top);
}
function unbindMovePopup(event, draggableWindow) {
    $(document).unbind('mousemove');
  draggableWindow.removeClass('dragging');
}
```

We start by watching for any <div> elements with a handle class in a draggable element. When the mouse is clicked and held, we call dragPopup(). This adds another observer for the mousemove event. Every time the mouse is moved, we update the position of the draggable_window. The event gives us the position of the mouse, but we need to set the position of the draggable <div>'s upper-left corner. To calculate this, we capture the offset between the initial position of the window and the position of the first click. That way, we can subtract those extra pixels from the mouse's position when moving the window in the observeMove() function.

Then, so we can finish the move event, we add an event handler for the mouseup event. When this event is triggered, we clean up the changes that we made since the mousedown event. This means we stop observing the mousemove event and remove an extra style class we added to the draggable_window.

Adding Mobile Functionality

Thankfully, with the hard part out of the way, it is easy to adapt this approach for mobile devices. Other than the use of mouse-related events, the dragPopup() function does most of what we want. So, it should be a matter of mimicking that mouse-related code and making it act on the touch events.

First we need a way to check that the touch events are supported. If we were to call a touch-related function on a desktop, our code would break. To prevent that, we wrap our touch code in isTouchSupported() if statements:

dragndrop/dragndrop.js
```
function isTouchSupported() {
  return 'ontouchmove' in document.documentElement;
}
```

Then we add an event handler for the touchstart event alongside our handler for the mousedown event. These both trigger the dragPopup() function. Then we trigger the dragPopup function from the touchstart event:

dragndrop/dragndrop.js
```
$('.draggable .handle').on('mousedown', dragPopup);
if (isTouchSupported()) {
  $('.draggable .handle').on('touchstart', dragPopup);
}
```

Since a user can touch multiple spots, the touch event returns an array of touches. But we're focused on only one-finger movements for now, so we use the first touch in the array to determine the position of the user's finger. We then pass in this location as the cursorPosition:

dragndrop/dragndrop.js
```
function dragPopup(event) {
  event.preventDefault();
  var handle = $(event.target);
  var draggableWindow = $(handle.parents('.draggable')[0]);
  draggableWindow.addClass('dragging');
  var cursor = event;
  if (isTouchSupported()) {
    cursor = event.originalEvent.touches[0];
  }
  var cursorOffset = {
    pageX: cursor.pageX - parseInt(draggableWindow.css('left')),
    pageY: cursor.pageY - parseInt(draggableWindow.css('top'))
  };

  if (isTouchSupported()) {
    $(document).bind('touchmove', function(moveEvent) {
      var currentPosition = moveEvent.originalEvent.touches[0];
      observeMove(moveEvent, cursorOffset,
        currentPosition, draggableWindow);
    });
    $(document).bind('touchend', function(upEvent) {
      unbindMovePopup(upEvent, draggableWindow);
    });
  } else {
    $(document).mousemove(function(moveEvent) {
```

```
      observeMove(moveEvent, cursorOffset,
        moveEvent, draggableWindow);
    });
    $(document).mouseup(function(up_event) {
      unbindMovePopup(up_event, draggableWindow);
    });
  }
}
function unbindMovePopup(event, draggableWindow) {
  if (isTouchSupported()) {
    $(document).unbind('touchmove');
  } else {
    $(document).unbind('mousemove');
  }
  draggableWindow.removeClass('dragging');
}
```

Unfortunately, jQuery doesn't fully support observing touch events using the on() function, so we can't access the touches array from the jQuery event. Instead, we have to get the position of the user's finger from the original event. Now we can also mimic the mousemove behavior with the touchmove event by calling observeMove(), which remains the same. The final difference is that on the touchend event, we unbind the touchmove event, just as we did with the mouseup and mousemove events, respectively.

Further Exploration

Now that we've seen how a single-touch event can be handled, it should be easy to figure out how to start handling multifinger gesture commands. Since the touch events return an array of touch positions, we can determine when a user has multiple fingers on the screen and where each finger is. This means we can know when users are pinching the screen, swiping side to side, or using a gesture that we invent. For more about what we can do with this API, check out HTML5 Rocks.[5]

Also See

• Recipe 24, *Touch-Responsive Drop-Down Menus* on page 168

---

5. http://www.html5rocks.com/en/mobile/touch.html

Recipe 26

Creating Interfaces with jQuery Mobile

Problem

Developing native applications for mobile devices isn't a simple task, and the programming knowledge required, and in some cases license fees, can create a barrier to entry. Android and iOS application development is typically done with Java and Swift, respectively. These are languages that many web developers don't have experience using.

Our catalog needs a mobile-friendly version. Native applications for the iOS and Android platforms would be ideal, but we don't have the time, resources, or knowledge to build them.

Ingredients

- jQuery
- jQuery Mobile[6]
- QEDServer (for our test server)[7]

Solution

To solve this problem, we can bring together the benefits of both web applications and native applications. With jQuery Mobile, we can use HTML5, JavaScript, and CSS3 to develop web applications that behave similarly to native applications for mobile platforms. jQuery Mobile makes it easy to develop native-feeling applications using the tools we're already familiar with.

We'll explore jQuery Mobile by creating a site to browse through our company's catalog. Our application will allow the user to view and search our merchandise. When we're done, we'll have built a mobile interface that looks like the figure on page 181.

Creating an application with jQuery Mobile relies on some semantic HTML and the data attributes available in HTML5. Using these attributes, we can build most of the application without writing any extra JavaScript.

---

6. http://jquerymobile.com/
7. A version for this book is available at http://webdevelopmentrecipes.com/.

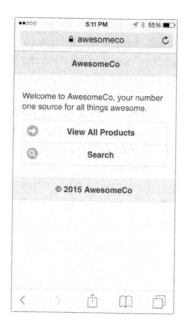

Building the Document

Let's set up an HTML file to use jQuery Mobile. Our application will run on QEDServer. In the `public` folder of the server, create a file called index.html and add this boilerplate HTML to get started:

jquerymobile/index.html

```
<!DOCTYPE html>
<html lang="en">
  <head>
    <meta charset="utf-8">
    <meta name="viewport" content="width=device-width, initial-scale=1">
    <title>Incredible Products from AwesomeCo</title>
    <link rel="stylesheet"
      href="http://code.jquery.com/mobile/1.4.5/jquery.mobile-1.4.5.min.css">
  </head>

  <body>
    <script
      src="http://ajax.googleapis.com/ajax/libs/jquery/1.11.1/jquery.min.js">
    </script>
    <script
      src="http://code.jquery.com/mobile/1.4.5/jquery.mobile-1.4.5.min.js">
    </script>
    <script src="products.js">
    </script>
  </body>
</html>
```

The boilerplate includes four files: the jQuery Mobile CSS, the jQuery library, the jQuery Mobile script itself, and a file for us to add our own JavaScript. Now we're ready to start adding pages and content to the application.

Creating Pages

A jQuery Mobile application consists of a set of pages. These pages can link to one another, but we can show only one page on the screen at a time, even though they all exist on the same HTML page. To build a page in jQuery Mobile, we use a <div> that has a data-role attribute set to page. When the framework runs, it loads whichever page comes first in the body of our HTML. Following that pattern. we'll start by creating our home screen. Let's add the following code below our opening <body> tag and above the <script> tags:

```
jquerymobile/index.html
<div data-role="page" id="home">
  <div data-role="header">
    <h1>AwesomeCo</h1>
  </div>
  <div data-role="main" class="ui-content">
  </div>
  <div data-role="footer">
    <h4>&copy; AwesomeCo</h4>
  </div>
</div>
```

Each page can have three sections: a header, content, and a footer. The header holds information about the current page in an <h1> tag. The header also can hold buttons for navigation within the application, as we'll see later. The content region can hold any number of paragraphs, links, lists, forms, and any other markup you would use on a normal web page. The footer is an optional section that can hold a copyright or any other information we want on the bottom of every page.

Now that our landing page is ready, let's create a few items to populate the content. We need some buttons to get to the other pages in our application, so let's place the following code inside our main <div>:

```
jquerymobile/index.html
<div data-role="main" class="ui-content">
  <p>Welcome to AwesomeCo, your number one source
    for all things awesome.</p>

  <div data-role="controlgroup">
    <a href="#products" class="ui-btn">View All Products</a>
    <a href="#search" class="ui-btn">Search</a>
  </div>
</div>
```

First we create a paragraph giving some information about the application. Then we make a <div> with a role of controlgroup. This role removes the margin between the links so they appear as one set, as you can see in the next figure. We also give the anchors a class of ui-btn so that they're styled accordingly. The two anchors link to other pages by setting the ID of the target page in the href attribute.

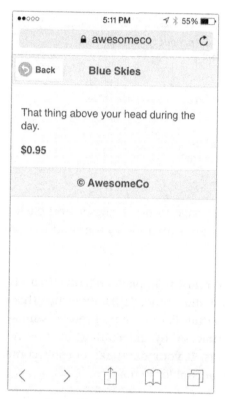

These buttons look great, but they could be enhanced to give some more feedback to the user. To add an icon to a button, we add a ui-icon-* class. The available icons can be found in the jQuery Mobile documentation,[8] but for our page we use the right-arrow icon and the search icon:

jquerymobile/index_icons.html

```
<div data-role="controlgroup">
  <a href="#products" class="ui-btn ui-icon-arrow-r ui-btn-icon-left">
    View All Products</a>
  <a href="#search" class="ui-btn ui-icon-search ui-btn-icon-left">
    Search</a>
</div>
```

---

8. http://api.jquerymobile.com/icons/

With these buttons, our home page navigation is complete. We've created a button group that will bring us to the various parts of our application and added customization to give some more feedback to the user.

The buttons we've added look good, but they don't go anywhere yet. We need to add another page to the markup so that we can be sure the links actually go somewhere:

```
jquerymobile/index.html
<div data-role="page" id="products">
  <div data-role="header">
    <h1>Products</h1>
  </div>
  <div data-role="main" class="ui-content">
  </div>

  <div data-role="footer">
    <h4>&copy; AwesomeCo</h4>
  </div>
</div>
```

Now when we load the page in our browser and click the product link, we should see the application transition to the products page.

Viewing Products

With the products-list markup in place, it's time to add the actual content so users can see what we offer. Since QEDServer has this data for us, we'll use jQuery to load the product list via Ajax. First let's make sure we have some products in the database by navigating to the nonmobile version at http://localhost:8080/products. If your database doesn't contain any records, feel free to create a few placeholder items.

Since we've already created the structure for the products page, let's create an empty <ul> in our content section to hold our list of products:

```
jquerymobile/index.html
  <div data-role="main" class="ui-content">
➤   <ul id="products-list" data-role="listview"></ul>
  </div>
```

The <ul> has a role of listview so that jQuery Mobile knows how to style it. We also set an ID so we can easily reference it with jQuery when we want to update the list. If we reload the application and navigate to the products page, it's pretty empty. To load some products, we use the custom events in jQuery Mobile to load the content dynamically when the user requests the page:

Testing jQuery Mobile

When it comes to testing jQuery Mobile, the browser on a computer mostly works, but the experience is different enough that another testing platform is warranted. But to see the application more realistically, we need a browser emulator. The emulator acts like a normal browser but has the same dimensions as a mobile device. Google Chrome has a great emulator for many devices, including iOS and Android.

To activate Chrome's mobile emulation mode, right-click anywhere on the page and choose Inspect Element. This opens the debug console. Then we can click the Toggle device mode button, which looks like a phone, to see options for the different devices we want to emulate and even what data speed we want to simulate, as shown in the following image:

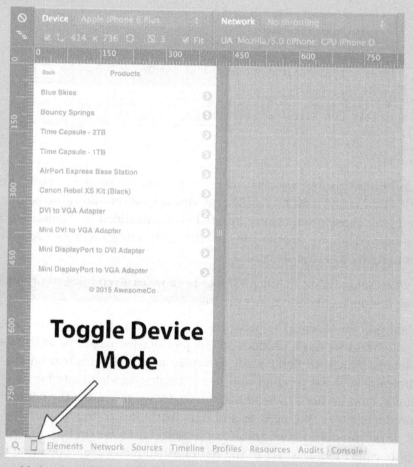

We could also use techniques explored in Recipe 33, *Testing Websites on Real Devices* on page 242, to verify our work on any physical devices we have handy.

jquerymobile/products.js

```
(function($) {
  var $products_page = $('#products'),
      $products_list = $('#products-list'),
      $product_page  = $('#product');

  $products_page.bind('pagebeforeshow', function() {
    $.getJSON('/products.json', function(products) {
      var $product_list_item;
      $products_list.html('');

      $.each(products, function(i, product) {
        $product_list_item = $('<li>').append(
          $('<a>')
            .attr('href', '#product')
            .text(product.name)
            .data('transition', 'slide')
        );
        $products_list.append($product_list_item);
      });

      $products_list.listview('refresh');
    });
  });
})(jQuery);
```

We bind to the page's pagebeforeshow event to load the product list before the page is shown. The getJSON() request queries the server and returns an array of products. Those products are iterated over and added to the list. Since we create new HTML, we refresh the listview, which tells jQuery Mobile to apply styles to newly inserted elements.

Now when we navigate to our products page we're given a list of products to browse that looks like the figure on page 187.

Our last goal for viewing the products is to create a show page for a specific product. When we tap a product on the product-list page, we want to show the details. Since we don't want to create a page for each product, we'll dynamically load the product and use a single-page template for all of our products. First we need to head back to where we generated the contents for the products listview. We need to add data attributes to the anchors to keep track of the product ID we want to navigate to, so we add a custom data attribute called data-product-id to the list of attributes we're appending to the list items:

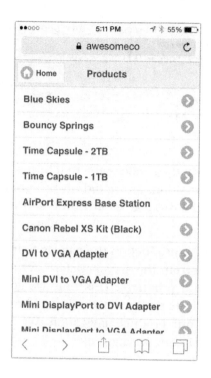

jquerymobile/products.js
```
$.each(products, function(i, product) {
  $product_list_item = $('<li>').append(
    $('<a>')
      .attr('href', '#product')
      .text(product.name)
      .data('transition', 'slide')
      .data('product-id', product.id)
  );
  $products_list.append($product_list_item);
});
```

Now that we're tracking the product ID for each of the links, we can create a page to show the product. Let's create the header, footer, and content <div>s for this page, as we did before with the list page:

jquerymobile/index_icons.html
```
<div data-role="page" id="product">
  <div data-role="header" id="product-header">
    <a href="#products" class="ui-btn ui-icon-back ui-btn-icon-left"
       data-role="back" data-direction="reverse"
       data-transition="slide">Back</a>
    <h1>Product</h1>
  </div>
```

```
<div data-role="main" class="ui-content" id="product-content">
  <p class="description"></p>
  <span class="price"><strong></strong></span>
</div>

<div data-role="footer">
  <h4>&copy; AwesomeCo</h4>
</div>
</div>
```

We create a back button in the header <div> that brings us back to the product list. We use the slide transition, as we did on the product-list page, but we add a reverse value for the data-direction attribute so the transition goes from right to left.

The last step to showing a product on the page is to intercept the navigation event and load the data from the server. Before, we asked the server to get information about several products. This time we get information about a single product and build the product view using the response. Let's write the JavaScript to complete our product navigation. We add the following code right above the last line in our products.js file:

jquerymobile/products.js
```
$products_list.on('tap', 'a', function(e) {
  requestProduct($(this).data('product-id'));
});

function requestProduct(product_id) {
  $.getJSON('/products/' + product_id + '.json', showProduct);
}

function showProduct(product) {
  $('#product-header h1').text(product.name);
  $('#product-content p.description').text(product.description);
  $('#product-content span.price strong').text('$' + product.price);
}
```

We start off by binding to the tap event, which is a custom event in jQuery Mobile. Since the raw tap events on mobile browsers differ so greatly, the jQuery Mobile tap event removes the inconsistencies and offers a single interface for managing touch events. Next we store a reference to the product ID so that we can make a call with getJSON(). On the success event we change the text of the product page to use the data we received.

Now we have a smooth interface that allows us to view products and their details. A single product page now looks like the image.

Further Exploration

We've only touched on a few of the features available through jQuery Mobile. Check out the API[9] for more details on other options this framework makes available to developers.

When we started this chapter, we added a search link on the home page that doesn't actually do anything. Following the patterns we've established, and by referencing the API, it would be relatively easy to implement this functionality.

Also See

- Recipe 20, *Accessing Cross-Site Data with JSONP* on page 144
- Recipe 23, *Targeting Mobile Devices* on page 164
- Recipe 24, *Touch-Responsive Drop-Down Menus* on page 168

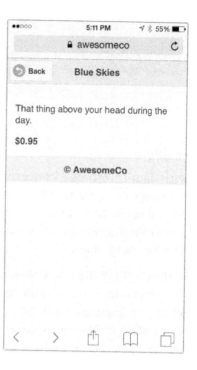

---

9. http://api.jquerymobile.com/

Recipe 27

Using Sprites with CSS

Problem

With data throttling a concern for many mobile users, the cost of loading lots of images on a phone or other mobile device can quickly add up in terms of time, money, and data. We want to minimize the impact we have on wireless carrier limitations so our users have a good mobile experience without eating up their data plans.

In Recipe 23, *Targeting Mobile Devices* on page 164, we built a mobile interface for the product list from Recipe 9, *Accessible Expand and Collapse* on page 53. We've been asked to add some color and graphics to the site. However, we want to make sure that we don't take up too much bandwidth with our new images, both so we don't use up our end users' limited data and to make sure the pages load quickly.

Ingredients

- CSS

Solution

CSS sprites let us reduce the number of files the user downloads by combining multiple icons into one and then using CSS properties to display only the portion of the image that we want. Just one file is downloaded, saving time and memory in HTTP requests, and we can use this image for multiple situations.

Our graphics department has created a sprite image like for us to use on the mobile site:

The sprite contains + and - images to replace the current text-based way of indicating if a list node is either expanded or collapsed. You can get this graphic by downloading the source code for the example projects from the book's website.[10]

---

10. http://webdevelopmentrecipes.com

> \\/ Joe asks:
>
> ᠊ᡭ **What Is a Sprite?**
>
> A sprite is a single image from a file that contains multiple images within it. We can show what appears to be a single image by selectively showing a part of the whole file. To visualize what we're doing in this recipe, imagine cutting a small hole in a piece of paper and laying it on top of a picture so only part of it shows at a time. To show part of the image that's farther down the picture, rather than move the piece of paper down, we keep it in place and move the picture up.

We need to create an images folder inside of the project and place expand_collapse_sprite.png inside of it. We'll do all of our work in mobile.css, which we originally created in Recipe 23, *Targeting Mobile Devices* on page 164.

In our style.css file from Recipe 9, *Accessible Expand and Collapse* on page 53, we have two CSS rules. These rules dictate what content is shown:

css_sprites/style.css
```
ul.collapsible li.expanded:before { content: '-'; }

ul.collapsible li.collapsed:before { content: '+'; }
```

We'll override the .expanded and .collapsed styles in mobile.css so the browser uses the graphics instead of the text we defined earlier. To use the sprites, we set the background CSS attribute along with some position adjustments to get the graphics aligned correctly so that only part of the total image is displayed:

css_sprites/mobile.css
```
ul.collapsible li.expanded:before {
  background: url(images/expand_collapse_sprite.png) 0 -5px;
  content: '';
  height: 20px;
  width: 30px;
}
ul.collapsible li.collapsed:before {
  background: url(images/expand_collapse_sprite.png) 0 -30px;
  content: '';
  height: 25px;
  width: 30px;
}
```

The first line in both of our CSS rules sets the content to a blank string. Without this, the CSS wouldn't allow us to specify the width or height of the pseudo :before block. When we specify the height and width, we need to make sure that we're matching these dimensions to the size of our individual sprites.

The background attribute also sets the x and y offsets so we can focus on a specific sprite.

Our current graphic has some extra whitespace at the top, so we can start our y position at -5 pixels. The graphic design team got the left edge pretty tight, so we will start that at 0. Our second image is below the first, so we slide down to -30 pixels so that the minus sign shows through, rather than the plus sign. We can see the fruits of our labor in the figure.

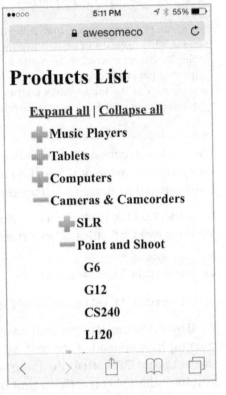

Further Exploration

Although CSS sprites let us streamline the process of downloading assets by consolidating multiple images into a single file, the downside is that we have to maintain that file. Any time we want to add or change an image, we must change the whole file and possibly all of the offsets within the CSS. Without a dedicated design team at your disposal, this can be cumbersome. Thankfully, tools such as node-sprite-generator[11] not only generate sprite images but also even provide the CSS file.

Also See

- Recipe 38, *Using Dropbox to Collaborate and Host a Static Site* on page 278
- Recipe 26, *Creating Interfaces with jQuery Mobile* on page 180
- Recipe 28, *Rapid, Responsive Design with Skeleton* on page 194
- *HTML5 and CSS3: Level Up With Today's Web Technologies [Hog13]*

---

11. https://github.com/selaux/node-sprite-generator

## CHAPTER 5

Workflow Recipes

The tools and processes we use ultimately make or break our productivity. As developers, we're used to looking at better ways to make our clients happy, but we should also look at ways to improve our own workflow. This collection of recipes explores different workflows for working with layouts, content, CSS, and JavaScript, as well as our code.

Recipe 28

Rapid, Responsive Design with Skeleton

Problem

We're often called on by clients or managers to provide a wireframe or a mock-up of a design (or multiple designs) before we do the actual implementation of a site. This process helps communicate design and layout ideas to our end users, especially when we're asked to design interfaces for mobile phones and tablets as well as desktop computers.

We have lots of options, from paper and pencil to full-blown mock-up tools like OmniGraffle, Visio, or Balsamiq Mockups, but we prefer to do these mock-ups in regular HTML and CSS. This way, we can code some interactivity, and we can use the code we write in our actual implementation.

Ingredients

- Skeleton[1]

Solution

By using one of the many available HTML and CSS frameworks, we can design layouts much more quickly than we could before, while avoiding some of the more troubling issues with CSS layout. And we can plan for different screen sizes, like mobile phones and tablets, from the beginning.

CSS grid frameworks provide a quick and simple way to lay out elements on a page without having to worry about floats, clears, and the like. We can choose among many great frameworks. For this recipe we'll use Skeleton because it's simple and easily supports multiple screen sizes.

We've been asked to provide a mock-up for a property-listing page. We need to show a few pictures of the property, its price, and some details from the property's Multiple Listing Service (MLS) listing. We need to make sure things are readable on a regular laptop and on the iPhone, so realtors can quickly reference the property information. This mock-up will eventually be turned into a template for an actual web application, so we'll use some hard-coded

---

1. http://getskeleton.com

text for our examples, and we'll use image placeholders for the property images. Before we start building the mock-up, let's explore what Skeleton is and how it works.

Skeleton's Structure

Skeleton, like other grid-based frameworks, divides a single centered container into twelve equal columns, creating a grid. We then use these columns to define the widths of our page regions. A header that stretches across all of these columns would be defined as twelve columns wide, while a sidebar that's only a third of the page would be defined as four columns wide. The main column would then be eight columns wide. The following illustration shows how a simple two-column page would work:

Using simple tried-and-true CSS techniques, Skeleton handles the task of floating and aligning elements for us and sets default line heights and font sizes so things flow across columns nicely. On top of all that, Skeleton makes it easy to make a layout work well on all screen sizes by taking advantage of CSS media queries, which we discuss in Recipe 23, *Targeting Mobile Devices* on page 164.

Skeleton provides more than some CSS to make layout easier. It provides us with a framework for our files. When we download and unpack the Skeleton files, we get a sample index.html file, a folder for our style sheets, and a sample Favorites icon.

Now that we know what Skeleton can do for us, let's get started with our mock-up.

Defining Our Layout

Our page will have a header with the property's address, a column with information about the property, and a column with some photographs. When we're done, we'll have a page that looks like the following figure:

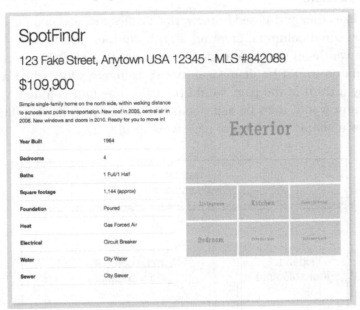

We'll use Skeleton version 2 for this recipe, which you can find in the book's source code. The Skeleton download gives us a default index.html file that we use as our base for our template. Let's open that file and delete everything between the opening and closing <div> with the container class. But we keep the container <div> itself, since Skeleton automatically sets that to a width of 960 pixels and centers it on the page.

Let's start by defining the header of the page, which will contain our site's title and the address of the property. To do this we need to define a new row and then divide that row into columns. So, we use a <div> tag to define the row, and we use the HTML5 <header> tag for the actual header:

skeleton/index.html
```
<div class="row">
  <header class="twelve columns">
    <h1>SpotFindr</h1>
    <h3>123 Fake Street, Anytown USA 12345 - MLS #842089</h3>
  </header>
</div>
```

Since we want a single column that stretches the width of the container, we use the twelve columns class for the <header>.

Next, we define the next section of the page, which will contain the left and right columns. Again, we define this region as a new row:

skeleton/index.html
```
<div class="row">
</div>
```

Inside this new region, we define the left column of the page, which holds the price and a brief property description. We use a <section> tag to contain this region. We want this one to stretch halfway across the page, so we define it as six columns wide:

skeleton/index.html
```
<div class="row">
  <section id="datasheet" class="six columns">
    <h2 class="price">$109,900</h2>
    <p>
      Simple single-family home on the north side, within walking
      distance to schools and public transportation. New roof in 2005,
      central air in 2006. New windows and doors in 2010. Ready for you to
      move in!
    </p>
  </section>
```

Now we define the right column by creating another region immediately after the previous <section> tag:

skeleton/index.html
```
<section class="photos six columns">
</section>
```

Skeleton automatically left-aligns regions until the total column count is twelve, when it then drops to the next line.

Since we don't have images yet, we'll use placeholder images that we'll generate using Placehold.it.[2] Using that simple API, we can have images generated for our mock-up on the fly, by pointing to the Placehold.it site. For example, we can make this request to insert an image that's 460 pixels wide by 200 pixels tall with the text Bedroom:

```
<img src="http://placehold.it/460x200&text=Bedroom">
```

For our mock-up, we use seven images, which we code up like this:

skeleton/index.html
```
<section class="photos six columns">
  <img class="u-max-full-width"
      src="http://placehold.it/460x320&text=Exterior"
```

---

2.   http://placehold.it

```
➤         alt="Exterior of house">
➤      <img src="http://placehold.it/150x100&text=Livingroom"
➤         alt="Livingroom">
➤      <img src="http://placehold.it/150x100&text=Kitchen"
➤         alt="Kitchen">
➤      <img src="http://placehold.it/150x100&text=Master+Bedroom"
➤         alt="Master Bedroom">
➤      <img src="http://placehold.it/150x100&text=Bedroom"
➤         alt="Guest Bedroom">
➤      <img src="http://placehold.it/150x100&text=Exterior+Side"
➤         alt="Exterior side">
➤      <img src="http://placehold.it/150x100&text=Exterior+Back"
➤         alt="Exterior back">
    </section>
```

When we shrink the browser window or view the page on a smaller device, we want our large image to scale down too. If we apply the u-max-full-width class to an image, Skeleton will crop the image for us by reducing its width and height to fit the available space.

The only thing we have left to implement is our two-column table of data for the house, which we want to place below the paragraph in the left column. We'll do that by defining columns within the left column we created earlier.

Mobile-Friendly Tables

Our next order of business is to define the data table for our details about the property. We define this with a standard HTML table, as Skeleton already has styles ready for us:

```
skeleton/index.html
<table class="u-full-width">
  <tr><th>Year Built</th><td>1964</td></tr>
  <tr><th>Bedrooms</th><td>4</td></tr>
  <tr><th>Baths</th><td>1 Full/1 Half</td></tr>
  <tr><th>Square footage</th><td>1,144 (approx)</td></tr>
  <tr><th>Foundation</th><td>Poured</td></tr>
  <tr><th>Heat</th><td>Gas Forced Air</td></tr>
  <tr><th>Electrical</th><td>Circuit Breaker</td></tr>
  <tr><th>Water</th><td>City Water</td></tr>
  <tr><th>Sewer</th><td>City Sewer</td></tr>
</table>
```

Skeleton's documentation says we should use the <thead> and <tbody> tags when we use tables, but since our headings are on the left side of the table rather than across the top, that markup doesn't work well. Fortunately, Skeleton works fine if we omit that extra markup. But if you have a table with headers across the top, it's a good idea to ensure that your table includes those tags.

In a short time, we have something that looks pretty nice. As we resize the screen, we see our elements restack vertically and look good on a small screen:

Let's finish this mock-up by adding a shadowed border around the container, but only when the full-width version is displayed. We'll also add a few more tweaks to ensure that things look great across a wide range of devices.

Styling with Media Queries

Skeleton makes things look pretty nice out of the box, but we can add our own customizations. Skeleton is designed to be lightweight and extendable. Let's add a background color to the main content area, set the background color of the page to white, and add a slight drop shadow around the content area. But we'll do this only on large screens.

To keep things organized, we add a new file to our project called css/custom.css. This keeps our code separate from the Skeleton library, in case we want to upgrade to a new version later. In this new file, we'll add a media query that targets desktop screen sizes only. Skeleton is built around the following media queries:

```
/* Mobile first queries */

/* Larger than mobile */
@media (min-width: 400px) {}

/* Larger than phablet */
@media (min-width: 550px) {}

/* Larger than tablet */
@media (min-width: 750px) {}

/* Larger than desktop */
@media (min-width: 1000px) {}

/* Larger than Desktop HD */
@media (min-width: 1200px) {}
```

Based on that, we target anything with a min-width of 750px for our styling:

skeleton/css/custom.css

```css
@media only screen and (min-width: 750px) {
  body {
    background-color: #ddd;
    margin-top: 20px;
  }

  .container {
    background-color: #fff;
    box-shadow: 5px 5px 5px #bbb;
    box-sizing: content-box;
    padding: 1%;
  }
}
```

To get this new style sheet to work, we need to add it to our HTML page, adding the reference below the existing CSS links:

skeleton/index.html

```html
<!-- CSS
-------------------------------------------------- -->
<link rel="stylesheet" href="css/normalize.css">
<link rel="stylesheet" href="css/skeleton.css">
➤ <link rel="stylesheet" href="css/custom.css">
```

One small detail remains, and that's that the images are all left-aligned, which doesn't look right on small screens. Let's center all of the images on all screen sizes to make things line up nicely. We can place this code right at the top of our custom style sheet, above any media queries. This way it applies to all styles and will be easy to override later if we need to adjust it for specific screen resolutions:

```
skeleton/css/custom.css
.photos{
  text-align: center;
}
```

From here we could make any number of additional customizations for various screen sizes, building off of what Skeleton gives us. And, of course, we're not restricted by those media queries. We can use any width we need to make things look the way we want.

Joe asks:
Aren't We Mixing Design and Implementation with Frameworks Like This?

To be honest, yes we are. When we have a `<div>` or `<section>` with a class of `four columns` and we decide that we need to reorganize things, we'll have to touch the markup. As a result, many purists will look at this as a bad idea in theory. While it's not nearly as bad as `class="redImportantText"`, it does couple the content with its presentation.

However, most site redesigns we've seen involve scrapping the existing structure and creating a new layout from scratch anyway, so the reusability of a template and its associated styles is often more theoretical than practical. With systems like this, you're trading strict semantic markup for a productivity gain. As you've seen in this recipe, frameworks like Skeleton are great for creating rapid prototypes of pages, even if you don't roll this markup into the actual site.

If you're still uncomfortable with this approach but like the idea of using these systems instead of rolling your own, you can investigate Sass (which we discuss in Recipe 30, *Building Modular Style Sheets with Sass* on page 213) and its advanced features to create an abstraction layer between the grid system and the HTML. Many other CSS frameworks offer this capability for advanced users.

Further Exploration

Skeleton's default template is worth a closer look because it starts us off with a great set of best practices. For example, it loads a web font from Google's

CDN, using a protocol-relative scheme so it supports both HTTP and HTTPS.[3] It includes all those other little things you might tend to forget, like a Favorites icon, <meta> tags for the description, and content encoding. And it includes a sensible <meta> tag to control the viewport on mobile devices.

Skeleton might not meet all of your needs, so you may want to look at Foundation[4] or Bootstrap,[5] which follow the same grid-based approach but offer many more advanced components, theming, and widgets—along with a steeper learning curve. However, both of these frameworks are similar enough to Skeleton that what you've learned here will help you greatly.

Also See

- Recipe 38, *Using Dropbox to Collaborate and Host a Static Site* on page 278
- Recipe 44, *Automating Static Site Deployment with Grunt* on page 304
- Recipe 30, *Building Modular Style Sheets with Sass* on page 213

---

3. http://paulirish.com/2010/the-protocol-relative-url/
4. http://foundation.zurb.com/
5. http://getbootstrap.com/

Recipe 29

Creating a Simple Blog with Enfield

Problem

We want to create a blog, but our server resources are limited. We don't have access to a database, and we aren't able to run PHP code. This makes solutions such as WordPress and Drupal impossible. We need a way to build a blog that's easy to manage and works around these barriers.

Ingredients

- Node.js[6] and npm
- Enfield[7]

Solution

To build a blog that doesn't require a database, we'll use a *static-site generator*—a tool that helps us build static sites quickly by reusing layout code. One of the more popular static-site generators, Jekyll,[8] is designed around creating blogs. Jekyll is powerful and easy to use, but it requires the Ruby programming language, which can be difficult to install. Fortunately, we can use Enfield, a Jekyll-compatible static-site generator written in Node.js.

Like Jekyll, Enfield relies on a rigid, opinionated file structure to form pages and articles. It has a simple and effective layout system, and although it isn't aimed at the average blogger, it's the perfect fit for a proof of concept or for a technical person who wants a fast yet simple blog without the overhead that comes from database-backed solutions. As an added bonus, our blog's infrastructure will be simpler. Database-driven sites make changing content easy but often require more complex caching solutions because they are slower than serving static pages to visitors. Static-site generators solve that problem, too, because they build regular HTML pages that can be uploaded anywhere.

We'll create a simple blog that details AwesomeCo's quest for world domination.

---

6. http://nodejs.org/
7. https://github.com/fortes/enfield
8. http://jekyllrb.com/

Installing Enfield

We install Enfield, like most Node.js libraries, by using npm:

```
npm install -g enfield
```

The installation process gives us an executable that we can use to build, test, and prepare our site for deployment.

Building the File Structure

To set up our blog, we run the enfield command and supply the new argument, followed by the name of the folder we want to create:

```
$ enfield new blog
Info enfield New site installed in /blog
```

This command creates the file and folder structure that Enfield relies on. Enfield expects a folder for layouts, a folder that will contain the posts, an index page, and a configuration file.

We can use the _config.yml configuration file to customize how our site is built. YAML[9] is a human-readable format for storing data that works across programming languages, similar to JSON. Enfield's generator already filled in some of the details, but let's modify it so it looks like this:

```
creatingablog/_config.yml
name: The Master Plan Blog
pygments: false
```

We specify the name of our blog, and we tell Enfield that we don't want to use the Pygments library to provide syntax highlighting. After all, we won't be showing off any of the top-secret code we're using to take over the world. (You can enable this feature for your own blog, but you'll need to have Python and the Pygments library installed on your machine before it'll work.)

Using Layouts

Let's start building our blog by creating our index page that lists recent posts. Pages in Enfield can be nested in a layout, so we'll create a layout that contains all the repetitive HTML on each page. This also enables us to easily change the HTML for the entire blog with one file. Enfield gives us a default layout, but let's create our own instead. In the _layouts folder, create a file named base.html and fill it with a standard HTML document and a few placeholders:

---

9.   http://yaml.org/

creatingablog/_layouts/base.html

```html
<!DOCTYPE html>
<html lang="en">
  <head>
    <meta charset="utf-8">
    <meta http-equiv="X-UA-Compatible" content="IE=edge,chrome=1">
    <title>{{ page.title }}</title>
  </head>
  <body>
    <div class="wrapper">
      <header>
        <h1>The Master Plan Blog</h1>
      </header>
      <section id="posts">
        {{ content }}
      </section>
      <footer>
        <small>Copyright AwesomeCo</small>
      </footer>
    </div>
  </body>
</html>
```

Enfield uses the Liquid template language[10] to create dynamic pages. Template tags are surrounded by double curly braces. In this case, any other layout file or post file that is rendered with our base.html layout will be inserted in place of the {{content}} area. The title of each page will get placed in the {{page.title}} area. We'll use other template tags later.

Our base layout is created, so we can now move on to creating the rest of the home page. We'll define the content in the index.html file in the root of our directory. The Liquid template language provides an iterator that we can use to create markup for each post. We use an unordered list to show the posts.

creatingablog/index.html

```
---
layout: base
---


<h2>Recent Posts</h2>
<ul>
  {% for post in site.posts %}
    <li>
      <!-- link to the post -->
    </li>
  {% endfor %}
</ul>
```

---

10. http://www.liquidmarkup.org/

The first three lines define a section that contains the YAML front matter, which is a special section where we can set some per-page metadata that Enfield will look for. The front matter is enclosed within three hyphens. We use this to tell Enfield that our layout for this page is the base.html file. Most of our files will render inside the base.html file that we made before.

```
creatingablog/index.html
<li>
  <span>{{ post.date | date_to_string }}</span>
  &raquo; <a href="{{ post.url }}">{{ post.title }}</a>
</li>
```

Within the context of this iterator, we have a template tag named post that contains the permalink for the post.

Creating Posts

Our home page is able to display posts now, but we haven't written any yet, so let's do that now. We can write posts in a variety of markup languages, including Markdown and regular HTML. For now, we'll use Markdown because it is simple and easy to read. The choice of markup language is flexible, but we must abide by a strict rule when naming our post files. Post files have to begin with a date followed by a title, and we must use hyphens to separate words in our title, like this:

2015-06-12-my-first-post.md

The post files reside in the _posts folder. Create a new file for the first post in that folder, and use today's date in the filename.

Posts, like the index.html file, require a YAML front matter. We use this front-matter section to define a layout to use and give our post a human-readable title. We haven't created a layout specifically for displaying a single post, but we will soon. Until then, we'll use the base layout. The content of the post comes after the front matter:

```
---
layout: base
title: Welcome!
---

Thank you for visiting our blog. We'll post daily updates
about our plans for global conquest. Be sure to check back often!
```

Building the Site

When we installed Enfield, we got a command-line utility that manages and builds out our site for us. In the root directory of our site, we run the following command, which generates the static files and puts them in a _site folder:

```
$ enfield build
```

When we're developing the blog, it's handy to serve these files through a web server so that we can ensure that our links work correctly. Enfield has this built in; all we need to do is use the server option:

```
$ enfield server
info enfield Configuration File: _config.yml
info enfield Source:
info enfield Destination: _site
info generate Begin generation
info generate Generated  -> _site
info enfield Generation done
info enfield Generation done
info enfield Running server at http://0.0.0.0:4000
```

This builds the site and starts a web server on port 4000. To view the site, we open a browser and navigate to http://localhost:4000.

Our blog shows the list of posts that we have created and allows us to view each post, as shown in the following image:

The Master Plan Blog

Recent Posts

- 12 Jun 2015 » Welcome!

Copyright AwesomeCo

We can shut down the server that we started by pressing Ctrl+C. Each time we edit the site, we must rebuild the site and restart the server before the changes appear in the browser. Keep in mind that the server is only for development purposes. When we deploy, we'll use the files that are generated in the _site folder.

Single-Post Layouts

If you follow the link to the post, you'll notice that viewing a post doesn't give us much information about the post, only its content. But we can create a specific layout for posts that lets us see more information. Create a file in the layouts folder called post.html. We're going to use it to display the post title along with the content and the author. Our new layout looks like this:

creatingablog/_layouts/post.html

```
---
layout: base
---

<article class="post">

  <h2>{{ page.title }}</h2>
  <section>
    {{ content }}
  </section>
  <footer>
    <p>Written by {{ page.author }}</p>
  </footer>

  <p><a href="/">Back</a></p>

</article>
```

Any variable we place in the YAML front matter is available via the page object in the template. Therefore, accessing the author of the post is as easy as referencing page.author. We could put any data we like in the front matter for a post and access it this way.

Before we're done, we need to tell our original post to use the new post layout. We edit the post we created earlier and change the layout in the front matter. Our new post looks like this:

creatingablog/_posts/2015-06-12-my-first-post.md

```
---
layout: post
title: Welcome!
author: Max Power
---

Thank you for visiting our blog. We'll post daily updates
about our plans for global conquest. Be sure to check back often!
```

When we rebuild the site and start the server, we can navigate to a post and see its title:

The Master Plan Blog

Welcome!

Thank you for visiting our blog. We'll post daily updates about our plans for global conquest. Be sure to check back often!

Written by Max Power

Copyright AwesomeCo

Of course, things are still a little rudimentary. Let's spice things up a bit.

Crafting Layouts

Enfield is a designer-friendly system. Using CSS and images in your layouts and posts is simple. Any folders and files we create in the root directory are automatically included in the site on generation. To spice up our home page, we'll write some CSS in an external file. Create a folder named css in the root directory, and create a file inside it named styles.css.

Let's write some simple styles in here to spice up the blog. We'll constrain the main content region, give the background some color, and set the footer apart from the rest of the site:

creatingablog/css/styles.css
```css
body {
  background: #DDD;
  color: #111;
  font-family: "Verdana", "Arial", sans-serif;
}

.wrapper {
  background-color: #FFF;
  max-width: 80%;
  margin: 0 auto;
}

.wrapper > header, .wrapper > section { padding: 1%; }

.wrapper > footer {
  background-color: #111;
  color: #DDD;
  text-align: center;
}

.wrapper > footer a { color: #DDD; }
```

Lastly, we need to change our base.html layout file to load the style sheet:

> ### Joe asks:
> ## Can I Exclude Files or Folders in My Root Directory?
>
> Yes! If you want to keep original assets like Photoshop files in the same folder as your images but you don't want to upload these to the server, you can tell Enfield to exclude them by modifying the _config.yml file we created at the beginning of the recipe.
>
> To exclude files, we use the exclude option in the configuration file. This option expects a list of files and folders to ignore. Enter the configuration option into the _config.yml file:
>
> ```
> exclude:
> - images/psd/
> - README
> ```
>
> You can learn more about the configuration options at the Jekyll wiki.[a] Enfield supports most of these options.
>
> ---
> a.   https://github.com/mojombo/jekyll/wiki/Configuration

creatingablog/_layouts/base.html
```
<link rel="stylesheet" href="/css/styles.css">
```

When we rebuild the site, we can see that the CSS is now applied to the page. When we pull up the page in our browser, our page looks like the following figure:

The Master Plan Blog

Recent Posts

• 12 Jun 2015 » Welcome!

Copyright AwesomeCo

The same concept applies for including images and JavaScript files. We can create folders named, for example, images and js and reference the files within them. And, of course, we don't have to craft things by hand; we can use CSS frameworks like Skeleton, which we cover in Recipe 28, *Rapid, Responsive Design with Skeleton* on page 194, to create a layout for our site that works nicely on mobile devices.

Static Pages

We can do more with Enfield than blogging. We can use the same layout and template system to create static pages too. Pages work nearly the same way that posts do; they have titles and layouts and can use template tags.

To create a static page, we create a new layout just for pages called page.html in the _layouts folder:

```
creatingablog/_layouts/page.html
---
layout: base
---


<h3>{{ page.title }}</h3>
{{ content }}
```

Now we can use this new layout to render a static page. In the root directory, create a file named contact.md. This file requires a YAML front matter that defines the layout for the page, as well as the page title:

```
creatingablog/contact.md
---
layout: page
title: Contact
---


If you would like to get in contact with us,
send an email to
[info@awesomeco.com](mailto:info@awesomeco.com).
```

Enfield generates static pages based on the filename of the Markdown page. Since we named ours contact.md, it generates a file named contact.html. Let's create a link to it on the index page in the footer:

```
creatingablog/_layouts/base.html
<footer>
  <small>Copyright AwesomeCo</small>
  <p><a href="/contact.html">Contact Me</a></p>
```

We need to fix the color of that link in the footer, too, so that it shows up as white instead of the default blue, which is too dark to be used with our dark gray footer color:

```
creatingablog/css/styles.css
.wrapper > footer a { color: #DDD; }
```

Now that our blog is ready, we can deploy it to a server by using the contents in the _site folder. And we can regenerate that content whenever we run the enfield build command.

Further Exploration

Static sites make it easy to serve your content quickly without the bottlenecks associated with databases. However, you do miss out on things that traditional blogs offer, such as comment systems. But you can quickly incorporate a system like Disqus.[11] You set up an account, add some code to your posts template, publish, and you've got a comments system ready to go.

Enfield's goal is to maintain full compatibility with Jekyll. If you're currently using WordPress, Drupal, or another blog framework, consult the Jekyll wiki[12] to find out how to easily transform your posts into a form that Jekyll or Enfield can digest. And like Jekyll, Enfield has a plug-in system you can use to develop your own ways to extend the platform.

If you do have the opportunity to use Ruby, you may want to look into Jekyll more, as it has some features that Enfield hasn't yet implemented, and has a larger community. And you may want to look into Middleman,[13] which offers even more power and flexibility for managing and generating content that doesn't need to change dynamically.

Also See

- Recipe 38, *Using Dropbox to Collaborate and Host a Static Site* on page 278
- Recipe 28, *Rapid, Responsive Design with Skeleton* on page 194
- Recipe 44, *Automating Static Site Deployment with Grunt* on page 304
- Recipe 28, *Rapid, Responsive Design with Skeleton* on page 194

---

11. https://disqus.com/websites/
12. https://github.com/mojombo/jekyll/wiki
13. https://middlemanapp.com/

Recipe 30

Building Modular Style Sheets with Sass

Problem

As web developers, we rely heavily on style sheets to create eye-catching interfaces, usable layouts, and readable typography. Style sheets are powerful but rudimentary. Even novice programmers tend to get frustrated that CSS doesn't provide things like variables and functions to reduce duplication. They turn to JavaScript and jQuery to fill in the gaps, which ends up creating a horrid mix of behavior and presentation in the code.

Ingredients

- Node.js[14] and npm
- Sass[15]

Solution

The Syntactically Awesome Style Sheets (Sass) CSS extension tool extends CSS, giving it the features we've longed for, including variables and reusable code. We can use the Sass language to build style sheets that are easier to maintain and build upon. We write our code using Sass's extended CSS syntax and then run this code through a precompiler that spits out regular CSS that web browsers understand. Sass's default syntax supports basic CSS3, so transitioning to Sass involves simply changing the extension for our style files' names from .css to .scss.

We developed some styled buttons in Recipe 1, *Styling Buttons and Links* on page 2, and some speech bubbles in Recipe 2, *Styling Stand-Alone Quotes with CSS* on page 6. In doing so, we created quite a bit of duplicated code. We'll use Sass and its features to build pieces we can share between the buttons and the speech bubbles, and then we'll stitch the pieces together into one master style sheet that we can include in our pages. We won't cover how the CSS code works in this recipe; refer to the other recipes for that.

---

14. http://nodejs.org/
15. http://sass-lang.com

Creating a Sass Project

Web browsers can't use Sass files, so we use a precompiler to convert Sass into regular CSS files. Some graphical tools will do this conversion, but we'll use a command-line version. We install this precompiler using npm:

```
$ npm install -g node-sass
```

We create folders for our Sass files and converted CSS files:

```
$ mkdir sass
$ mkdir stylesheets
```

Then we create a file in the sass folder called style.scss. This is the file we'll write our code in.

The node-sass command-line tool can monitor a file we specify for changes and convert it into a CSS file that our browser understands. We tell it to watch the sass/style.scss file and place the output in the stylesheets/style.css file:

```
$ node-sass sass/style.scss -o stylesheets/ --watch
```

Now node-sass watches sass/style.scss for changes and, when the file changes, will create or update stylesheets/style.css. It keeps watching until we press Ctrl+C or until we restart the computer. But don't shut the watcher down yet.

That's all there is to setting up our simple project. We can write our styles in Sass, and the CSS will be automatically generated for us. Let's start exploring Sass by taking a look at a simple yet powerful Sass feature: variables.

Using Variables and Imports

Our button has a background color and a border color. When we're working with CSS, we often use the same HTML color codes repeatedly in our style sheets, which makes changing these colors difficult. In programming languages like JavaScript, we solve problems like this by using variables, but regular CSS doesn't have them. Sass does, and they're easy to use.

In the sass/style.scss file, we add two variable declarations, one for the background color and one for the border color:

sass/sass/style.scss
```
$button_background_color: #A69520;
$button_border_color: #282727;
```

In Sass, variables start with a dollar sign and get their values assigned the same way we'd assign a value to a CSS property.

To keep our code organized, we'll keep the definition for our CSS button in its own file, called _buttons.scss, and we'll place it in the sass folder. Naming it with the underscore prefix does two things. First, it lets Sass know that it's not a style sheet of its own, so it won't generate a CSS file from this file directly. Second, it lets other developers know that it's a partial file. We put the basic styles for our button in this file, using our two variables for the button's border and background color:

sass/sass/_buttons.scss
```
.button {
    background-color: $button_background_color;
    border: 1px solid $button_border_color;
    color: #000;
    cursor: pointer;
    display: inline-block;
    font-family: "Verdana";
    font-weight: bold;
    font-size: 1.2em;
    line-height: 1.22em;
    padding: 6px 20px;
    text-transform: uppercase;
    text-decoration: none;
}

input::-moz-focus-inner {
        border: 0;
        padding: 0;
}

input.button {
    outline: none;
}
```

We can then import this partial Sass file into our style.scss file using the @import statement, which we place after our variable declarations:

sass/sass/style.scss
```
@import "buttons";
```

When we process our files, the Sass compiler will see the @import statement, pull in the contents of our other file, and create one CSS file. This is a great way to keep sections of style sheets organized during the development process. Better yet, we can take organization a step further by reducing duplication.

Using Mixins to Share Code

Our buttons and our speech bubbles both have gradient backgrounds and rounded corners. In addition, our button has a different gradient-background definition when the user hovers over the button. Defining these gradients and rounded corners requires a lot of CSS because we have to support different definitions for the various browsers. On top of that, our buttons also have a drop shadow that we need to define, and we may want to share that code with other elements on the page so we have consistent shadows.

We can define these rules as *mixins* that we can share across style definitions. Let's create a new file called _mixins.scss to hold the mixins that we define, and then add the @import statement to style.scss *above* our other @import statement:

```
sass/sass/style.scss
$button_background_color: #A69520;
$button_border_color: #282727;
@import "mixins";
@import "buttons";
```
➤ (arrows pointing to the two @import lines)

In _mixins.scss, let's first define a mixin for the rounded corners. A mixin looks a lot like a function declaration in JavaScript, with parentheses for the parameters and curly braces for the content:

```
sass/sass/_mixins.scss
@mixin rounded($radius){
    background-clip: padding-box;
    border-radius: $radius;
}
```

With the mixin declared, we can add it to our .button definition in _buttons.scss by using the @include statement, which we place after the other declarations we've added inside the .button rule:

```
sass/sass/_buttons.scss
padding: 6px 20px;
text-transform: uppercase;
text-decoration: none;
@include rounded(12px);
```
➤ (arrow pointing to the @include line)

It fits in like any other CSS property.

Next, let's create a mixin for our gradients, which are a little more complex:

```
sass/sass/_mixins.scss
@mixin gradient($color1, $color2, $alpha1: 100%, $alpha2: 100%){
    background-image: -webkit-linear-gradient(top, $color1 $alpha1, $color2 $alpha2);
    background-image: linear-gradient(to bottom, $color1 $alpha1, $color2 $alpha2);
}
```

Since WebKit-based browsers like Google Chrome, Safari, and those on many mobile devices support alpha transparency for the gradients, we'll make our mixin take those as parameters too. Our button styles don't make use of the alpha transparency, but our speech bubbles do, so we assign these default values of 100 percent. Now we can include this mixin into our _buttons.scss file right below the mixin we placed for the rounded corners:

sass/sass/_buttons.scss
```
@include gradient(#FFF089, #DBC73C);
```

We also need to use the gradient code when we hover over the button. Let's look at how Sass handles pseudoclasses.

Reducing Duplication with Nesting

With regular CSS, we end up duplicating selectors. To define styles for a hyperlink, we often end up writing code like this to handle the regular state and the hover state:

```
a{
  color: #300;
}
a:hover{
  color: #900;
}
```

With Sass, we can nest the pseudoclass definition *within* the parent rule:

```
a{
  color: #300;
  &:hover{
    color: #900;
  }
}
```

This nesting doesn't save us a lot of keystrokes in this case, but it does help us keep things more organized.

In _buttons.scss, we'll use this nesting technique to include our gradients mixin for the hover pseudoclass. Place this code inside of the .button rule after the previous @include statement:

sass/sass/_buttons.scss
```
&:active, &:focus {
  @include gradient(#DBC73C, #FFF089);
  color: #000;
}
```

When developing a more complex style sheet, we often use this nesting feature to dramatically reduce repeating selectors, turning this:

```
#sidebar a{
  color: #300;
}
#sidebar a:hover{
  color: #900;
}
```

...into this:

```
#sidebar a{
  color: #300;
  &:hover{
    color: #900;
  }
}
```

This way, we use nesting for the scope of the selectors, instead of repeating the selection hierarchy over and over.

With these mixins created, we can create the file _speech_bubble.scss and define the bubbles like this:

```
sass/sass/_speech_bubble.scss
blockquote {
    background: #FAF205;
    margin: 0;
    padding: 15px 30px;
    position: relative;
    width: 225px;
    @include gradient(#FAF205, #FFFC9C, 20%, 100%);
    @include rounded(20px);

    p {
      font-size: 1.8em;
      margin: 5px;
      position: relative;
      z-index: 10;
    }

    + cite {
      display: block;
      font-size: 1.1em;
      margin: 3em 0 0 3em;
    }

    &:after {
      content: "";
      border-color: transparent #FFFC9C;
      border-style: solid;
      border-width: 0 15px 50px 0px;
      display: block;
      bottom: -50px;
      left: 40px;
      position: absolute;
      width: 0;
      z-index: 1;
    }
}
```

We call our mixins starting on line 7, and on line 17, we use Sass's nesting support to keep things organized. Now we can tell style.scss to import this new file as well:

```
sass/sass/style.scss
@import "mixins";
@import "buttons";
@import "speech_bubble";
```

If we glance back at the pure CSS implementation of the buttons, we see that we need to write one last bit of code to finish up our buttons—the drop-shadow code. We can make this a mixin too, just like the one we did for the rounded corners. In _mixins.scss, we add this code after our other @mixin declaration:

```
sass/sass/_mixins.scss
@mixin shadow($x, $y, $offset, $color){
  box-shadow: $x $y $offset $color;
}
```

Then, to apply the shadow, we invoke the mixin by adding a call to the bottom of the _buttons.scss file:

```
sass/sass/_buttons.scss
@include shadow(1px, 3px, 5px, #999);
```

As we've been working, the Sass command has been stitching all of our individual style sheets together, producing a single style.css file that we can include in our page. Our Sass files can stay in our source code repository, nicely organized. And best of all, we have reusable components that will let us add consistent rounding, shadows, and gradients to elements with ease.

Further Exploration

With the powerful features that Sass brings to the table, it's hard to imagine doing style sheets any other way. We managed only a small amount of CSS in this recipe, but imagine how much more maintainable the style sheets for a large content-management system would be. You could define your own library of mixins that you share across the various functional pieces of the site, and you could use variables to hold the values for measurements, colors, and font choices so you can quickly alter them when needed.

Sass is just the beginning. With Compass, a CSS framework built on Sass, you can take advantage of many prebuilt mixins and plug-ins for things like grid frameworks and CSS3.[16]

---

16. http://compass-style.org/

A Tale of Two Syntaxes

Sass actually has two syntaxes—the SCSS syntax that we used in this recipe and another syntax commonly referred to as Indented Sass or Sass Classic. Instead of curly braces, it uses indentation and is aimed at developers who favor conciseness over similarity to regular CSS. It also eliminates semicolons from the definitions. A Sass style sheet that defines different link colors for sidebar and main regions of a page would look like this, using this alternative syntax:

```
#sidebar
  a
    color: #f00
  &:hover
    color: #000
#main
  a
    color: #000
```

You only need to use the .sass extension instead of the .scss extension. The end result and workflows don't change. Both of these syntaxes are interoperable and will be supported well into the future, so the choice is yours.

Also See

- Recipe 1, *Styling Buttons and Links* on page 2
- Recipe 2, *Styling Stand-Alone Quotes with CSS* on page 6
- Recipe 31, *Cleaner JavaScript with CoffeeScript* on page 221
- Recipe 44, *Automating Static Site Deployment with Grunt* on page 304
- *Pragmatic Guide to Sass [CC11]*

Recipe 31

Cleaner JavaScript with CoffeeScript

Problem

JavaScript is the programming language of the web, but it's often misunder-
stood, which leads to poorly written and terribly performing code. Its rules
and syntax can lead to developer confusion and frustration, which slow down
productivity. Since JavaScript is everywhere, we can't simply remove it or
replace it with a language with a more comfortable syntax.

Ingredients

- CoffeeScript[17]
- Node.js[18] and npm
- QEDServer (for our test server)[19]

Solution

We *can* use other languages to generate good, standard, and well-performing
JavaScript. Several solutions make writing JavaScript more enjoyable,
including the forthcoming ECMAScript 6 standard (ES6), which brings new
syntax and language features. Another is Microsoft's TypeScript, which brings
static typing to JavaScript. But CoffeeScript lets us write JavaScript in a more
concise format, similar to languages like Ruby or Python. To use CoffeeScript,
you write your code in CoffeeScript's syntax and then run your code through
a transpiler that emits standard JavaScript that you use on your pages.

Although interpretation adds a step to your development process, the productivity gains are worth the trade-off. For example, you won't accidentally forget
a semicolon or miss a closing curly brace, and you won't forget to declare
variables in the proper scope. CoffeeScript takes care of those issues and
more, so you can focus on the problem you're solving.

We'll take CoffeeScript for a spin by using it with jQuery to fetch the products
from QEDServer's API.

---

17. http://coffeescript.org/
18. http://nodejs.org/
19. A version for this book is available at http://webdevelopmentrecipes.com/.

CoffeeScript is a language of its own, so you need to learn a new syntax for declaring things like variables and functions. The CoffeeScript website and Trevor Burnham's book, *CoffeeScript: Accelerated JavaScript Development, Second Edition [Bur15]*, explain these fundamentals in excellent detail. Let's take a look now at a couple of basic CoffeeScript concepts you need to understand to move forward.

> **\\//**   **Joe asks:**
> **ʾʃ**
> # Does CoffeeScript Still Matter Now That ES6 Transpilers Exist?
>
> In our opinion, yes, but not because of the language features. ES6 incorporates many of the things that CoffeeScript provides, such as classes, comprehensions, and somewhat shorter syntax for defining functions. But CoffeeScript's syntax is where it really shines. The fact that variables get declared for you in the proper scope, the extremely simple list comprehensions, and the fact that indentation is a part of the language instead of just a readability aid are some of the things we like about the language.
>
> To use ES6, you still need a transpiler that converts the code back to JavaScript that works across browsers, and because browsers still have to work with JavaScript that was written in 1995, you'll probably need that transpiler for a long time. The promise is that eventually, if you use ES6, you'll be able to remove the transpilation step. But based on the way the web works and the way standards are adopted, that reality may be years away.
>
> And as ES6 matures, CoffeeScript is sure to adapt its output to support the new features that ES6 provides. It's our responsibility as developers to stay up to date with those changes.

CoffeeScript Basics

CoffeeScript's syntax is designed to be similar to JavaScript but with much less noise. For example, take this JavaScript function declaration:

```
var hello = function(){
  alert("Hello World");
}
```

We can express it with CoffeeScript like this:

```
hello = -> alert "Hello World"
```

We don't need to use the var keyword to declare our variables. CoffeeScript figures out which variables we've declared and adds the var statement in the appropriate place for us.

Second, we use the -> symbol, often called the *skinny arrow*, instead of the function keyword to define functions in CoffeeScript. Function arguments come before the -> symbol, and the function body comes after, with no curly braces. If the function body goes for more than one line, we indent it:

```
hello = (name) ->
  alert "Hello " + name
```

Also, instead of concatenating strings like this in JavaScript:

```
var fullName = firstName + " " + lastName;
```

...we can use #{} within double-quoted strings:

```
fullname = "#{firstName} #{lastName}"
```

The expressions within the #{} markup are evaluated and converted to strings. This makes string concatenation a breeze.

While there are many more powerful expressive features of CoffeeScript, those two make it possible to turn something like this:

```
$(function() {
  var url;
  url = "/products.json";
  $.ajax(url, {
    dataType: "json",
    type: "GET",
    success: function(data, status, XHR) {
      alert("It worked!");
    }
  });
});
```

...into this:

```
$ ->
  url = "/products.json"
  $.ajax url,
    dataType: "json"
    type: "GET"
    success: (data, status, XHR) ->
      alert "It worked!"
```

The CoffeeScript version of the code is a little easier on the eyes, and it takes less time to write. If we make syntax errors, we find out as soon as we try to convert our CoffeeScript to JavaScript, so we won't be spending time hunting the errors down in the web browser.

CoffeeScript is whitespace-sensitive, meaning we have to indent lines consistently or our code won't compile. But that shouldn't be a problem, because

consistent indentation in code is important for readability, and we should
indent our code consistently regardless of the programming language we use.

Installing CoffeeScript

We can get CoffeeScript running in numerous ways, but the simplest way to
test it is through the browser. This way, we don't have to install anything on
our machines to try a quick demo. We download the CoffeeScript interpreter[20]
and include it on our web page:

coffeescript/browser/index.html

```
<script src="coffee-script.js"></script>
```

Let's run through a trivial example to show how CoffeeScript works. We'll
write a small bit of code that creates a new paragraph element that, when
clicked, shows a JavaScript alert box. To do this in JavaScript, we'd write
this code:

```
var element;

element = document.createElement("p");
element.innerHTML = "Click me to see an Alert box";

element.addEventListener("click", function() {
  return alert("This came from clicking the paragraph!");
});

document.body.appendChild(element);
```

This code first finds the body element on the page. It then creates a new p
element with some text, registers a click event handler on the new element,
and appends the new element to the body of the page.

But instead of using JavaScript, we use CoffeeScript, and we place our CoffeeScript code in a <script> block:

coffeescript/browser/index.html

```
<script type="text/coffeescript">
  element = document.createElement "p"
  element.innerHTML = "Click me to see an Alert box"

  element.addEventListener "click", ->
    alert "This came from clicking the paragraph!"

  document.body.appendChild element
</script>
```

---

20. http://coffeescript.org/extras/coffee-script.js

Since the web browser doesn't know how to handle <script> elements with a type of text/coffeexcript, it ignores them. But when we include the CoffeeScript interpreter on the page, it finds these <script> elements and evaluates their contents. It then writes the resulting JavaScript to the page, where the browser executes it. CoffeeScript's interpreter is *written* in CoffeeScript, which is then compiled down to JavaScript.

When we run our page, we can click on the text of the paragraph and see our alert show up.

Compare the CoffeeScript version to the JavaScript version. Notice that we don't have to declare our variables using the var keyword; CoffeeScript will add it in for us when the code gets compiled to JavaScript. Also notice that we don't always need to use parentheses around the arguments to our functions. It's optional, except in places where it's unclear, like when we fetch the first <body> element from the page. Finally, notice how much more simple the event-listener callback looks without the function keyword and the curly braces. Instead, we use the skinny arrow and indentation.

This in-browser approach is great for experimenting, but you won't ever want to roll it out in production: the CoffeeScript interpreter is a large file that end users would have to download, and interpreting CoffeeScript on the client machine would be too slow. We want to convert our CoffeeScript files ahead of time and serve only the resulting JavaScript files from our website. For that, we need to install a CoffeeScript interpreter, and we need a good workflow to go along with that.

We install the CoffeeScript interpreter using npm. Type this on the command line:

```
$ npm install -g coffee-script
```

This installs a command-line tool that turns CoffeeScript into JavaScript code. Now we can set up our project and get a demo going.

Working with CoffeeScript

Let's use CoffeeScript and Handlebars templates to make an Ajax request for some products and display those products on a web page. We'll use QEDServer and its product-management API as our development server. We'll place all of our files in the public folder that QEDServer makes for us so our development server will serve them properly and our Ajax requests will work without any same-origin policy issues.

Since we're going to turn CoffeeScript files into JavaScript files, let's create folders for each of those file types:

```
$ mkdir coffeescript
$ mkdir javascriptf
```

Now, let's create a simple web page that loads jQuery; the Handlebars library you learned about in Recipe 11, *Rendering HTML with Handlebars Templates* on page 69; and app.js, which will contain the code that fetches our data and displays it on the page:

coffeescript/compiled/index.html
```html
<!DOCTYPE html>
<html lang="en">
  <head>
    <meta charset="utf-8">
    <title>Products</title>
  </head>
  <body>
    <script
      src="http://ajax.googleapis.com/ajax/libs/jquery/2.1.4/jquery.min.js">
    </script>
    <script
      src="http://cdnjs.cloudflare.com/ajax/libs/handlebars.js/3.0.3/
handlebars.min.js"></script>
    <script src="javascript/app.js"></script>
  </body>
</html>
```

We're linking to javascript/app.js, which will be generated from our CoffeeScript.

Now we add two Handlebars templates to the page. The first will display the products, and the second will display any error message that we get if our connection to the products API fails. We place these *above* the scripts we just added, because we need these templates to be on the page before we execute our code that tries to use them:

coffeescript/compiled/index.html
```html
<script id="product_template" type="text/x-handlebars-template">
  <div class="product">
    {{#products}}
      <h3>{{name}}</h3>
      <p>{{description}}</p>
    {{/products}}
  </div>
</script>

<script id="error_template" type="text/x-handlebars-template">
  <p>{{error}}</p>
</script>
```

Next, we create the coffeescript/app.coffee file, which contains our logic, and where we place the code that makes the request for data and renders the templates:

```
coffeescript/compiled/coffeescript/app.coffee
$.ajax "/products.json",
  type: "GET"
  dataType: "json"
  success: (data, status, XHR) ->
    template = Handlebars.compile $("#product_template").html()
    html = template {products: data}
    $('body').append html

  error: (XHR, status, errorThrown) ->
    template = Handlebars.compile $("#error_template").html()
    html = template {error: "Can't load data: #{errorThrown}"}
    $('body').append html
```

We call jQuery's ajax() function, rendering the products template if we get a response and rendering the error template when we don't. The logic and flow are identical to a pure JavaScript implementation, but the code is several lines shorter. Of course, this code won't work yet because our page is requesting a JavaScript file that we still need to generate.

Convert CoffeeScript Automatically

When we installed CoffeeScript, we got the coffee command-line tool. This tool makes it easy to convert files from CoffeeScript to JavaScript. It can convert a single file or a folder of files, and it can even watch files for changes and run the conversion when it sees a change.

We want to watch for changes to the coffeescript folder and then write the output to the javascript folder. To do that, we run this command:

```
$ coffee -o javascript/ -w -c coffeescript/
```

This command immediately converts what it finds for us:

```
09:44:08 - compiled /Users/bstinson/code/coffeescript/app.coffee
```

And when we save the coffeescript/app.coffee file, the coffee command notices and does the conversion. This process keeps watching until we stop it with Ctrl-C.

If we open the page in our browser, though, we get an error because we can't make a request to our back-end API unless we run the code from the same domain. That's why we're using QEDServer, which can act as a web server for our pages. When we view the page at http://localhost:8080/index.html, everything works! If we inspect the generated app.js file, we see that all of the required curly braces, parentheses, and semicolons are where they should be. We now have a workflow we can use to write better JavaScript, so we can continue making changes to our application. When we're done, we can deploy the javascript folder and leave the coffeescript folder in our source-code repository.

You should know one more thing about CoffeeScript. Throughout this book we wrapped our JavaScript code inside Immediately-Invoked Function Expressions (IIFEs). By default, CoffeeScript wraps our output in those expressions. If you look at the code in the app.js file, you can see it's been wrapped with an IIFE:

```
➤ (function() {
    $.ajax("/products.json", {
      type: "GET",
      ...

    });
➤ }).call(this);
```

You can turn this option off, but if you leave it alone, it's one less thing you have to think about when working on your own projects.

Further Exploration

Quite a few popular projects[21] use CoffeeScript as a development platform because of its ease of use and because it provides some of the niceties of Ruby, Python, and more functional programming languages, including list comprehensions.

For example, when you're working with arrays or lists of items, you may often find yourself writing code like this:

```
var colors = ["red", "green", "blue"];
for (i = 0, length = colors.length; i < length; i++) {
  var color = colors[i];
  alert(color);
}
```

Using CoffeeScript's support for list comprehensions and its simplified syntax, you can write the logic like this:

```
alert color for color in ["red", "green", "blue"]
```

This produces the same result but in a more direct and clear syntax. You can use JavaScript libraries like Lodash[22] to achieve the same kind of effect, but in that case you make your end users download additional code so you can

---

21. https://github.com/jashkenas/coffeescript/wiki/In-The-Wild
22. https://lodash.com/

write less of it. CoffeeScript's output is regular, standard JavaScript that works anywhere JavaScript works, without any additional libraries. In fact, CoffeeScript produces JavaScript code that looks almost identical to the original result with the for loop and incrementing variable.

CoffeeScript makes a great companion to Sass, which we talk about in Recipe 30, *Building Modular Style Sheets with Sass* on page 213. Using Sass and CoffeeScript together gives you a powerful workflow for managing your sites. And if you want to integrate CoffeeScript into your web development workflow, you can use a tool like Harp, which makes building static sites with Sass and CoffeeScript a breeze.[23] Combining that with an automated deployment strategy like the one we talk about in Recipe 44, *Automating Static Site Deployment with Grunt* on page 304, can create an efficient and enjoyable development experience.

To get more comfortable with CoffeeScript, try to implement some of the recipes in this book in CoffeeScript. For example, in Recipe 37, *Testing JavaScript with Jasmine* on page 267, you'll learn how to write tests for your JavaScript code. CoffeeScript's syntax can make those tests easier to write and easier to read.

Be sure to keep an eye on ES6. It's got some of the features that CoffeeScript uses, including string interpolation and support for list comprehensions, but using the more traditional JavaScript syntax with curly braces and parentheses. Like CoffeeScript, ES6 isn't compatible with current browsers, but you can use Babel[24] to convert the code you write into code browsers understand.

Also See

- *CoffeeScript: Accelerated JavaScript Development, Second Edition [Bur15]*
- Recipe 30, *Building Modular Style Sheets with Sass* on page 213
- Recipe 37, *Testing JavaScript with Jasmine* on page 267
- Recipe 44, *Automating Static Site Deployment with Grunt* on page 304

---

23. http://harpjs.com/
24. https://babeljs.io/

Recipe 32

Managing Files with Git

Problem

As web developers, we're often in situations in which we need to juggle multiple versions of our code. Sometimes we need to experiment with the latest and greatest plug-in. Then there are the times when we're in the zone, cranking away on a new feature, but get sidetracked because we need to fix a critical bug. Even if you've never used a formalized version-control system, you've probably created multiple copies of a file with small variations in the filename to differentiate between different problems you were working on. But that multiple-file system breaks down quickly because it's all on our machine and isn't easy to manage. We need something that's fast, robust, and modern—something that we can use to manage our code as well as collaborate with others.

Ingredients

• Git[25]

Solution

Today we have many options for version control. Git is popular among developers because it's local and fast—faster than making local copies. Git also allows us to work on multiple versions in parallel. We can save changes often, which gives us many restore points. All of these features make it the version-control system of choice for many of today's open-source projects.

During our morning meeting, our boss turned to us and said, "I need you to take those two mocks you presented last week and develop actual versions of the site using those templates. Oh, and while you're working on that, we also need a few bugs fixed in the existing site."

Now we have three versions of our site to maintain. Let's use Git to keep our files organized and in sync.

---

25. http://git-scm.com/

Setting Up Git

Let's get started by installing Git. Head over to Git's website[26] and download the appropriate packages for your operating system. Or, if you're running Windows, use MsysGit[27] and choose the option to use Git Bash. Windows users need to use Git Bash, instead of the normal Windows command prompt, to follow along with this recipe.

Git tracks the person who makes a code change based on that person's configured Git username. This makes it easy to see who made what changes and when. Let's configure Git by specifying our name and email address. Open a new shell and type the following:

```
$ git config --global user.name "Firstname Lastname"
$ git config --global user.email "your_email@youremail.com"
```

Now that we have Git installed and configured, let's get comfortable with the basics.

Git Basics

We'll start by turning our project into a Git repository. Let's create a folder called git_site for this web project and initialize it as a Git repository. From the command line (or from Git Bash, if you're on Windows), type:

```
$ mkdir git_site
$ cd git_site
$ git init
```

We get a confirmation message:

```
Initialized empty Git repository in /Users/webdev/Sites/git_site/.git/
```

Initialization creates a hidden folder named .git in the root of our directory. All of the history and other details about our repository will go in this folder. Git will track changes to our folder and store *snapshots* of our code, but first we have to tell Git which files we want to track.

Let's copy our website files into our new git_site folder. You can find these files in the git folder of the book's source code.

With the files in place, let's add them all to the Git repository so we can get them back to an earlier state if something goes wrong. To add all the files, run the following command:

```
$ git add .
```

---

26. http://git-scm.com/
27. http://msysgit.github.io

The add command doesn't display any output; for that we need to use the git status command. We can run git status at any time to see the current status of our Git repository. The output looks like this:

```
# On branch master
#
# Initial commit
#
# Changes to be committed:
#   (use "Git rm --cached <file>..." to unstage)
#
#       new file:   index.html
#       new file:   javascripts/application.js
#       new file:   styles/site.css
#
```

Running git add *stages* files in Git. It declares what files and changes are ready to be committed to the repository. git status tells us what is going to be committed, so we can verify that we're committing everything we want and nothing we don't. Everything looks good, so let's commit these changes.

$ git commit -m "initial commit of files"

The two flags we pass in are -a and -m. The -a tells Git that we want to add all the changes before committing, and the -m specifies a commit message. Unlike other version-control systems, Git requires every commit to have a commit message. This helps when identifying commits, so make commit messages informative. Git easily shows us what has changed, so we should try to explain why we are making the changes we are in each commit. After our commit finishes, we get confirmation of what it did, as shown in the following example:

```
[master (root-commit) 94c75a2] Initial Commit
1 files changed, 17 insertions(+), 0 deletions(-)
create mode 100644 index.html
create mode 100644 javascripts/application.js
create mode 100644 styles/site.css
```

We can run git status to verify that the files were committed, and we see that everything is up to date:

```
# On branch master
nothing to commit (working directory clean)
```

We now have a snapshot of our code, which means we can start making and tracking changes.

Working with Branches

Branching allows us to simultaneously work on multiple features of our website. Effectively, we can develop a new feature while maintaining our current deployed code. With Git—unlike with other version-control systems —branching is an easy and commonly used feature.

Our boss wants us to start work on implementing two site layouts, which we'll call *layout_a* and *layout_b*. Let's create a branch for *layout_a*:

```
$ git checkout master
Switched to branch 'master'
Your branch is up-to-date with 'origin/master'.
$ git checkout -b layout_a
Switched to a new branch 'layout_a'
```

Now when we run git status we see that our current branch is layout_a. Let's open the index.html file, change the text in the <h1> tag to say Layout A, and save the file. Now when we run git status, we see the following:

```
$ git status
# On branch layout_a
# Changed but not updated:
#   (use "Git add <file>..." to update what will be committed)
#   (use "Git checkout -- <file>..." to discard changes in working directory)
#
#        modified:   index.html
#
no changes added to commit (use "Git add" and/or "Git commit -a")
```

Let's commit the changes to the layout_a branch:

```
$ git commit -m "beginning update to Layout A"
```

While we were working on our branch, our boss sent an email that says, "On the home page, it says that we offer one-day shipping. We no longer offer that promotion. We need to update it to two-day shipping, and we have to do it right now before anyone else holds us to that option!" Let's switch back to our *master* branch and make that change:

```
$ git checkout -b remove_shipping_promotion
```

Now when we open index.html we don't see the text we changed in the layout_a branch. The changes we made are in another branch, and instead of moving files around, we let Git alter the file's contents when we change branches. Now we can make the changes to the home page that our boss wanted, and then we can commit back to the master branch:

```
$ git commit -m "shipping promotion has ended, removing it"
 [remove_shipping_promotion d00d2de] shipping promotion has ended, removing it
 1 files changed, 1 insertions(+), 1 deletions(-)
$ git checkout master
$ git merge remove_shipping_promotion
```

This takes anything that wasn't changed in a branch and applies it to the active branch.

We made our change on the remove_shipping_promotion branch and then merged it into master. However, if we change to another branch we won't see the change. Although this is a small change, it will be good to have it in our other branches. Let's get these changes into our layout_a branch so we can get back to working on it with the latest copy:

```
$ git checkout layout_a
$ git merge master
```

> **Joe asks:**
> ## Why Are We Committing Changes So Often?
>
> Think of commits as snapshots, or restore points, for your project. The more commits you make, the more powerful and flexible Git becomes. If we keep our commits small and focused on a particular feature, we can use Git's *cherry-pick*, which lets us take a single commit from one branch and apply it to other branches. If the idea of lots of small commits seems messy, you can squash commits together using the rebase command when you've completed a feature.

Next let's create a branch for our *layout_b* option. We want this to start off based on our current production site, not our layout_a version, so we need to switch back to the master branch and then create a branch for layout_b:

```
$ git checkout master
$ git checkout -b layout_b
```

This time we change the text inside of the <h1> tag to say Layout B. Let's save and commit this change:

```
$ git commit -a -m "beginning update to Layout B"
```

This version of our layout requires us to add a products.html file and an about_us.html file. Let's create those files and then stage those files for check-in:

```
$ touch products.html
$ touch about_us.html
$ git add .
```

Now if we run git status, we see that we have two new staged files:

```
# On branch layout_b
# Changes to be committed:
#   (use "Git reset HEAD <file>..." to unstage)
#
#       new file:   about_us.html
#       new file:   products.html
#
```

Let's commit those files:

```
$ git commit -m "setting up products and about_us, no content"
```

Now, let's add an <h1> to products.html with the text of Current Products to comply with our design.

While we were doing that, we got another email from our boss that says, "We need to change the shipping time on the home page back to one day. We struck a deal with a major shipping company. Get these changes made ASAP!!!" We need to make these changes and get them pushed out right away. However, we're not ready to commit the changes we just made.

Git's stash command is meant for situations like this. We can use stash to store our changes so we can switch branches. Stashes are a great way to store things you're working on without having to commit them:

```
$ git stash
```

Now if we do a git status, we see that no changes need to be committed. Let's switch over to the master branch and create a new add_shipping_promotion branch from it:

```
$ git checkout master
$ git checkout -b add_shipping_promotion
```

Now we can make our changes to the shipping information in index.html and commit the changes, then merge them into master:

```
$ git commit -a -m "updated shipping times for new promotion"
$ git checkout master
$ git merge add_shipping_promotion
```

Let's switch back to our layout_b branch with git checkout layout_b and explore what we can do with stashes. We see what stashes are available by using the git stash list command:

```
$ git stash list
stash@{0}: WIP on layout_b: f8747f4 added products and about_us, no content
```

When we open up the products.html file, we see that it's empty. Let's get the changes we made to that file back. We do that with this command:

```
$ git stash pop
```

Now when we look at our products.html file, we'll see the <h1> tag that we added before we got sidetracked.

After several more tweaks to both layouts (and several other "important" distractions), our boss decided that the layout_b option was the best and wants to roll that out into production. Let's commit those changes and then merge this work into our master branch:

```
$ git commit -a -m "updated products page"
$ git checkout master
$ git merge layout_b
```

In traditional version-control systems, it's common to leave branches in a repository indefinitely. Git differs in that both branches and tags refer to a commit. With Git, when we delete a branch, Git doesn't remove any of the commits; it removes only the reference. Because we've merged our changes back into master, we can delete the branches that we used for development.

Let's use the git branch command to look at the branches we currently have. It shows us that we are on master and lists the other available branches: layout_a, layout_b, remove_shipping_promotion, and add_shipping_promotion. Let's delete those branches:

```
$ git branch -d layout_a
$ git branch -d layout_b
$ git branch -d remove_shipping_promotion
$ git branch -d add_shipping_promotion
```

Git warns us if a branch has not been merged into the current branch. We can override this by using -D to force-delete the branch.

Working with Remote Repositories

So far we've worked only with a local repository. It's great to keep our local code under version control, but having a remote repository allows us to collaborate with others and have redundant copies of our code in multiple locations.

We can set up a remote Git server using the development virtual machine (VM) created in Recipe 39, *Setting Up a Virtual Machine* on page 282. By creating SSH keys, we can save ourselves the extra step of having to type our password whenever we log in or transfer files. Creating an SSH key and placing it on the server will allow us to authenticate quickly and without a password every time we want to push to our remote repository.

SSH keys consist of two components: a private key that we keep to ourselves and a public key we give to another server. When we log in to that server, it checks to see whether our key is authorized, and then our local system proves that we're who we say we are by matching the public key with the private key. With Git, this handshaking process is all done transparently during the login process.

Before we continue, you should check to see whether you have any SSH keys on your system. Try to change directories into ~/.ssh. If you get a message saying the directory doesn't exist, then you need to generate keys. If you see files like id_rsa and id_rsa.pub, then you already have keys, and you can skip the next step.

Let's run the ssh-keygen command to generate a new SSH key. We pass in our email address, which is placed into the key as a comment:

```
$ ssh-keygen -t rsa -C "webdev@awesomeco.com"
```

The comment helps us or other server administrators quickly identify who owns the key when it's uploaded to a server.

The ssh-keygen program asks you for a place to store the SSH key; you can press the `Enter` key to save it in the default location. It also asks you to enter a passphrase. This adds an additional layer of security to the key, but we'll leave it blank for now. Press `Enter` again.

Now that we have our keys, let's add them to our VM. We can pipe our local public key into the authorized_keys file on the server. This lets the VM know that our machine has access to the server:

```
$ cat ~/.ssh/id_rsa.pub | ssh webdev@192.168.1.100 \
"mkdir ~/.ssh; cat >> ~/.ssh/authorized_keys"
```

After executing this command, the server asks for our password to make sure this is a legitimate request. After the command finishes, we can test our key by trying to ssh into the VM:

```
$ ssh webdev@192.168.1.100
```

And this time it doesn't ask us for our password.

Now that we're logged in to our VM, we use Ubuntu's package manager to install Git on the server:

```
$ sudo apt-get install git-core
```

Now we can create a *bare* repository on the VM. A bare repository is nothing more than a directory usually named with a .git extension to make it easier for us to identify as such. Then, inside the directory, we use the git command to initialize the folder, using the --bare switch:

```
$ mkdir website.git
$ cd website.git
$ git init --bare
```

With the repository created on the remote machine, we can log out of the VM by typing exit.

Back on our local machine, let's add the location of our remote repository and push up our master branch:

```
$ git remote add origin ssh://webdev@192.168.1.100/~/website.git
$ git push origin master
```

Let's say we wanted to work on a new feature with another developer. We can create a branch for this new feature called new_feature and then work on our design implementation. When our design work is done, we can push the branch to the remote repository:

```
$ git checkout -b new_feature
$ git push origin new_feature
```

Now that we've pushed our branch, let's see what branches are out on the remote repository:

```
$ git branch -r
```

We end up with a list of branches. We don't see the branches that we deleted locally earlier, because we never pushed them out before they were deleted:

```
origin/HEAD -> origin/master
origin/new_feature
origin/master
```

To give our developer colleague access to our Git repository, we can have him clone the full project. After he clones the whole project, we can have him check out the new_feature branch. Lastly, he can make sure he's up to date on the project by pulling the remote branch from the server into his local branch:

```
$ git clone ssh://webdev@192.168.1.100/~/website.git
$ git checkout -b new_feature
$ git pull origin new_feature
```

With the branch on the developer machine also, the cycle begins again. Git gives us the power to work side by side on the same code and merge the changes with ease, as we did locally earlier in the recipe.

Further Exploration

Now that you've explored the basics of Git, you might start seeing other uses for it. In this recipe, we worked only with text files, but Git supports any type of file. You could use Git to version-control your Photoshop files, so you can easily maintain multiple versions as you build out designs. You can explore how to pull out previous versions of files, so you can recover that change your boss didn't like last week but wants to look at one more time.

You can also use Git to collaborate on open source projects with others. For example, you can go to GitHub[28] and find an open-source project such as jQuery (or one of the other libraries you've learned about in this book) and clone it, which pulls it down to your computer as a Git repository. You can then use techniques such as branching to develop new features for that project, which you can then submit back to the original maintainers to help the community grow.

Also See

- Recipe 38, *Using Dropbox to Collaborate and Host a Static Site* on page 278
- Recipe 39, *Setting Up a Virtual Machine* on page 282
- *Pragmatic Version Control Using Git [Swi08]*

---

28. http://www.github.com

## CHAPTER 6

Testing Recipes

We need to ship, but we have to ship code that *works*. We often ensure that our apps do what we want them to do by testing them in the browser manually. Sometimes we get other people to test things for us. In these recipes, we'll explore how to test our code as we build it and also how to create repeatable *acceptance tests*—test that we can run whenever we make changes to our code—so we can see whether things still work the way they did before. And we'll look at how we can test our assumptions.

Recipe 33

Testing Websites on Real Devices

Problem

We're building a new web app that needs to work on iOS and Android, not to mention all of the major desktop web browsers. We need a simple way to manage all of the web browsers throughout the design process, so we can test things out as we go without tons of extra effort.

Ingredients

- BrowserSync[1]

Solution

BrowserSync is a free, open-source tool that, as its name suggests, syncs browsers. When you point all of your browsers at BrowserSync's server, the links, refreshes, and scroll position are updated on every connected browser. Best of all, it supports watching files for changes, so when we update CSS, the new CSS is injected into the page for us. And when we change HTML or JavaScript, the page is refreshed. This makes it easy to develop user interfaces that work across devices.

BrowserSync works by injecting a bit of JavaScript on pages it serves, which lets it communicate with the connected clients. You don't need to change your code, add browser plug-ins, or do lots of configuration. Let's use it to develop a simple site design.

First, let's install BrowserSync using npm:

```
$ npm install -g browser-sync
```

Then let's create a new index.html file with an HTML skeleton:

```
browsersync/index.html
<!DOCTYPE html>
<html>
  <head>
    <meta charset="utf-8">
```

---

1. http://www.browsersync.io/

```
  <meta name="viewport" content="width=device-width">
  <title>Simple Site</title>
  <link rel="stylesheet" href="css/style.css">
</head>

<body>
</body>
</html>
```

Then let's add just a small amount of markup to the page so we have something to look at. We add a header, a navigation section, a small bit of main content, and a footer:

browsersync/index.html

```
<div class="container">
  <header>
    <h1>Responsive Template</h1>
  </header>
  <nav>
    <ul>
      <li><a href="#">About</a></li>
      <li><a href="#">Products</a></li>
      <li><a href="#">Services</a></li>
    </ul>
  </nav>

  <main>
    <h2>Main Content</h2>
    <p>
      Lorem ipsum dolor sit amet, consectetur adipisicing elit, sed do
      eiusmod tempor incididunt ut labore et dolore magna aliqua. Ut enim
      ad minim veniam, quis nostrud exercitation ullamco laboris nisi...
    </p>
  </main>

  <footer>
    <small>Copyright &copy; AwesomeCo</small>
  </footer>
</div>
```

This file links to css/style.css, so let's create that too:

browsersync/css/style.css

```
*, *:before, *:after {
    -webkit-box-sizing: border-box;
       -moz-box-sizing: border-box;
            box-sizing: border-box;
}
```

We're using the box-sizing property to change how the box model affects all elements. The default behavior for the box model is that the element's width is a combination of its margin, border, and padding. But adding this rule forces the content area of elements to be constrained by the width we specify. This makes the math much simpler.

Now let's fire up BrowserSync and tell it to watch our index file and our stylesheet for changes:

```
$ browser-sync start --server --files="index.html, css/style.css"
[BS] Access URLs:
-----------------------------------
Local: http://localhost:3000
External: http://192.168.1.2:3000
-----------------------------------
UI: http://localhost:3001
UI External: http://192.168.1.2:3001
-----------------------------------
[BS] Serving files from: ./
[BS] Watching files...
```

Running this command displays the URLs we can access and also opens a web browser for us. We can use the Local address on our machine, but we'll use the External address for our physical devices such as an iPhone. The figure on page 245 shows what things look like in Firefox, Chrome, and Chrome on an iPhone.

Right away we can see that our rudimentary site looks pretty good across these devices. We spend a lot of time using CSS to make web pages work across multiple browsers, but it's good to reflect on the fact that by default, the content in a browser is always as wide as the browser window. So in reality, we only need to apply styles that constrain and align elements for our desktop displays.

So let's test out BrowserSync's live-reloading feature. In the stylesheet, add a rule to constrain the content on devices larger than 768 pixels wide:

browsersync/css/style.css

```css
@media screen and (min-width: 768px) {

  body {
    background-color: #ddd;
  }

  .container {
    background-color: #fff;
    margin: 0 auto;
    padding: 1em;
    width: 80%;
  }
}
```

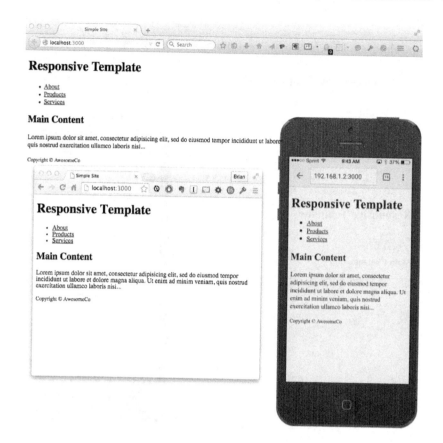

Saving the file triggers BrowserSync to push the new CSS into the browsers of all connected devices, including the local machine. When we look at our devices again, we see that only the desktop size is affected, as shown in the figure on page 246, even though all the devices have the updates:

We don't see any changes on our iPhone because the style we used didn't target the smaller screen size. So let's go a step further and style the navigation. We design the navigation mobile-first, so we set the buttons to be stacked vertically and have a width of 100%:

browsersync/css/style.css

```
nav ul {
  list-style: none;
  padding: 0;
}

nav li {
  border: 1px solid #ddd;
  text-align: center;
  width: 100%;
```

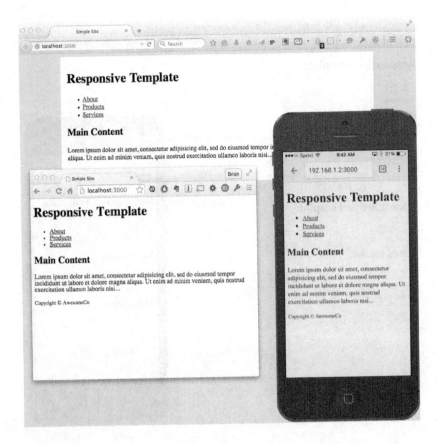

```
    margin-bottom: 0.5rem;
}

nav li a {
  display: block;
  text-decoration: none;
}
```

And then, for screen sizes wider than 480 pixels, we make the buttons line up horizontally like a navigation bar:

browsersync/css/style.css
```
@media screen and (min-width: 480px) {
  nav li {
    float: left;
    width: 33%;
  };
}
```

We can glance at our interface again and see if the changes we made, shown in the following figure, work for us:

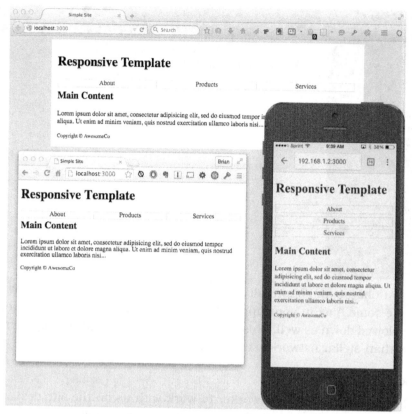

We can continue to iterate on our design, tweaking navigation and other elements until we get what we're looking for. And when it comes time to test on Internet Explorer or any other browser, we point that browser at the server too.

Using the BrowserSync User Interface

BrowserSync includes a user interface that runs on port 3001, and we can use it to control which connected devices reload, view the history of links we've looked at, and enable or disable scroll synchronization across devices.

One of the most useful features for mobile testing is BrowserSync's ability to introduce latency into the responses from the server. Our apps may appear to load quickly in our test environment, but in the real world, people often have slow or sometimes unreliable mobile Internet access. BrowserSync lets us simulate that latency.

When you visit http://localhost:3001 and choose the Network Throttle menu, you see several options that let you simulate different connection speeds:

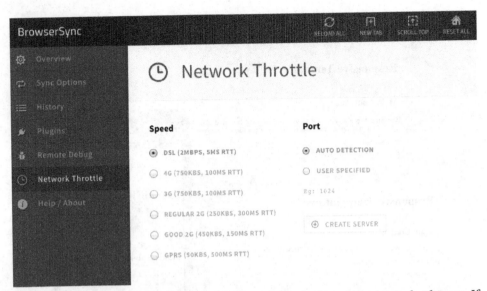

Once you choose an option, all requests will start seeming much slower. If you have some Ajax in your app that's fetching records, those connections will be slowed down as well. This is a great way to see what the experience is on less-than-stellar networks so you can try to optimize it.

Collaborating with Others

We need to allow a remote coworker to work with us on the site design. We can fire up BrowserSync with the --tunnel option, which gives us an external URL that we can provide to anyone who needs to collaborate with us:

```
$ browser-sync start --server --files="index.html, css/style.css" --tunnel
BS] Access URLs:
-------------------------------------------------
     Local: http://localhost:3000
  External: http://192.168.1.2:3000
    Tunnel: https://yyqanajlou.localtunnel.me
-------------------------------------------------
        UI: http://localhost:3001
UI External: http://192.168.1.2:3001
```

We give the Tunnel URL to our collaborator. When we make changes on our end, anyone looking at it sees those changes happen in real time.

Each time you start the server, you'll get a fresh new random URL, so keep that in mind. BrowserSync does have additional configuration options for using a specific URL for tunneling, though; configuring that is beyond the scope of this book, so consult the documentation.

Further Exploration

In this chapter we used BrowserSync and its own static web server. But you may be doing development using PHP, Java, Ruby, ASP.NET, or some other tool where an application sever is already in use and your files are dynamic. You still want to be able to test your designs and interactions on a range of devices. BrowserSync includes a -proxy option that lets you use your existing app sever.

In Recipe 16, *Creating Client-Side Apps with Angular.js* on page 107, and Recipe 15, *Creating a Search Interface with React* on page 97, we used QEDServer as the back end for our data. If we wanted to use BrowserSync to reload the pages when we change the code, all we'd need to do is launch BrowserSync like this:

```
$ browser-sync start --proxy http://localhost:8080 --files "*.html, css/*.css"
```

When you visit http://[your_address]:3000/index.html on your devices, the request will be forwarded to your application server, and you'll have the same features we used with the local server—including the ability to test network latency, which will help you identify and fix those trouble spots your visitors might face.

Also See

- Recipe 16, *Creating Client-Side Apps with Angular.js* on page 107
- Recipe 14, *Snappier Client-Side Interfaces with Knockout.js* on page 87
- Recipe 15, *Creating a Search Interface with React* on page 97
- Recipe 31, *Cleaner JavaScript with CoffeeScript* on page 221
- Recipe 28, *Rapid, Responsive Design with Skeleton* on page 194
- Recipe 30, *Building Modular Style Sheets with Sass* on page 213

Recipe 34

Tracking User Activity with Heatmaps

Problem

When running a promotion or redesigning a site, it's helpful to know what works and what doesn't so we know where to spend our time. We need a way to quickly identify the most used regions of our page or to find out which parts of our interface people aren't using.

For example, we need to resolve an internal dispute. One of our clients is launching a new product, and the two partners are at odds about whether the Sign Up button or the Learn More button is more useful. These buttons are placed right next to each other on the interface. We want to add some tracking to this page to see which button is getting clicked more.

Ingredients

- A server running PHP
- ClickHeat[2]

Solution

We can track where our users click the page and display the results in a graphical overlay called a *heatmap*, giving us an at-a-glance idea of the most-used parts of our page. Several commercial products can create heatmaps, but we'll use the open-source ClickHeat script because setting it up on modern web hosts is almost as easy as using a commercial solution.

Setting Up ClickHeat

ClickHeat has two components: a client-side piece that sends data and a server-side piece that processes it. ClickHeat's server-side piece needs PHP to work, but we can use ClickHeat to monitor any website as long as we can add a little bit of JavaScript to that site. We need to download ClickHeat from the project's web page and place ClickHeat's scripts in a PHP-enabled folder on our server. For this recipe, we'll use a virtual machine running on our own

---

2. http://www.labsmedia.com/clickheat/index.html

network at http://192.168.1.100. Check out Recipe 39, *Setting Up a Virtual Machine* on page 282, to learn how to build your own virtual machine for testing.

When we unzip the ClickHeat archive, we find a clickheat folder. We upload this folder into /var/www, the folder on our virtual machine that contains our existing web pages. Since our virtual machine has SSH enabled, we can copy the files up with a single command by using scp:

```
scp -R clickheat webdev@192.168.1.100:/var/www/clickheat
```

Or we can transfer them over to the server's /var/www folder with an SFTP client like FileZilla.[3]

Now that we've copied the code out to the server, we need to modify the permissions on a few folders within the clickheat folder structure so that we can write the logs and modify permissions. We log in to our server and use the chmod command to make the config, tmp, and logs folders writeable:

```
$ ssh webdev@192.168.1.100
$ cd /var/www/clickheat
$ chmod -R 766 config logs cache
$ exit
```

With the files in place, we can complete the configuration by browsing to http://192.168.1.100/clickheat/index.php. ClickHeat will verify that it can write to the configuration folder, and then we'll be able to follow the link to configure the rest of the settings.

We'll enter values for the administrator username and password. After we click the Check Configuration button and we see no errors, we can save the configuration. Now that the server component is configured, we can configure our web page to capture some data.

Tracking Clicks and Viewing Results

To begin tracking clicks, we add a few lines of JavaScript to our home page, right above the closing <body> tag:

heatmaps/index.html
```
<script src="clickheat/js/clickheat.js"></script>
<script>
  clickHeatSite = 'AwesomeCo';
  clickHeatGroup = 'buttons';
  clickHeatServer = 'http://192.168.1.100/clickheat/click.php';
  initClickHeat();
</script>
```

---

3.   https://filezilla-project.org/

We define a *site* and a *group* for this heatmap so we can track multiple sites.

When we redeploy the page to our server, clicks from our users will be recorded to ClickHeat's logs. After a few hours, we can visit http://192.168.1.100/ clickheat/index.php to see the results of our test, shown in the following figure:

It looks like more people are clicking the Sign Up button, whereas the other button isn't getting a lot of attention. We can let this script run for a few more days and see if things change. Now we have a graphical way of looking at user engagement, which will help the business make better decisions going forward.

Further Exploration

ClickHeat is relatively low maintenance once it's running. But it has a lot of options we can adjust, such as the number of times we'll record a click from the same user. We can also configure ClickHeat to record its results to the Apache logs and then parse them out with a script, which is a great approach for servers where PHP might be too slow to invoke on each request. Finally, ClickHeat can be set up on its own server, so it can collect data from more than one site or domain. Check out the documentation at the ClickHeat website for more options, or just explore its interface.

If you'd like something with a little more power, you might want to investigate hosted commercial solutions such as CrazyEgg,[4] which has similar functionality. Unlike ClickHeat, which stores your results on your own servers, these third parties collect your data on your behalf; for security and privacy reasons, this might not be something all organizations can use.

Finally, when you're looking at heatmaps of your own sites, you might get a little unexpected guidance from your users. If you notice a bunch of click activity on part of your page that doesn't have a link, consider making that region active. Heatmaps can often show you things you never saw before, such as the fact that you have elements in your design that people think they should click. These visitors might get frustrated or think things are wrong or broken. Use heatmaps to monitor and address those issues.

Also See

- Recipe 39, *Setting Up a Virtual Machine* on page 282

---

4. http://www.crazyegg.com/

Recipe 35

Browser Testing with Selenium

Problem

Testing is a hard and tedious process. As websites become more complex, it becomes more important to have tests that are repeatable and consistent. Without automated testing, our only chance at having a consistent working website is to have a top-notch quality-assurance person who works long hours and has checklists. That process could be painfully slow. We need to speed up the testing process and create tests we can run on demand so we can verify that things work the way we want today, as well as several months from now when we start adding new features.

Ingredients

- Firefox[5]
- Selenium IDE[6]
- QEDServer (for our test server)[7]

Solution

We can use automated tools to test our web projects, in addition to manual testing. The Selenium IDE plug-in for Firefox lets us build tests in a graphical environment by recording our actions as we use a website. As we move through a site, we can create *assertions*—little tests that ensure that certain things exist on the pages. We can then play them back any time we want, creating a set of automated, repeatable tests.

Our development team has built a product-management website, and our boss wants some safeguards in place to ensure that this will always work. The development team has added some unit testing to its business logic underneath, but we're tasked with building some automated tests for the user interface. Automated testing will give both the development team and us peace of mind if we make changes to the user interface down the road.

---

5. http://getfirefox.com
6. http://seleniumhq.org/download/
7. A version for this book is available at http://webdevelopmentrecipes.com/.

Setting Up Our Test Environment

First, we need to install the Firefox web browser. Go to the Firefox website and follow the instructions for your operating system.

Once we have Firefox working, we need to get the Selenium IDE installed. Open Firefox, visit the Selenium website,[8] and download the latest version.

With the tools installed, let's write our first test.

Creating Our First Test

We'll create our test by recording our movements with the Selenium IDE against our test server, which we'll run on our own machine using QEDServer. Start QEDServer and then launch Firefox. Go to http://localhost:8080 to bring up the test server, where you see an interface like the one in the following figure:

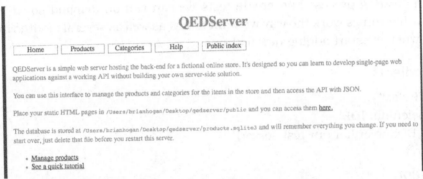

Since this is a product-management application, we'll start off with a test to make sure we always have the Manage products link on the home page and that the link goes where we expect it to go.

Open the Selenium IDE by selecting it from the Tools menu in Firefox. To start recording, we need to make sure the Record button is active. Then, in the browser, we click the Manage products link. When we click the link, we see some items begin to show up in the Selenium IDE:

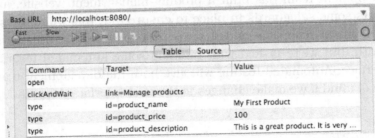

---

8.   http://seleniumhq.org/download/

Let's explore the Selenium IDE and see what it's doing for us.

At the top, the Base URL is now set to http://localhost:8080, and then we see one of the most useful commands in the Selenium IDE: the clickAndWait() method. When we use web applications, we spend a lot of time clicking links or buttons and waiting for pages to load. That's exactly what this command does. Every time we click a link, the Selenium IDE adds this method to our test, along with some text that identifies the link. When we play the test back, it uses this method and the associated link text to drive the browser.

The Selenium IDE shows us the three parts of a Selenium test action. The first is Command, which is the action that Selenium is performing. The second is Target, which is the item that Selenium is performing the action on. The third is Value, which we'll use to set a value for fields that take inputs, such as when we're filling out a text box or selecting a radio button.

A powerful part of Selenium is its locator functions. We can use these to find an element on the page not only by its id but also via the DOM, an XPath query, a CSS selector, or even plain text. When we clicked Manage products, the target we used is link= Manage products. The link= is the selector that allows us to choose a block of text to perform an action on. One thing we should keep in mind is that locators default to looking for an id first, followed by that string of text. Identifying elements for testing with IDs is a great way to speed up your tests and improve accuracy, but it can make tests harder to read.

Now that you have an understanding of locators, let's look at what the commands do. Commands are the actions that Selenium performs when we run a test. Selenium can do anything a human would do, with one small exception —it can't upload a file without some significant modifications. The ability to manipulate a browser the way a human would allows us to simulate human interaction, giving our tests the ability to flex our code realistically.

Let's test that clicking Manage products takes us to a page where the word *Products* is present. First we need to click the Manage products link. Next we want to make sure that the word Products is on the screen. To add a test for that, locate the word Products on the web page and right-click it. Choose the verifyText command from the context menu. We could also do this by using the Selenium IDE and clicking in the whitespace just below the clickAndWait() command and using the form fields to choose our command, target, and value. But the Selenium IDE adds some test helpers to the context menu, which makes the process much faster.

We can save this test by choosing Save Test Case from the Selenium IDE's File menu. We can then run the test by clicking the play button below the

Base URL window. As the test runs, the browser moves through our pages, and the background color for each step changes to green as it passes. If a step fails, it turns red and also shows some bold red text in the log window below with descriptions of what went wrong so we can address it.

Creating an Advanced Test

We want to make sure that our product-management application functions and that we can create a new product and delete a product. We also want to make sure we can view the details of a product. This is a multistep process; let's use Selenium to automate it.

Let's go back to the home page at http://localhost:8080, start up the Selenium IDE, and begin recording. Click the Manage products link and wait for the page to load. Then select the New Product text, right-click it, and select verifyText New Product. Next, leave the product form blank and click the Add Product button. The application we're testing requires that we fill in at least some of the product details; because we submitted a blank form, we now see an error message on the screen.

Let's make this part of our test. Right-click the "The product was not saved" error message and use the verifyText command to add an assertion that verifies that the error message shows up on the Products page.

Now that we've shown that our error message works, we can fill out all of the information in the form and submit it. The Selenium IDE adds a row to our test for each field we fill out. It also shows the value we typed in.

When we submit the form this time, it takes us back to the products page, where we see the message "Created." We can use the verifyText command again to make sure this text is displayed.

Now we have a feature-rich test that we can save and run later. If anyone changes the site, we'll know what's broken, simply by replaying the test.

Further Exploration

Now that we have test coverage, we can take this to the next level by automating our entire test suite. We currently have to run each test individually by loading it into the Selenium IDE, and this breaks down when we have a lot of tests. You'll want to investigate Selenium Remote Control and Selenium Grid,[9] which let you build automated test suites that run against multiple browsers.

---

9. http://selenium-grid.seleniumhq.org/

And although Selenium IDE is primarily a testing tool, you could use it as an automation tool as well. For example, if you have a process that has a less-than-friendly user interface, such as a time-tracking system or a repetitive and clunky management console, you might try using Selenium IDE to save you some keystrokes and mouse clicks.

With many of today's JavaScript-intensive applications you may also want to look at Nightwatch (explored in Recipe 36, *Testing Web Interfaces with Nightwatch* on page 258) to programmatically create your browser tests. Tools like Nightwatch are designed with these types of applications in mind but also require a bit more setup.

Also See

- Recipe 36, *Testing Web Interfaces with Nightwatch* on page 258
- Recipe 37, *Testing JavaScript with Jasmine* on page 267

Recipe 36

Testing Web Interfaces with Nightwatch

Problem

Browser testing can be a tedious and time-consuming activity. In Recipe 35, *Browser Testing with Selenium* on page 253, we learned how to build tests using the Selenium IDE. Unfortunately, that limits our tests to Firefox. We want to make sure that we can test in all of the browsers that might be used to visit our site. Manually testing sites in multiple browsers would require having access to installations of every browser we want to test. We need a way to automate testing across multiple browsers without having to keep our own versions installed.

Ingredients

- Node.js and npm[10]
- Nightwatch[11]
- QEDServer (for our test server)[12]
- BrowserStack Trial account[13]

Solution

Nightwatch is an end-to-end testing library that uses Selenium under the hood but lets us write tests in JavaScript that we can then run in a number of browsers or in the cloud.

To use Nightwatch, we first have to install it with npm:

```
$ npm install -g nightwatch
```

Then we need to grab the latest version of the Selenium Standalone Server, which we can get from the Selenium download site.[14] Specifically, we're looking for a file called selenium-server-standalone-[VERSION].jar, which we place this in a folder called jar within our project.

---

10. *Node.js*, on page xii
11. http://nightwatchjs.org/
12. A version for this book is available at http://webdevelopmentrecipes.com/.
13. http://browserstack.com
14. http://selenium-release.storage.googleapis.com/index.html

Next we need to configure our testing environment by creating a file called nightwatch.json:

nightwatch/first_test/nightwatch.json
```
{
  "src_folders" : ["test"],
  "output_folder" : "reports",

  "selenium" : {
    "start_process" : true,
    "server_path" : "jar/selenium-server-standalone-2.45.0.jar",
    "log_path" : "",
    "host" : "127.0.0.1",
    "port" : 4444
  },

  "test_settings" : {
    "default" : {
      "launch_url" : "http://localhost",
      "selenium_port"  : 4444,
      "selenium_host"  : "localhost",
      "silent": true,
      "desiredCapabilities": {
        "browserName": "firefox",
        "javascriptEnabled": true,
        "acceptSslCerts": true
      }
    }
  }
}
```

Creating Our First Test

To learn how to write end-to-end tests with Nightwatch, you'll work with QEDServer's product-management interface and write some tests to ensure it works the way it should. Start QEDServer and then launch Firefox. Go to http://localhost:8080 to bring up the interface:

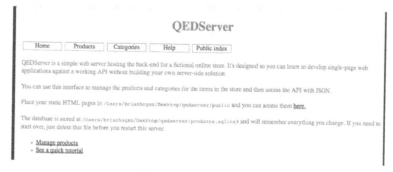

One of the easiest tests we can write is a test to ensure that when the page loads, we see the word QEDServer at the top of the page. If we right-click that text in our browser and choose Inspect Element, the debugging console shows us that this text is inside of an <h1> element, as in the following figure:

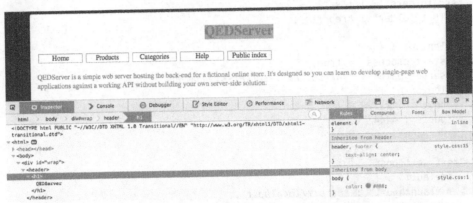

Let's write a test in the test/qedserver.js file that looks for the <h1> and text:

nightwatch/first_test/test/qedserver.js
```
module.exports = {
    "Test QEDServer title" : function (browser) {
        browser
            .url("http://localhost:8080")
            .waitForElementVisible('body', 1000)
            .assert.containsText('h1', 'QEDServer')
            .end();
    }
};
```

This test specifies the URL we're going to visit on the server and then waits for the page body to appear on the screen. Then it looks for the text on the page but ensures it's within the <h1> tag. Nightwatch uses CSS selectors to locate elements on the page.

When we run the test with the nightwatch command, we see this output:

```
$ nightwatch
[Qedserver] Test Suite
=======================

Running:  Test QEDServer title
✓ Element <body> was visible after 136 milliseconds.
✓ Testing if element <h1> contains text: "QEDServer".

OK. 2 total assertions passed. (3.073s)
```

When we ran this test, Firefox opened for a tiny bit and then closed. Nightwatch ran our actual site through its test and captured the results for us.

Interacting with Elements

Now that we know how to run a simple test, let's build a test that clicks the Manage products link, adds a new product, and tests to see if the product was created successfully. To do that, we need to gather some information about our interface.

First, we need to know where the Manage products link is on the page. Using the Web Inspector again, we find that it's located in an unordered list within the #main section of the page.

When we click that link, we're taken to a page that contains a form with three fields: one for the name of the product, another for the price, and a third for the description. If we inspect these three fields, we find out that each has an ID. The name field is product_name, the price field is product_price, and the description field is...you guessed it, product_description. Hurray for consistency.

Using this knowledge, we can construct a test that fills in this form and submits it. Let's remove the current test we have and replace it with this:

```
nightwatch/product_test/test/qedserver.js
module.exports = {
  "Test adding a product" : function (browser) {
    browser
      .url("http://localhost:8080")
      .waitForElementVisible('body', 1000)
      .click("#main ul li a:first-child")
      .pause(1000)
      .setValue('#product_name', 'Widget')
      .setValue('#product_price', '25')
      .setValue('#product_description', 'A simple widget')
      .click('input[type=submit]')
      .pause(1000)
      .assert.containsText('#notice', 'Created Widget')
      .end();
  }
};
```

Nightwatch can't find elements on the page by the text, so we have to locate that Manage products link by using a CSS selector. A huge downside to this approach is that if we reorder the links on this interface, it'll break the test. If we had access to the code for this app, we could add a unique ID or class to this link to make it easier to locate.

We find the form fields by using their IDs and use setValue() to fill in the values. We locate the submit button for the form and click it, and then we wait a little bit for a response. Then we check to see if we see a success message on the page.

When we run the test with nightwatch again, we see the browser open and our tests run, producing a result like this:

```
$ nightwatch
[Qedserver] Test Suite
=======================

Running:  Test adding a product
✓ Element <body> was visible after 135 milliseconds.
✓ Testing if element <#notice> contains text: "Created Widget".

OK. 2 assertions passed. (6.306s)
```

However, if we run the test again, we'll get an error. Our interface prevents us from creating duplicate records in the database. One of the biggest drawbacks to doing testing through the browser is that you have to have a way to reset the database when you do these kinds of tests. Or you have to include something in your tests that undoes what your test does.

QEDServer has a script called fresh_start that removes the existing database and sets things back to the way they were. So if you're following along, stop QEDServer and start it again with the fresh_server command. Or use the user interface to delete the record that the test just added.

Let's modify the existing test to delete the record we just found. New records get added to the top of the table, so we can grab the record at the top of the table and delete it:

nightwatch/product_test/test/qedserver.js
```
       .assert.containsText('#notice', 'Created Widget')
➤      .assert.containsText('table tr:first-child td:first-child', 'Widget')
➤      .click('table tr:first-child input[value=Delete]')
➤      .pause(1000)
➤      .assert.containsText('#notice', 'Widget was deleted')
       .end();
```

First, we check to see if the first row actually is the Widget record. If the assertion fails, the rest of the test won't run, and we won't accidentally remove something we shouldn't have. Then we locate and click the button that deletes the widget by looking in the first row of the table for an input element with a value of Delete...with a *capital D*. Make sure it matches, or the test will fail to delete the record.

As a final step, we check the message to ensure the record was deleted. When we run this test, the new record is created and then deleted:

```
[Qedserver] Test Suite
======================

Running:  Test adding a product
✓  Element <body> was visible after 143 milliseconds.
✓  Testing if element <#notice> contains text: "Created Widget".
✓  Testing if element <table tr:first-child td:first-child>
contains text: "Widget".
✓  Testing if element <#notice> contains text: "Widget was deleted".

OK. 4 total assertions passed. (7.224s)
```

We now have a repeatable test. But we're only testing in one browser. Let's run our test against multiple browsers.

Testing in Multiple Browsers

Our tests run in Firefox by default, but we can add in support for Chrome if we install the Chrome webdriver and alter our configuration. We install the Chrome webdriver with npm:

```
$ npm install -g chromedriver
```

Our configuration changes slightly too. After our default section, we add a new section for Chrome:

nightwatch/multiple/nightwatch.json

```json
{
  "src_folders" : ["test"],
  "output_folder" : "reports",

  "selenium" : {
    "start_process" : true,
    "server_path" : "jar/selenium-server-standalone-2.45.0.jar",
    "host" : "127.0.0.1",
    "port" : 4444
  },

  "test_settings" : {
    "default" : {
      "launch_url" : "http://localhost",
      "selenium_port"  : 4444,
      "selenium_host"  : "localhost",
      "silent": true,
      "desiredCapabilities": {
        "browserName": "firefox",
        "javascriptEnabled": true,
        "acceptSslCerts": true
```

```
      }
    },

    "chrome" : {
      "desiredCapabilities": {
        "browserName": "chrome",
        "javascriptEnabled": true,
        "acceptSslCerts": true
      }
    }
  }
}
```

With this new configuration, we can run our test using Chrome by passing the -e flag when we run the nightwatch command:

```
$ nightwatch -e chrome
```

This time the test runs in Chrome rather than Firefox.

Nightwatch supports running tests in parallel too. We can run tests in Chrome and Firefox like this:

```
$ nightwatch -e default,chrome
```

But in our case, that test fails because we run into a race condition. It tries to create two items called Widget and fails miserably. Worse, it'll probably have trouble deleting the records we created, because now with parallel tests there's no guarantee that the last record in our table will be the record we want to delete. Is this a showstopper? Not at all. It just means that the tests we built to demonstrate this tool aren't as robust as they could be.

In your applications, you'll need to develop methods that make it easy to reset the database from the test. For example, your application could have a special URL that you hit at the end of each test run that puts the database back to its original state by dropping the database and re-creating it. Or you could write your own code as part of your test suite that does that. You can come up with lots of strategies for this that are outside the scope of this book.

Testing on BrowserStack

We can test our site in Internet Explorer or other browsers by using BrowserStack's automatic testing API. After we sign up for an account, we can get a username and a key from our account page and use them use with Nightwatch to run our tests against /briwser/stcj;s Selenium server instead of our local one.

To make this work, we need two components: the local driver and Browser-Stack's tunneling software. We use npm to install the driver:

```
$ npm install -g browserstack-webdriver
```

BrowserStack's tunneling software lets BrowserStack's cloud services talk to our local server. We can download it for our OS from the BrowserStack web-site.[15] We'll download the BrowserStackLocal app to the bin folder of our project.

After we set up the prerequisites, we can create a configuration file specifically for BrowserStack that specifies the connection info we want, as well as the OS and browser we're testing. We could add it to our existing configuration file, but we've found it's best to add it to a specific configuration file all by itself:

nightwatch/multiple/browserstack.json

```
{
  "src_folders": ["test/"],
  "selenium" : {
    "start_process" : false,
    "host" : "hub.browserstack.com",
    "port" : 80
  },
  "test_settings" : {
    "default" : {
      "launch_url" : "http://hub.browserstack.com",
      "selenium_port" : 80,
      "selenium_host" : "hub.browserstack.com",
      "silent": true,
      "desiredCapabilities": {
        "project": "QEDServer",
        "browserName": "internet explorer",
        "version": 10.0,
        "javascriptEnabled": true,
        "acceptSslCerts": true,
        "browserstack.user": "bstinson",
        "browserstack.key": "abcdefg",
        "browserstack.local": true
      }
    }
  }
}
```

To run the tests, we have to start up BrowserStack's local tunnel by using our key. To do this, open a new terminal window, because this program has to stay running while we run our tests:

---

15. https://www.browserstack.com/local-testing#command-line

```
$ bin/BrowserStackLocal YOUR_KEY
BrowserStackLocal v3.5
```

You can now access your local server(s) in our remote browser.

Press Ctrl-C to **exit**

Finally, we can run our test:

```
$ nightwatch -c browserstack.json
```

Our test runs in the cloud against Internet Explorer 10. When we're done writing tests, we can shut down the BrowserStackLocal program.

Further Exploration

BrowserStack supports multiple browsers and operating systems, including mobile platforms. If you look at the capabilities list,[16] you'll see how to configure tests against iOS devices or Android devices.

Also, as we mentioned previously, Nightwatch has some limitations on how it can test your sites. Since it can only identify things based on IDs, you may need to modify the HTML of your interfaces to ensure you can more easily locate things. For example, adding unique classes or IDs on elements can make integration testing like this easier. Of course, you don't want to design your application solely for tests. You have to strike a balance between maintainable code and testable code.

Also, explore ways you can reset your database between test runs. You might consider testing your application against a blank database, rather than one that contains default data. This way it's easy to put things back.

Finally, make sure you test things at a lower level too. Acceptance testing like this looks at the application only from the end-user point of view. Don't forget about testing things with something like Jasmine or other unit-testing frameworks. And of course, don't discount the value of occasional old-fashioned user testing. Quality apps are the result of a multipronged approach to testing.

Also See

- Recipe 35, *Browser Testing with Selenium* on page 253
- Recipe 37, *Testing JavaScript with Jasmine* on page 267

---

16. http://www.browserstack.com/automate/capabilities

Testing JavaScript with Jasmine

Problem

JavaScript can be difficult to test accurately, because its flexibility and dynamic nature make it moving target. We can do browser testing with the Selenium IDE (Recipe 35, *Browser Testing with Selenium* on page 253), but that still requires manual JavaScript debugging with the console and doesn't give us direct information about functions that are broken. What we need is a full testing framework for JavaScript.

Ingredients

- jQuery
- Jasmine[17]
- Jasmine-jQuery[18]
- Firefox[19]

Solution

Jasmine is a JavaScript testing framework created by Pivotal Labs to allow behavior-driven development (BDD) in JavaScript. Jasmine's syntax is similar to that of Ruby's RSpec testing framework.[20] (You can find out more about RSpec and BDD in *The RSpec Book [Nor10]*.) BDD is an outside-in approach to testing that focuses on behaviors rather than structure.

For our first fully tested JavaScript application, let's build a to-do application using jQuery. Even though Jasmine is a BDD testing framework, we'll still use the test-driven development (TDD) approach by writing a test and then implementing the code to make that test pass—but we'll describe behaviors instead of specific elements of code.

To get started, let's create a folder for our application and then download and extract Jasmine testing libraries from GitHub inside of our application folder.

---

17. https://github.com/jasmine/jasmine/releases/download/v2.3.4/jasmine-standalone-2.3.4.zip
18. https://raw.githubusercontent.com/velesin/jasmine-jquery/master/lib/jasmine-jquery.js
19. http://www.mozilla.com/en-US/firefox/new/
20. http://rspec.info/

We also want to get the Jasmine-jQuery plug-in and put that in the jasmine/lib/jasmine-2.3.4 folder. The Jasmine-jQuery plug-in gives us some additional functionality that we'll use later when we work with fixtures.

Inside the Jasmine folder we find three folders and a SpecRunner.html file. We can remove the two .js files inside the spec and src folders. These are sample files that come with the Jasmine libraries, so we don't need them.

Now we can build out our tests and application. We'll start with the basics and add items as we need them. Let's add add_todo_spec.js inside the spec folder. Our directory structure should look like the following figure:

To get oriented, let's take a look at the mock-up of the application in the following figure:

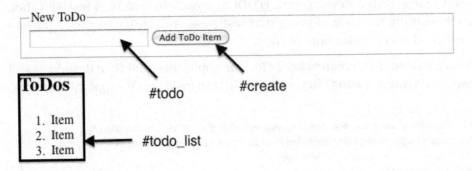

Writing Our First Test

Let's start off by calling the describe() function, which is a way to group related tests. As shown in the preceding figure, the primary function of our application is to add an item to a to-do list. Here you may notice the similarities to Ruby's RSpec framework. We have a describe() function that takes a message and another function. Inside of the describe() function we add our examples that describe specific behaviors:

jasmine/jasmine/spec/add_todo_spec.js

```
Line 1  describe('Add ToDo', function () {
     2    it('calls the addToDo function when create is clicked', function () {
     3    });
     4    it('triggers a click event when create is clicked.', function() {
     5    });
     6  });
```

Our first example, on line 2, describes what to do when we click the create button. With this test we're saying that when the button is clicked, the to-do application should call a function to add the to-do item. Our second example describes what event should be fired when the create button is clicked. In this situation, we want to make sure that the click() event is called.

Before we can use Jasmine, we need to tell it where our test, application, and third-party libraries are. To configure Jasmine, we modify SpecRunner.html, removing references to the spec files we deleted earlier and adding the location of add_todo_spec.js:

jasmine/jasmine/SpecRunner.html

```html
<script src="lib/jasmine-2.3.4/jasmine.js"></script>
<script src="lib/jasmine-2.3.4/jasmine-html.js"></script>
<script src="lib/jasmine-2.3.4/boot.js"></script>

<script
  src="http://ajax.googleapis.com/ajax/libs/jquery/2.1.4/jquery.min.js">
</script>
<script src="lib/jasmine-2.3.4/jasmine-jquery.js"></script>

<!-- include source files here... -->
<script src="../add_todo.js"></script>

<!-- include spec files here... -->
<script src="spec/add_todo_spec.js"></script>
```

To run our specs, open SpecRunner.html in a modern browser. Everything is green, and it looks like all the tests have passed! Well, not quite. The tests that we wrote don't do anything. We actually want to test things, so now we'll write some tests that'll fail and then implement the actual code and watch them go green.

Let's work on our first test. We want to make sure that the addToDo() function gets called when we click the create button:

jasmine/jasmine/spec/add_todo_spec.js
```
$('#create').click();
expect(ToDo.addToDo).toHaveBeenCalledWith(mocks.todo);
```

Then we want to test that the click() event triggers the addToDo() function. To call the click() event, we need some HTML to execute the JavaScript against. One benefit of the Jasmine-jQuery plug-in is its *fixture* support, which lets us create pieces of HTML code that we can rely on to be consistent and make our tests repeatable. Since our application is going to be a form with one text box and a create button, followed by a list, we can mock up the application in a fixture file. Jasmine looks for fixtures in the jasmine/spec/javascripts/fixtures/ directory of our application. Let's create an index.html file in that location to represent our to-do application:

jasmine/jasmine/spec/javascripts/fixtures/index.html
```
<!DOCTYPE html>
<html lang="en-US">
<title>Fixture</title>
<fieldset title="">
  <legend>New ToDo</legend>
    <form action="">
      <input type="text" id="todo"/>
      <button id="create">Add ToDo Item</button>
    </form>
</fieldset>
<h2>ToDos</h2>
<ol id="todo_list"> </ol>
</html>
```

Now that we've created a fixture, we need to tell our tests to use it. We'll use Jasmine's beforeEach() function to do some setup before each one of our tests. We want the beforeEach() function inside of the describe() function, and we use the loadFixtures() function to load our fixture:

jasmine/jasmine/spec/add_todo_spec.js
```
beforeEach(function () {
  loadFixtures("index.html");
});
```

Because the beforeEach() function is inside the describe() function, Jasmine will execute the code for all of the tests that are inside the same describe() function.

The beforeEach() function is the perfect place to put any code you need executed for each of the tests below it.

We'll want to test our application's functionality of adding a to-do item. Let's get some mock data to work with the fixture we just created. *Mocks* are objects that simulate real data and are consistent for every test run. Let's start by creating a blank mocks object that we can attach different values to. Right above the beforeEach() we need to initialize a variable that's accessible to each of our tests:

jasmine/jasmine/spec/add_todo_spec.js
```
var mocks = {};
```

Creating a global variable in the top of our test gives us an object that we can add functions and values to. Since our Jasmine test interacts with our application code, using a mock object will keep the test objects separated.

Inside of the beforeEach(), we add a todo variable to the mocks object. We can use jQuery to set the value of the to-do text box with the mocked todo. We know from our wireframe that the text box needs to have an ID of todo:

jasmine/jasmine/spec/add_todo_spec.js
```
mocks.todo = "something fun";
$('#todo').val(mocks.todo);
```

Here we're giving our todo a value of something fun and then filling the textbox with that value.

Since we're using a TDD approach, we write our test first and then the code to make it pass. We haven't written any actual code yet, so the test will fail when we run it, and we'll get output similar to the figure on page 272.

Going Green

In TDD and BDD, we create tests first and then try to get them to pass by implementing code. Tests that don't pass are often represented in red, as you've seen. Tests that pass usually show up green in reporting tools. So now that we have a broken test, let's implement the code to make it pass.

We need a place to keep our application code. Let's create a file named add_todo.js in the root of the application. We use a JavaScript object called ToDo to organize our functions and make them more testable. Inside of our ToDo object, we add three functions:

jasmine/add_todo.js
```
var ToDo = {
  setup: function(){
  },
```

```
  setupCreateClickEvent: function(){
  },
  addToDo: function(todo){
  }
};
```

With our add_todo.js file in place, we need to add all of the functionality to make the application work. We start with a setup() function, which we invoke in both our application and our tests. Its job is to call the setupCreateClickEvent() function, which binds a click() event to the create button. When a user clicks the create button, the browser fires a click() event, which triggers the addToDo() function:

jasmine/add_todo.js

```
var ToDo = {
  setup: function(){
    ToDo.setupCreateClickEvent();
  },
  setupCreateClickEvent: function(){
    $('#create').click(function(event){
      event.preventDefault();
      ToDo.addToDo($('#todo').val());
      $('#todo').val("").focus();
    });
  },
  addToDo: function(todo){
    $('#todo_list').append("<li>" + todo + "</li>");
  }
};
```

In the setupCreateClickEvent() function, we call preventDefault() on the event that's passed into the click() function, which prevents the button from submitting the form. We then call the addToDo() function, passing in the value from our todo text field. Then we set the value of todo to a blank string and set the cursor's focus to the text field so it's ready for the next to-do. In our addToDo() we are adding the to-do to our list using jQuery's append() function.

Let's jump to our spec and add the ToDo.setup() call to the beforeEach() function:

jasmine/jasmine/spec/add_todo_spec.js
```
ToDo.setup();
```

Now before every test, our ToDo.setup() function will be called, which will bind a click() event to the create button in our fixture.

The main focus of our first test is that the ToDo.addToDo() gets called. To assert that the function was called, we need to use a Jasmine *spy*.[21] A spy is a multiuse test double, which can be used as a *stub, fake,* or *mock*. A stub is a predefined response to something, usually a method that returns a specific value. The stub doesn't care what parameters are passed into it and always returns the predefined response. A fake is an object that still has working parts but takes shortcuts—it pretends to be a method that exists but only does a shorthand version of the original. A mock is similar to a fake but does more: it inspects what's going on, such as who's calling it and how many times it was called and with what parameters, in addition to responding the same every time it is called.

Attaching a spy to a function enables assertions for that function, such as checking to see whether the function was called, the number of times it was called, and even the arguments from each call. For our expect(ToDo.addToDo).toHaveBeenCalledWith(mocks.todo); to perform an assertion, and not call the function, we need to add a spyOn() to the top of the test. In this case, the spy will hijack our addToDo() function when it gets called. Then it'll check that the toHaveBeenCalledWith(mocks.todo) assertion is true—or, in other words, check that the function was called with whatever value is in mocks.todo:

jasmine/jasmine/spec/add_todo_spec.js
```
spyOn(ToDo, 'addToDo');
```

We're spying on the ToDo object's addToDo() function. Our assertion is that we are expecting the function to be called with the value in mocks.todo. This test is giving us a clear picture of the code we need to implement to make this pass.

---

21. http://jasmine.github.io/2.0/introduction.html#section-Spies

Now that you know what spies do, let's work on our second test and make sure a click() event is triggered when the create button is clicked. Our test needs to spy on the click() event, then click the create button, and assert that the click() has been called. Let's add this code inside of our second test:

```
jasmine/jasmine/spec/add_todo_spec.js
spyOnEvent($('#create'), 'click');
$('#create').click();
expect('click').toHaveBeenTriggeredOn($('#create'));
```

We don't want to execute the click() function, but we want to make sure that it was called. By using spyOnEvent(), we are using Jasmine again to hijack the click() event so our assertion can be evaluated.

Now that we've completed our tests and related code, let's watch the tests pass. Open SpecRunner.html in Firefox. We see the specs passing, as in the following figure:

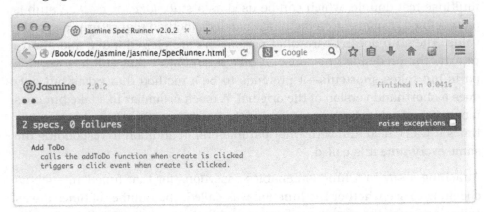

See? Our reporting tool is now all nice and green, signifying that we're on the right track. With working tests, let's finish up the last part and build the index.html page and have a functioning to-do list.

Finishing Touches

To finish up, we'll create a JavaScript file to hold our DomReady() function. Creating a separate file for this little bit of JavaScript ensures that we can set the state of our tests and not have them influenced by outside sources. At the root of the project, let's create app.js:

```
jasmine/app.js
ToDo.setup();
```

Here we are just calling our ToDo.setup() function. This gives us the most flexibility, because we're keeping most of the code in add_todo.js.

Lastly, let's create the index.html based on our fixture. We need to include both the app.js and the add_todo.js files. Let's start off our index.html by including the script tags at the bottom of the body:

jasmine/index.html

```
<script
  src="http://ajax.googleapis.com/ajax/libs/jquery/2.1.4/jquery.min.js">
</script>
<script src="add_todo.js"></script>
<script src="app.js"></script>
</body>
```

For the body of the page, we want to grab the code from our fixture. This way, our tests are executing against the same code as our application:

jasmine/index.html

```
<!DOCTYPE html>
  <head>
    <title>My Great ToDo List</title>
  </head>
  <body>
    <fieldset>
      <legend>New ToDo</legend>
      <form action="#" method="post" accept-charset="utf-8">
        <input type="text" id="todo"/> <button id="create">Add ToDo Item</button>
      </form>
    </fieldset>

    <h2>ToDos</h2>
    <ol id="todo_list">
    </ol>

    <script
      src="http://ajax.googleapis.com/ajax/libs/jquery/2.1.4/jquery.min.js">
    </script>
    <script src="add_todo.js"></script>
    <script src="app.js"></script>
  </body>
</html>
```

Now when we open index.html in a browser, we see something like the following figure:

We've now gone through a cycle of the TDD process and brought our tests to green, and we have a working application to show for it.

Further Exploration

To expand on our Jasmine exploration, try adding some tests to other recipes in this book, such as Recipe 10, *Interacting with Web Pages Using Keyboard Shortcuts* on page 61, or Recipe 12, *Displaying Information with Endless Pagination* on page 76. You could continue this recipe by adding tests and functionality to restrict adding blank to-dos. You can also use Jasmine with CoffeeScript (see Recipe 31, *Cleaner JavaScript with CoffeeScript* on page 221), which gives you testable JavaScript with the syntax safety of a compiler.

If refreshing a browser isn't your cup of tea, take a look at PhantomJS[22] and see how you can test an application by running a headless browser. Or take a look at Recipe 36, *Testing Web Interfaces with Nightwatch* on page 258, to see how you can test your application by driving a virtual browser.

Also See

- Recipe 35, *Browser Testing with Selenium* on page 253
- Recipe 36, *Testing Web Interfaces with Nightwatch* on page 258
- Recipe 31, *Cleaner JavaScript with CoffeeScript* on page 221

---

22. http://phantomjs.org/

Hosting and Deployment Recipes

We want to get our work out there for others to see, but that's only the beginning. Once our sites are live, we have to make sure they're secure. In this collection of recipes, you'll learn how to deploy your work and how to work with the Apache web server to redirect requests, secure content, and host secure sites.

Recipe 38

Using Dropbox to Collaborate and Host a Static Site

Problem

Our company and our partner company, AwesomeCableCo, are sponsoring Youth Technology Days. AwesomeCableCo has its own designer, Rob, who works remotely. We need a way to work with Rob on this site and show our bosses the progress we're making. Rob doesn't have virtual private network (VPN) access to our server farm, and our firewall allows deployment only from within our network.

Ingredients

* An active Dropbox account and the Dropbox desktop client[1]

Solution

We can use Dropbox to collaborate on static HTML files and host them so they can be viewed by external users. With Dropbox we don't need to worry about firewalls, FTP servers, or emailing files. Because Dropbox is cross-platform, we don't have to waste time with different applications for each OS, making Dropbox a productivity win.

Let's walk through the Dropbox client installation so we can document it and send it off to Rob. First, we head to the Dropbox website and get the installer.

Once installed, we can go to the Dropbox folder on our local computer. Dropbox automatically creates a Public folder, as shown in the following figure:

Photos   Public   Getting Started.pdf

---

1.   http://www.dropbox.com

We can use this Public folder to distribute files to anyone in the world. Let's make a youth_tech_days folder inside of that Public folder.

Now that we have a folder created, we need to invite Rob to collaborate with us. When we right-click the folder we created, we see a context menu that gives us the option to share this folder, as shown in the following figure:

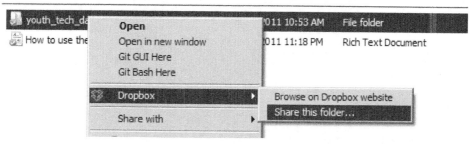

When we choose Share this folder, we're taken to the Dropbox website to finish the sharing process, as shown in the following figure:

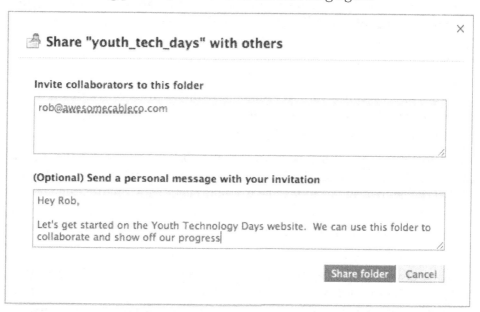

We fill out the information to share this folder with Rob.

Now we can move the files for the website into the youth_tech_day folder, which you can find in the book's source code in the dropbox folder. Now the directory looks like the following figure:

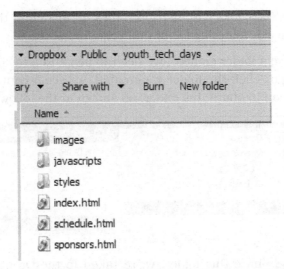

Whenever we drop files into this folder, they'll show up on Rob's computer as well. When Rob updates the files, our copy will be updated to stay in sync. As we work on the files, we'll want to communicate with Rob about what we're doing so that we don't overwrite his work. Dropbox has checks in place to handle conflicts if we edit a file at the same time as Rob, saving multiple copies of the file and appending a message to the filename indicating the conflict. This works fine for our simple situation, but if we are doing heavy active collaboration, we would should be using Git, as mentioned in Recipe 32, *Managing Files with Git* on page 230.

Now we need to show our bosses what we've done. Since we put the files in the public folder, they're available on the web to anyone who knows the URL. To find the address of our index file, we right-click it and choose Copy public link, which saves the URL to our clipboard. We can test the URL—one similar to http://dl.dropbox.com/u/33441336/youth_tech_days/index.html—by opening it in a browser.

This is a great, simple way to collaborate with people outside our company and easily show progress without the need for an FTP server, web server, or VPN connection. We can add other contributors to our project and share the URL with anyone who's interested in our progress.

Further Exploration

We can further explore by sharing nonpublic folders with coworkers and friends. We can also use nonpublic folders to back up files and share them among several of our own computers. In addition, we can use the public folder to send Mom an Internet Explorer patch she just can't seem to find on her own or provide our clients with a place to send us photos or other assets they'd like us to post on their sites. Other uses include the following:

- Hosting files you want to share on a blog post
- Sharing a folder with each of your clients for easy collaboration
- Forwarding a vanity domain to a public site
- Creating a blog with Enfield and hosting it from Dropbox

If your registrar or DNS provider supports redirection, you could set up a URL that's easier for people to remember when they want to check out your pages on Dropbox.

Also See

- Recipe 32, *Managing Files with Git* on page 230
- Recipe 29, *Creating a Simple Blog with Enfield* on page 203

Recipe 39

Setting Up a Virtual Machine

Problem

We want to test PHP scripts and configurations on a local server that looks like our production server. We need to set up an environment in which it's safe to experiment.

Ingredients

- VirtualBox[2]
- Ubuntu Server LTS image[3]

Solution

We can use virtualization and open-source tools to create a server playground that runs on our laptop or workstation. We'll use the free VirtualBox software and the Ubuntu Server Linux distribution to build this environment, and we'll then set up the Apache web server with PHP so we can use this environment to test some PHP web projects.

Creating Our Virtual Machine

We need to grab two pieces of software: the Ubuntu server operating system and VirtualBox, an open-source virtualization program. VirtualBox lets us create virtual workstations or servers that run on top of our operating system, giving us a sandbox that we can play in without modifying our actual OS.

First, we need to visit the Ubuntu download page[4] and grab the *server* version of Ubuntu 14.04 LTS instead of the most recent release. LTS stands for Long-term Support, which means we can get updates for a much longer period without having to do a complete OS upgrade. The LTS releases don't always have the most up-to-date features, but they're perfect for servers.

---

2. http://www.virtualbox.org/
3. http://www.ubuntu.com/download/server
4. http://www.ubuntu.com/download/server/download

While that's downloading, we can go to the VirtualBox web page[5] and download the latest edition of VirtualBox for our platform. Once it's downloaded, install it using the defaults, and then launch the VirtualBox program.

With VirtualBox launched we'll want to create a new virtual machine by clicking the New button. Virtual Box provides a wizard. With the first menu, we name our virtual machine, choose Linux as a type, and then leave version as Ubuntu (64bit). The RAM setting is next; it defaults to 512 MB, which is enough RAM for our machine. We can then complete the wizard using the provided defaults.

With our virtual machine created, we can click the Settings button to configure additional options. We need to change our network type from NAT to Bridged, so that we can access our servers from our host machine. The settings are shown in the following figure:

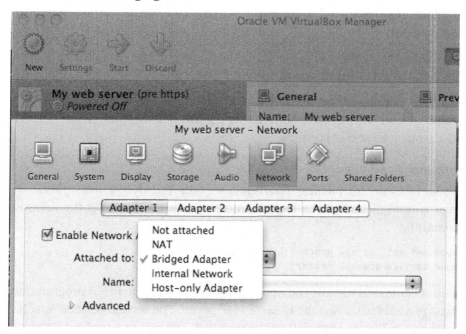

Now we can click the Start button to fire up the new virtual machine. VirtualBox detects that we're running it for the first time and walks us through the steps to get the Ubuntu OS installed. It asks us to choose either virtual or physical installation media. Since we downloaded the ISO image from Ubuntu's website, we can use that directly by clicking the Select icon and locating the ISO file on our computer. VirtualBox also allows for the use of

---

5. http://www.virtualbox.org/

physical media, so if we wanted to save some space on our hard drive, we could burn the ISO image to a DVD and use that for future installations. Once we select our installation media, the virtual server starts and the installation of Ubuntu is underway.

For our purposes, we can accept all of the default settings in the Ubuntu installation process. When asked for a hostname you can enter whatever you like, but the default will work fine. When asked about disk partitioning, accept the defaults and answer yes whenever you're prompted to write changes to disk. Since this is a virtual machine, you're not going to erase data on your computer's actual hard drive.

Toward the end of the process, we're asked to create a user account. This is the user we'll use to log in to our server and do our web server configuration, so let's call it webdev. We can use that value for both the full name and the username. We also need a password, which you can create on your own. Don't forget it!

When asked whether you'd like to install any predefined software, choose Continue. We'll install things ourselves at the end of the process.

When the installation finally ends, the virtual machine restarts, and we're prompted to log in with the username and password we created. Let's do that and get our web server running.

Configuring Apache and PHP

Thanks to Ubuntu's package manager, we can quickly get the Apache web server running with PHP by logging into our server and typing the following commands:

```
$ sudo apt-get install apache2 libapache2-mod-php5
$ sudo service apache2 restart
```

The first command installs the Apache web server and the PHP5 programming language and sets up Apache to serve PHP pages. The second reloads Apache's configuration files to ensure that the new PHP settings are enabled. Now let's set up our virtual private server (VPS) so we can copy files into our web server's directory.

Getting Files to Our Virtual Server

To work with our virtual server, we need to set up services so we can copy our files there.

Joe asks:
Do I Need to Perform Operating System Updates on My Virtual Machine?

Yes. Because packages can have different requirements, it's a good idea to keep your system up to date. Also, because this virtual machine is running on your computer, make sure all security patches have been applied.

To make sure your system is up to date, use the following two commands:

```
$ sudo apt-get update
$ sudo apt-get upgrade
```

The first command refreshes the list your server will use to find and install packages. The second command upgrades any existing installed packages and their dependencies.

Apache is serving all of the web files out of the /var/www/html folder, and the only user who can put files into that folder is the root user. Let's change that by taking ownership of that folder and all its contents with this command:

```
$ sudo chown -R webdev:webdev /var/www/html
```

Now, let's set up OpenSSH so we can use an SFTP client to copy files, just as we would if we were using a hosting company:

```
$ sudo apt-get install openssh-server
```

And now we can log in using any SFTP client. We'll use the IP address of our virtual machine, which we can find by typing the following:

```
$ ifconfig eth0
```

Our IP address is the one that looks like this:

```
inet addr: 192.168.1.100
```

We can now use an SFTP client to connect to that address with the username and password we set when we built the virtual machine. From a Windows machine, we could use FileZilla.[6] From a Mac we can use Cyberduck[7] or even use scp from the command line to transfer a file. For example, if we had an HTML file in our home directory, we could transfer it to our server like this:

```
scp index.html webdev@192.168.1.100:/var/www/html/index.html
```

---

6. https://filezilla-project.org/
7. https://cyberduck.io/

We specify the source filename, followed by the destination path, which is the username we want to connect with, followed by the @ sign, the IP address of the server, a colon, and then the full path where we'll place the file.

With our virtual machine in place, we can start using it as a testing playground. When it comes time to deploy our code to our production environment, we'll have had enough practice.

Further Exploration

Virtual machines give us a playground where we can test, experiment, and break things, but we can do more than that. The *snapshot* feature in Virtual-Box lets us create restore points that we can revert to if we goof something up. This is perfect for those times when we're interested in playing with a new piece of technology. In addition, we can create *appliances*—specific virtual machines with preloaded packages. We could create a PHP appliance, which has PHP, MySQL, and Apache already configured, and then share that virtual machine with others so they can get started quickly.

We can go a step further and automate this process using tools like Puppet, as shown in Recipe 45, *Configuring a Virtual Machine with Puppet* on page 317, and then keep all the configuration files stored in source control, as we see in Recipe 32, *Managing Files with Git* on page 230. This way we can share only configuration files with our team, rather than full virtual-machine images.

Virtual machines are useful for deploying applications. For example, in production we can take snapshots before upgrading an application or patching a security exploit, and revert if the upgrade or patch fails. And we can clone virtual machines to scale things out. Closed-source products such as VMware provide enterprise-level solutions for hosting multiple virtual machines on a single physical server.[8] VMware even provides some tools for converting a physical machine to a virtual one.[9]

Also See

- Recipe 41, *Configuring Secure Websites with Apache* on page 292
- Recipe 45, *Configuring a Virtual Machine with Puppet* on page 317

---

8. http://www.vmware.com/virtualization/
9. http://www.vmware.com/products/converter/

Changing Web Server Configuration Files with Vim

Problem

Many production servers use Linux and don't give us access to a graphical interface. When we have to make changes to our server's configuration files, it's inefficient to download a file, make the change on our development workstation, and then upload the file back to the server. To save time, we need a way to edit files directly on the server.

Ingredients

- Our virtual machine (VM), created in Recipe 39, *Setting Up a Virtual Machine* on page 282[10]
- The Vim text editor

Solution

We can use Vim, a powerful Terminal-based text editor, to make the changes we need quickly. Vim is designed with efficiency in mind. It's a great choice for working with files on a server because it's lightweight, highly configurable, and almost always available.

We recently deployed a site to our client's production server, but we forgot to configure the web server to display a proper 404 Page Not Found error page. The default Page Not Found message is a little more technical than our client would like, so we'll modify the message by configuring Apache to serve up a custom 404 page.

For this recipe, we'll use the VM we built in Recipe 39, *Setting Up a Virtual Machine* on page 282. Before we customize our error page, let's get acquainted with editing files in Vim.

Editing Files with Vim

Let's start by starting our VM and logging in through its console. Once logged in, we can start Vim by typing the following at the server's prompt:

---

10. You can grab a premade VM from http://www.webdevelopmentrecipes.com/.

```
$ vim
```

When we open Vim without specifying a file, we see a screen that gives us a little introduction to the editor, as in the following figure:

```
                  VIM - Vi IMproved

                    version 7.4.430
                 by Bram Moolenaar et al.
         Vim is open source and freely distributable

              Help poor children in Uganda!
         type  :help iccf<Enter>        for information

         type  :q<Enter>                to exit
         type  :help<Enter>  or  <F1>   for on-line help
         type  :help version7<Enter>    for version info

              Running in Vi compatible mode
         type  :set nocp<Enter>         for Vim defaults
         type  :help cp-default<Enter>  for info on this
```

We'll use the keyboard for absolutely *everything* in Vim, from moving our cursor around the screen to saving and opening files. We do this through Vim's various *modes*.

Vim has four main modes: normal, insert, command, and visual.

- Normal mode is for navigating around a file and switching to other modes.

- Insert mode is for entering text or making changes to the file.

- Command mode is where we execute specific commands, such as saving and opening files.

- Visual mode is for selecting text so we can manipulate it.

When we first open Vim, we start in normal mode. We can go into insert mode by pressing i. When we do that, we'll see -- INSERT -- at the bottom of the screen.

In insert mode, type *Welcome to Vim*, press the Enter key, and then type *Let's have some fun!* We should now have a file that looks like this:

```
Welcome to Vim
Let's have some fun!
```

We're done adding text, so we want to go back to normal mode, which we do by pressing the ESC key. In normal mode we can navigate around our file character by character using either the arrow keys or the h, j, k, and l keys.

These navigation keys keep your fingers on the keyboard's home row and, with practice, will let you move around files quickly. The `h` key moves the cursor left; the `l` key moves right. The `k` key moves up one line, and `j` moves down. If you need help remembering which key moves up and which key moves down, imagine that the `j` key looks like an arrow pointing downward, so pressing that key moves the cursor down one line.

From normal mode, we can save and close this file. We press `:` to switch to Vim's command mode. To save a file, we use :w (write). We can pass a filename to this command, so to save this file as test.txt, we use the following command:

```
:w test.txt
```

Any time we're editing an existing file, we can use :w to save the file we are working on, so we don't always have to pass the filename.

Finally, we can quit Vim with the :q command.

Vim includes a lot more than these simple commands, but we now know enough to modify our configuration to show a friendlier error page to our client's users.

Creating and Serving a Custom Error Page

We have a few ways to customize the error pages Apache displays to our end users. We could modify the main Apache configuration file, we could change the configuration file for our website, or we could use a special file called .htaccess. Using an .htaccess file lets us configure the Apache web server on a per-directory basis, giving us more flexibility. In some hosting environments, this is often the only way for us to configure things like error pages, since we may not have permission to edit the other configuration files. Let's configure Apache to use .htaccess files.

First, we need to enable the mod_rewrite extension to Apache, which we discuss in more detail in Recipe 43, *Rewriting URLs to Preserve Links* on page 300. We do this by typing this command at the server's prompt:

```
$ sudo a2enmod rewrite
```

Next, we need to tell Apache to allow overriding of configuration properties for this site. If we don't do this, Apache will ignore anything we put in our .htaccess file. Let's use Vim to modify the configuration file for the default website:

```
$ sudo vim /etc/apache2/apache2.conf
```

Instead of the arrow keys, let's use Vim's navigation keys (h, j, k, and l) to move down and change the AllowOverride value for our web directory /var/www/html. Navigate to the end of AllowOverride None and press i to go into insert mode. Then delete None and replace it with All. Our file should now look like this:

```
<Directory /var/www/>
        Options Indexes FollowSymLinks
        AllowOverride All
        Require all granted
</Directory>
```

Before we can save the file, we have to press the ESC key to leave insert mode. Then we can save the file with :w. We can then quit Vim with :q. After quitting Vim we want to restart Apache:

```
$ sudo service apache2 restart
```

Next we need to create a file to use as our 404 page. Let's navigate to the root of our sample website and use Vim to create a new 404 page called 404.html:

```
$ cd /var/www/html
$ vim 404.html
```

We're presented with a blank file, so we can press i to enter insert mode and then type in some basic markup for this page:

```
<h1>We're sorry</h1>
<p>
  The page you are looking for can't be found.
  It may have been moved to a new location.
</p>
<p>
  You might be able to find what you're looking for
  <a href="/">here</a>.
</p>
```

Once again, we press the ESC key to leave insert mode. We can then type :wq to save and close Vim with a single command.

Now that our 404 page is created, we need to tell the web server to display it. We'll create the .htaccess file in the same directory, /var/www/html, that contains our other web files:

```
$ vim .htaccess
```

Then we add a *directive*, or *configuration rule*, to define the location of our 404 page. Press i to enter insert mode, and enter this rule:

```
ErrorDocument 404 /404.html
```

The location of the file is relative to the site's URL, not the location of the file on the server's disk.

We press `ESC` to leave insert mode and then type `:wq` again to save the file. We can test it by trying to load a page that doesn't exist on our site with a browser. We see our custom 404 page. With our friendlier 404 page online, we've bought ourselves some time to fix the application and make a real 404 page that matches our site's theme. Using Vim like this allows you to create a stopgap while you implement a more permanent solution.

Further Exploration

Saying that Vim is just a text editor is like saying that bacon is just meat. Bacon is more than meat—it's super tasty. By using the right mixture of plug-ins, we can turn Vim into a full-fledged super-tasty IDE. A Vim installation is available for every major OS,[11] so you can download and install it on your development machine. Then you can find some plug-ins that relate to your daily activities by visiting VimAwesome, a directory of plug-ins and scripts.[12]

Once you've found some plug-ins that interest you, you might consider using Vundle[13] or Pathogen[14] to manage those plug-ins. Normally, you install Vim plug-ins into specific folders, but these tools make managing plug-ins easier by letting you keep the plug-ins in a central location so you can update them easily. Vundle contains an automatic installer and updater for plug-ins, whereas Pathogen gives you more manual control. Both are well-maintained and excellent solutions for easily extending Vim.

To learn more about using Vim for different tasks, look at Drew Neil's book *Practical Vim [Nei12]*, or check out Vimcasts.[15] Vimcasts posts screencasts that go into detail about using Vim and various plug-ins. You can also customize Vim further by writing your own plug-ins, which you can learn about in Ben Klein's *The VimL Primer [Kle15]*.

Also See

- Recipe 39, *Setting Up a Virtual Machine* on page 282
- Recipe 41, *Configuring Secure Websites with Apache* on page 292
- Recipe 43, *Rewriting URLs to Preserve Links* on page 300

---

11. http://www.vim.org/download.php
12. http://vimawesome.com/
13. https://github.com/gmarik/Vundle.vim
14. https://github.com/tpope/vim-pathogen
15. http://vimcasts.org/

Recipe 41

Configuring Secure Websites with Apache

Problem

When our applications and websites deal with people's information, we owe it to those people to safeguard it. We want to make sure our servers and databases safely store that information, but we also need to protect that data during its trips from their computers to our servers and back. We need to configure our web server so that it uses SSL to connect to web browsers.

Ingredients

- A virtual machine running Ubuntu for testing
- The Apache web server with SSL support

Solution

To set up a secure web server, we need to set up SSL certificates. Production websites use signed SSL certificates that are verified by a third-party authority. This verification gives customers a sense of security.

Signed SSL certificates cost money, and we don't want to pay for certificates for our development environments. For testing purposes, we can create *self-signed* certificates, which are ones we verify ourselves.

We'll use the virtual machine we created in Recipe 39, *Setting Up a Virtual Machine* on page 282, so we can get some practice.[16] That way, when we have to set up our production machine, we'll know exactly what to do. Run all of the commands in this recipe from your virtual machine's console, *not* on your local machine.

Creating a Self-Signed Certificate for Development

The process for getting an SSL certificate is the same whether we're getting a verified one or a self-signed one. We start by creating a certificate request. This request usually gets sent to a certificate authority along with a payment, and it then sends back a verified SSL certificate that we can install on our

---

16. To save time, you can grab a pre-made VM from http://www.webdevelopmentrecipes.com/.

server. In our case, we'll be acting as both the certificate requester and the certificate authority.

To create the request, we fire up our virtual machine, log into the console, and type the following:

```
$ openssl req -new -out awesomeco.csr
```

This creates both a certificate request and a private signing key that requires a passphrase.

We'll need to provide a passphrase for this new key, and we'll be asked for our company name and other details. You'll want to fill these out with real data, especially if you plan to use this to request a key from a certificate authority!

The key we created requires that we enter a passphrase every time we use it. If we request a certificate with this key, we'll have to enter that passphrase every time we restart our web server. This is secure but inconvenient. It's also not manageable in a production environment. Let's create a key we can use that doesn't require a password:

```
$ sudo openssl rsa -in privkey.pem -out awesomeco.key
```

Now that we have our request, we can sign it by passing both our request and our key:

```
$ openssl x509 -req -days 364 -in awesomeco.csr \
-signkey awesomeco.key -out awesomeco.crt
```

The certificate we created will be good for one year.

Finally, we need to copy our certificate and our keyfile to the appropriate locations:

```
$ sudo cp awesomeco.key /etc/ssl/private
$ sudo cp awesomeco.crt /etc/ssl/certs
```

Now let's modify the default Apache website to use SSL.

Configuring Apache for SSL Support

We need to enable the Apache module for SSL support on our server. To do that, we can either manually edit the list of installed modules or type the following:

```
$ sudo a2enmod ssl
```

This will do the modification for us.

Now we need to tell Apache to serve web pages using SSL.

Let's create a separate configuration file for our SSL site. Create the /etc/apache2/sites-available/ssl_example.conf file and add the following configuration to the file:

```
<VirtualHost *:443>
  ServerAdmin webmaster@localhost
  DocumentRoot /var/www/html
  <Directory /var/www/html/>
    Options FollowSymLinks
    AllowOverride None
  </Directory>
  SSLEngine on
  SSLOptions +StrictRequire
  SSLCertificateFile /etc/ssl/certs/awesomeco.crt
  SSLCertificateKeyFile /etc/ssl/private/awesomeco.key
</VirtualHost>
```

We're creating a new virtual host on port 443, listening on all addresses. The document root specifies where our web pages are, and the directory section sets up some basic permissions.

The last few lines set up the actual SSL connections, turning on SSL support, ensuring it's strictly enforced, and ensuring that it knows where our self-signed certificate and key are located.

With this new configuration file saved, we need to enable it and tell Apache to reload its configuration:

```
$ sudo a2ensite ssl_example
$ sudo service apache2 restart
```

Now we can visit our website's URL over SSL. We'll get some warnings from the browser, though, because a certificate we created by ourselves isn't considered safe for the average user. And that makes sense. If anyone could create a certificate that was automatically trusted by every browser, it wouldn't really be secure. We need to get a third party involved to get a trusted certificate. That's where a certificate provider comes in.

Working with a Certificate Provider

We don't want our users thinking we're trying to steal their credit card information or do other evil things with their data, so we need to get a trusted certificate. To do that, we generate a certificate request and a key in the same fashion we did for our self-signed certificate. We then send the certificate request to the certificate authority along with our payment, and it sends back a certificate we can install along with other instructions.

Some certificate authorities do more than take your money in exchange for a certificate that removes the error message. Some also verify that your entity is a legitimate business. When your users review the details of the certificate in their browsers, they can see this information, which adds an additional layer of trust. It also adds extra costs for you, but depending on your industry, it may be worth it.

Many certificate authorities exist. Thawte[17] and VeriSign[18] are well-known and trusted certificate authorities, but you'll need to research some on your own to find ones that meet your needs. If you're working with a hosting provider, you can often work with it to get a signed certificate for your site.

Further Exploration

We can use several types of SSL certificates. We can get certificates that cover a single server, or we can get a *wildcard* certificate that we apply to all servers within our domain. Wildcard certificates are much more expensive than single-server certificates.

Finally, Server Name Indication (SNI) certificates are a much cheaper option, but they work only with the most modern browsers and operating systems. SNI certificates are great for internal organizations where you have control over the browsers your clients use, but you'll want to rely on more traditional host- or IP-based certificates for the general public.

Also See

- Recipe 39, *Setting Up a Virtual Machine* on page 282

---

17. http://www.thawte.com
18. https://www.verisign.com/

Recipe 42

Securing Your Content

Problem

When we put files on our web server, they're available for anyone to see. But we don't want the entire world to have access to any important documents we're storing. When we want a select group of people to be able to access the files, we need a way to lock certain files or folders and create basic authentication.

Ingredients

- Development server with Apache
- Apache2-Utils

Solution

Apache allows us to create configuration files that specify which directories and files shouldn't be served without authentication. We'll take a look at how we build these configuration files to secure our server.

Using Basic HTTP Authentication

When Apache is serving up files, it's always looking for the .htaccess file. This special file tells Apache the configuration for a specific folder on your server. With the .htaccess file, we can enable password protection of files, block users based on certain criteria, set redirects and error documents, and much more.

Let's start by creating a file to ask for authentication. If you haven't already, be sure to read through Recipe 39, *Setting Up a Virtual Machine* on page 282, so that you have a development server to test with. After we log into our development server, let's also make sure that Apache is running and that we have the most up-to-date apache2-utils package:

```
$ sudo service apache2 restart
$ sudo apt-get update
$ sudo apt-get install apache2-utils
```

We'll also want to make sure that our website is configured correctly. Open the default site configuration /etc/apache2/sites-available/000-default.conf and make sure the following code exists. The key piece we need here is the AllowOverride All so that our .htaccess can be used by the web server for this site.

```
<Directory /var/www/html/>
  Options FollowSymLinks
  AllowOverride All
</Directory>
```

Now that Apache is running, we can start to build the authentication. For basic HTTP authentication, we need to create a file to hold the usernames and passwords that are allowed to log in. We can use the htpasswd command to generate a username with an encrypted password. Let's create the username and password now, and let's keep the file in our home directory:

```
$ htpasswd -c ~/.htpasswd webdev
New password:
Re-type new password:
Adding password for user webdev
```

When we call htpasswd, we pass a location for the file and our username. We use the -c flag to create a new file if one doesn't exist. When we press Return, we're prompted to enter the password we want to encrypt. If we want, we can use the cat command to check what's in that file so far, and we'll see something similar to the following:

```
$ cat .htpasswd
webdev:$apr1$9rQfRhOd$ZJJpVrhFVlWvYrn3vVrtI0
```

Now that our user is created, we can start locking down directories. Let's navigate to the document root and create an .htpasswd file:

```
$ cd /var/www/html
$ touch .htaccess
```

Let's open up our new file with our text editor and add some directives to lock down the root directory:

```
AuthUserFile /home/webdev/.htpasswd
AuthType Basic
AuthName 'Our secure section'
Require valid-user
```

Because we created this file in the top level of the document root, we've locked down every document on our server. Let's use our browser and navigate to http://192.168.1.100/. You should see an authentication modal dialog like the one in the following figure:

To view this page, you must log in to area "OurSecureSection" on 192.168.1.110:80.
Your password will be sent unencrypted.

Name: webdev
Password: ••••

☐ Remember this password in my keychain

Cancel   Log In

Thanks to Apache's HTTP authentication, we have an easy method for securing the content on our servers.

Where Should I Keep My .htpasswd Files on a Live Server?

With most shared hosts, you're limited to working only in your home directory. This means that the document root for Apache is set up to point most often to something like /home/webdev/mywebsite.com/public_html. Since you'll often be hosting multiple websites, it's nice to have each website in its own folder. For security reasons, you should place each site's .htpasswd file in that site's folder. For example, to generate the file for mywebsite.com, we'd run something like this:

```
$ htpasswd -c ~/mywebsite.com/.htpasswd webdev
```

This allows us to keep the users for different websites separate from one another.

Denying Off-Site Image Requests

We're paying a pretty penny for our hosting plan, so bandwidth and server load are always a concern. Also, we don't want anyone to be able to use our images without the correct rights and permissions. Thankfully, we can write a rule in .htaccess that will block off-site linking of images.

First, we need to enable Apache's mod_rewrite, since we'll want to use it to deliver a broken image to the request:

```
$ sudo a2enmod rewrite
```

To learn more about mod_rewrite, refer to Recipe 43, *Rewriting URLs to Preserve Links* on page 300.

We'll add a rule that rewrites the URLs for incoming requests to instead deliver an image that doesn't exist. Let's open up our .htaccess file and add these lines:

```
RewriteEngine on
RewriteCond %{HTTP_REFERER} !^http://(www\.)?mywebsite.com/.*$ [NC]
RewriteRule \.(jpg|png|gif)$ - [F]
```

The first line tells Apache to use mod_rewrite. Next, we add a condition that applies our rewrite rule only if the referring website is different from our own URL. Last, we create a rewrite rule to look for any requests that end in an image extension. We use the [F] flag to tell Apache that these URLs are forbidden.

With that, any image request to our server returns a broken image in place of the image that was being used.

Further Exploration

When it comes to locking down a server, we can use many methods to keep information and content hidden. Aside from password protection and rewrite rules, we can also block users by IP address or even by the website they are coming from. With Apache's configuration files, we can secure our content in many ways. To see more advanced applications of the rewrite engine, read through Recipe 43, *Rewriting URLs to Preserve Links* on page 300. Also, you can refer to Apache's own .htaccess tutorial.[19]

Also See

- Recipe 39, *Setting Up a Virtual Machine* on page 282
- Recipe 40, *Changing Web Server Configuration Files with Vim* on page 287
- Recipe 43, *Rewriting URLs to Preserve Links* on page 300
- Recipe 44, *Automating Static Site Deployment with Grunt* on page 304

---

19. http://httpd.apache.org/docs/current/howto/htaccess.html

Recipe 43

Rewriting URLs to Preserve Links

Problem

We plan to redesign our site around a new content-management system (CMS), and our URLs are going to change as a result. We have a lot of incoming links to pages and don't want to lose out on that traffic. Trying to figure out who links to us and asking them to change the links would take a lot of work and isn't a reasonable plan; nor is leaving the old pages around with a link to the new ones. We need a way to redirect users from the old URLs to the new ones with as little overhead as possible.

Ingredients

- The Apache web server
- mod_rewrite

Solution

The Apache web server and mod_rewrite—an Apache module that lets you make custom and simplified URLs—enable us to tell the server to load a specified file when another is requested. This will let us dictate what to load when a user visits our site. We can even use regular expressions so that we don't have to write an entry for every page in the site. Additionally, we can set headers so that search engines know to direct users to the new locations.

In this recipe, we'll work with a virtual machine with Apache on it, as covered in Recipe 39, *Setting Up a Virtual Machine* on page 282. If you're using a server hosted by another company, you may have to contact a server admin to set up mod_rewrite.

The first thing we need to check is whether mod_rewrite has been installed. The easiest way to do this is by making a page called phpinfo.php that contains one line of code:

```
<?php phpinfo(); ?>
```

Joe asks:

Why Can't I See the .htaccess File?

Just because you don't see the file in your file browser doesn't mean it's not there. Files that begin with a period (.) may not show up because they're typically system or configuration files and are hidden. Enabling the display of hidden files in the file browser will allow you to see them. You can see a list of all files by running ls -la in Terminal on OS X or Linux or by running dir /a on Windows.

We place this file on our server with the rest of our web pages and then load it in the browser. We'll see all sorts of information about our environment, but we're looking for mod_rewrite in the apache2handler section labeled Loaded Modules, as in the following figure:

Configuration

apache2handler

Apache Version	Apache/2.4.7 (Ubuntu)
Apache API Version	20120211
Server Administrator	webmaster@localhost
Hostname:Port	127.0.1.1:80
User/Group	www-data(33)/33
Max Requests	Per Child: 0 - Keep Alive: on - Max Per Connection: 100
Timeouts	Connection: 300 - Keep-Alive: 5
Virtual Server	Yes
Server Root	/etc/apache2
Loaded Modules	core mod_so mod_watchdog http_core mod_log_config mod_logio mod_version mod_unixd mod_access_compat mod_alias mod_auth_basic mod_authn_core mod_authn_file mod_authz_core mod_authz_host mod_authz_user mod_autoindex mod_deflate mod_dir mod_env mod_filter mod_mime prefork mod_negotiation mod_php5 mod_rewrite mod_setenvif mod_status

If you're checking on a production server, you should remove this file after you finish checking, because it exposes details of your server configuration that are best kept private. If mod_rewrite is there, we're good to go. If not, we'll ssh to the server and install it by issuing the following command:

```
$ sudo a2enmod rewrite
```

Next, we'll also want to make sure that our website is configured correctly. Open the default site configuration /etc/apache2/sites-available/000-default.conf and make sure the following code exists. The key piece we need here is the AllowOverride All so that our .htaccess can be used by the web server for this site.

```
<Directory /var/www/html/>
  Options FollowSymLinks
  AllowOverride All
</Directory>
```

Restart Apache with this command:

```
sudo /etc/init.d/apache2 restart
```

Now mod_rewrite is ready to use.

mod_rewrite uses an .htaccess file to know how to handle requests for files and redirect them to the appropriate location:

```
RewriteEngine on
RewriteRule ^pages/page-2.html$ pages/2
```

Our initial .htaccess file handles only the display of a single page, but it's enough to ensure that everything is set up correctly. The first line activates the RewriteEngine, allowing us to use mod_rewrite. The second line creates a RewriteRule, which consists of three parts. First we declare that we're creating a RewriteRule, and then we use a regular expression to identify URLs that match the incoming request by the user; finally, we tell Apache what it should load instead. The rule takes any request for pages/page-2.html and renders the content from pages/2 instead. As far as users can tell, they're still on pages/page-2.html.

We can use regular expressions to avoid having to create a URL for every page. Let's assume that we're deploying a new version of a site. The old URLs were at pages/page-2.html, while the new CMS uses pages/2:

```
RewriteRule pages/page-(\d+) pages/$1 [L]
```

This rule tells the server to find the first set of numbers in the URL after matching the pages/page- string and use the match for the path to the page it should load. pages/page-3.html will load pages/3, and pages/678.html will try to load the old pages/678.html file, since it doesn't match the regular expression. The final option we're passing—[L]—tells Apache that it should not apply any more RewriteRules if this one had a successful match.

Now that our new content is loading through the old URLs, we realize that having the same content available at two URLs—pages/page-2.html and pages/2—isn't ideal, because it's not clear which page should be linked to, and it's making updating pages more difficult. Instead, we'd like to redirect the browser to the new URL entirely and make sure that any search-engine robots also know to update their records.

To do this, we open .htaccess again and add the R=301 option to our RewriteRule:

```
RewriteRule pages/page-(\d+) pages/$1 [R=301,L]
```

This option makes Apache respond with a 301 Redirect header when the original URL is requested, which means that the resource at the given URL has been moved permanently. In addition, the new URL, which .htaccess has determined, is passed along so that browsers and search-engine robots can continue along to the new location and still access the information.

With some regular expressions and a few RewriteRules, we can move to a new website without being restricted by its previous content structure or fear of breaking existing inbound links.

Further Exploration

How could we use mod_rewrite and .htaccess to redirect requests to a new domain name? We can specify a full URL in RewriteRule, so what would it look like to redirect users from a.com to b.com? What if a section of our site was moved from a directory to a subdomain?

Also, what if we changed server-side languages from PHP to Ruby on Rails? What would it take to preserve all of our URLs from /display.php?term=foo&id=123 while loading content from /term/foo or /term/123? Executing this well could mask the fact that we ever changed our back end.

Also See

- Recipe 40, *Changing Web Server Configuration Files with Vim* on page 287
- Recipe 39, *Setting Up a Virtual Machine* on page 282
- Recipe 41, *Configuring Secure Websites with Apache* on page 292

Recipe 44

Automating Static Site Deployment with Grunt

Problem

Web developers working with static sites typically use tools like FTP to transfer web pages and associated assets into production. This practice works on a small scale, but as things get more complicated, manual processes break down. A file might be left out accidentally or copied to the wrong location. In addition, practices such as *asset packaging*—combining multiple JavaScript files into a single, compressed file—are required to improve download speed. We want to add this process easily to an automated deployment process. We need to develop a simple workflow that's easy to maintain yet flexible enough to extend.

Ingredients

- Node.js[20] and npm
- Grunt[21]
- Our virtual machine, created in Recipe 39, *Setting Up a Virtual Machine* on page 282[22]

Solution

As developers, we spend a lot of time automating the processes for our customers and clients, so it makes sense for us to invest some time in automating our own processes. Nearly every command shell has its own scripting language that we could use to automate website deployment, but we can leverage some powerful JavaScript-based tools that work whether we're deploying from Windows, OS X, or Linux.

At AwesomeCo, we're getting ready to expand our newly acquired daily deals to some new markets, and we've been asked to develop a simple microsite to collect email addresses from people so we can let them know when the service is available in their area. When we're done, it'll look like the following figure:

---

20. http://nodejs.org/
21. https://gruntjs.com
22. You can grab a premade VM from http://www.webdevelopmentrecipes.com/.

AwesomeCo Deals
is coming to your area!

Sign up to be notified when we're ready to launch and be one of the first in your area to get in on the action!

Enter your email [   ] **Sign Me Up**

We'll build a quick prototype of the site, and we'll use Grunt to combine and compress our JavaScript and style sheet files. Then we'll set things up so that we can quickly push updated versions of the site to the server. Let's start by taking a quick look at how we can develop our project with asset management in mind.

Improving Performance with Asset Packaging

Loading a web page containing two JavaScript includes, a style sheet link, and a single image takes a total of five requests to the server. The browser first pulls down the page and then makes additional requests to the server to grab the other assets. Some browsers are limited in the number of simultaneous requests they can make to the same server at a time. Instead of including multiple JavaScript files on a page, we can combine them into a single file. We can reduce the loading time even further by *minifying* that file, which means we remove comments and whitespace. This makes the file size smaller so there's less data to transfer to the client. Instead of including two JavaScript files on our page, we include a single, minified one. The same goes for our CSS.

To avoid losing our clean indentation, our comments, and our well-organized files, we write regular JavaScript and then minify it automatically when we save. This is similar to how we work with CoffeeScript in Recipe 31, *Cleaner JavaScript with CoffeeScript* on page 221. When we're ready to publish to the server we'll upload only the minified file. We'll use Grunt to manage this process for us. Grunt is a task runner that has many powerful plug-ins that we'll use to construct the perfect workflow for minifying and deploying our website.

Setting Up the Project

In our project folder, we create a folder for JavaScript files, a folder for style sheets, and a public folder that'll contain all the files we'll be pushing to production:

```
$ mkdir public
$ mkdir javascripts
$ mkdir stylesheets
```

To use Grunt, we have to first set up our project with a file called package.json. This file includes information like our project's name, version number, and any dependencies our project needs. We can generate that file with the npm init command, which runs a little wizard that asks us for the details:

```
$ npm init
This utility will walk you through creating a package.json file.
It only covers the most common items and tries to guess sane defaults.

See `npm help json` for definitive documentation on these fields
and exactly what they do.

Use `npm install <pkg> --save` afterwards to install a package and
save it as a dependency in the package.json file.

Press ^C at any time to quit.
name: (deploy) awesomeco_deals
version: (1.0.0) 1.0.0
description: Our Deals site
entry point: (Gruntfile.js) index.html
test command:
git repository:
keywords:
license: (ISC)
About to write to package.json:

{
  "name": "awesomeco_deals",
  "version": "1.0.0",
  "description": "Our Deals site",
  "main": "index.html",
  "scripts": {
    "test": "echo \"Error: no test specified\" && exit 1"
  },
  "author": "Max Power <maxpower@awesomeco.com>",
  "license": "ISC"
}

Is this ok? (yes) y
```

Now we can add Grunt as a dependency to our project and install the grunt command-line program systemwide:

```
$ npm install grunt --save-dev
$ npm install -g grunt-cli
```

The --save-dev flag installs Grunt and then places an entry for Grunt as a development dependency in the package.json file. The -g flag installs a Node.js package globally. The Grunt developers separated the Grunt command-line interface from the rest of the Grunt codebase, so we install the command-line interface globally on our system and install the parts of Grunt that do the work as a dependency of our project.

We're going to use a few more Grunt plug-ins in this recipe:

- grunt-contrib-uglify will merge and minify our JavaScript files.

- grunt-contrib-cssmin will merge and minify our CSS files.

- grunt-scp will transfer our files to our web server.

We install these plug-ins the same way as Grunt itself and make sure that we link them to the project:

```
$ npm install grunt-contrib-uglify grunt-contrib-cssmin grunt-scp --save-dev
```

Finally, our project relies on jQuery. Up until this point we've always brought jQuery in from a CDN. But we want to reduce the number of requests for JavaScript files, so we'll bundle jQuery with our own JavaScript code. To do that, we need a local copy of jQuery that we install by using Bower, a package manager for front-end code:

```
$ npm install -g bower
$ bower install jquery
```

The first command installs the bower command-line utility on our system. The second uses Bower to fetch jQuery, which it places in our project in a folder called bower_components/jquery. In this way, Bower eliminates the need for us to manually download, unzip, and manage popular libraries.

With everything downloaded, we can start configuring our workflow.

Creating a Gruntfile

Grunt looks for a file called Gruntfile.js, so we create one in our project. In this file, we write out some JavaScript code that configures the plug-ins we've installed. First, we put in the Gruntfile skeleton:

```
static/deploy/Gruntfile.js
'use strict';
module.exports = function(grunt){
};
```

Next, we configure Grunt to combine and minify the JavaScript files in our project, placing them in the public/assets folder. We load the grunt-contrib-uglify plug-in and then set the source and destination configuration:

```
static/deploy/Gruntfile.js
grunt.loadNpmTasks('grunt-contrib-uglify');
grunt.config('uglify', {
    'public/assets/app.js': [
      'bower_components/jquery/dist/jquery.js',
      'javascripts/form.js'
    ]
});
```

If we had more JavaScript files, we would add them to the source file array.

The configuration for combining and minifying CSS is similar. We load the grunt-contrib-cssmin plug-in and configure it:

```
static/deploy/Gruntfile.js
grunt.loadNpmTasks('grunt-contrib-cssmin');
grunt.config('cssmin', {
  'public/assets/app.css': ['stylesheets/*.css']
});
```

With these two plug-ins in place, we can execute the tasks with Grunt:

```
$ grunt cssmin uglify
```

But we'll most likely run these tasks together, so let's add a new task to our configuration called build that runs both of those commands for us:

```
static/deploy/Gruntfile.js
grunt.registerTask('build', ['cssmin', 'uglify']);
```

Now all we have to do is run grunt build to do both the CSS and JavaScript minification.

Running the build task by hand isn't the best approach, though. We can configure Grunt to watch files in the stylesheets and javascripts folders for changes and automatically execute the cssmin and uglify tasks for us. That way we don't have to run our build task manually anymore.

First, we install the grunt-contrib-watch plug-in using the process we've already used:

```
$npm install grunt-contrib-watch --save-dev
```

And then we configure the plug-in in Grunt to watch for changes and fire off the appropriate tasks when files change:

```
static/deploy/Gruntfile.js
grunt.loadNpmTasks('grunt-contrib-watch');
grunt.config('watch', {
  js: {
    files: ['gruntfile.js', 'javascripts/*.js'],
    tasks: ['uglify' ]
  },
  css: {
    files: ['stylesheets/*.css'],
    tasks: ['cssmin' ]
  }
});
```

We could have configured this so that it runs the build task, but we're being explicit here; we only want to run the specific tasks associated with the kind of file we're changing. We can use the build task to build the site before we deploy things, and this watch task while we develop.

With the config in place, we kick things off with the grunt watch command:

```
$ grunt watch
Running "watch" task
Waiting...
```

When we save a file, Grunt executes the tasks we associated with the files it's watching. It will continue to watch for changes until we stop it with CTRL-C. Let's keep it running though.

That was a *lot* of initial setup. But now that our tools are installed, let's get to work on our page.

Building Our Landing Page

First, we create the basic structure for our landing page, which we place in public/index.html:

```
static/deploy/public/index.html
<!DOCTYPE html>
<html>
  <head>
    <title>AwesomeCo Deals</title>
➤   <link rel="stylesheet" href="assets/app.css" >
  </head>
  <body>
➤   <script src="assets/app.js"> </script>
  </body>
</html>
```

Notice the <head> section of our page: we're including the CSS from a folder called assets rather than our stylesheets folder. And at the bottom of the page, we're also loading the JavaScript file from the assets folder instead of from the javascripts folders. This is because our workflow with Grunt builds this folder and these files for us by stitching the files in the javascripts and stylesheets folders.

Next we add the markup for our form to index.html:

static/deploy/public/index.html
```
<div class="container">
  <h1><span class="name">AwesomeCo Deals</span> is coming to your area!</h1>

  <form method="post" action="">
    <p>
    Sign up to be notified when we're ready to launch and be one of the
    first in your area to get in on the action!
    </p>
    <div>
      <label>
        Enter your email
        <input type="email" placeholder="email@example.com">
      </label>
      <input type="submit" value="Sign Me Up">
    </div>
  </form>
</div>
```

When a visitor fills in an email address and submits the form, we'll capture the form submission and send the result to the server with Ajax. We'll then hide the form and display a confirmation message. For this demo, we'll leave the actual Ajax piece out.

We'll place our JavaScript code in the javascripts folder of our project, *not* in the public folder of our project. Remember, Grunt will pluck the file out of the javascripts folder and combine it with jQuery, placing the resulting file in the public/assets folder. In javascripts/form.js, we add this code:

static/deploy/javascripts/form.js
```
(function() {
  $(function() {
    return $("form").submit(function(event) {
      var element;
      event.preventDefault();
      element = $("<p>You've been added to the list!</p>");
      element.insertAfter($(this));
      return $(this).hide();
    });
  });
})(this);
```

Grunt is watching our files for changes, so when we save the JavaScript file, Grunt updates the public/assets/app.js file. This file now contains our form-handling code, as well as the jQuery library it depends on, all in a single minified file. We don't change our workflow at all; Grunt makes this all transparent.

All that's left to do is add some simple CSS to stylesheets/style.css. First we center the page and set some font sizes:

```
static/deploy/stylesheets/style.css
.container {
  border: 1px solid #ddd;
  box-shadow: 5px 5px 5px #ddd;
  margin: 0px auto;
  text-align: center;
  width: 960px;
}

.container h1 {
  font-size: 72px;
}

.container h1 span.name {
  color: #900;
  display: block;
}

.container p {
  font-size: 24px;
}
```

Then we change the borders and text sizes on the form fields:

```
static/deploy/stylesheets/style.css
.container form {
  margin-bottom: 20px;
}

.container input,
.container label {
  font-size: 36px;
  height: 50px;
}
.container input {
  border: 1px solid #ddd;
}

.container input[type=submit] {
  background-color: #900;
  color: #fff;
}
```

Saving the CSS file triggers Grunt again, this time creating the public/assets/app.css file for us.

When we open index.html in our browser, we can see everything working together. But now let's extend this a step further by turning this development workflow into a deployment workflow.

Automating Deployment with SCP

Using Grunt and the grunt-scp plug-in, we can add a task to package up our assets and push all of our files to our server. We'll use the virtual machine we created in Recipe 39, *Setting Up a Virtual Machine* on page 282, as our server for this recipe. If you don't have that one handy, feel free to use your own server or download the virtual machine from the book's website.[23]

Joe asks:

What About Deploying to Windows Servers?

The configuration we whipped up in this recipe will let us send files from our Windows, Mac, or Linux machine to any box running SSH. Windows servers don't have SSH installed, but you can install OpenSSH[a] on your Windows servers and use the same scripts we're building in this recipe to push your files to Windows-based servers. If that's not an option, you could mount the server's disks as network drives on your client machine and copy the files over instead of using SCP. We've used both of these approaches successfully. We highly recommend automating your deployment regardless of your target platform.

a.   http://sshwindows.sourceforge.net/

We configure the plug-in for SCP just like the rest of our file. However, the plug-in needs connection information from our server, and we don't want to store sensitive data in our script. So let's make a new file called servers.json that contains details about the server we're going to connect to:

static/deploy/servers.json

```
{
  "production": {
    "host" : "192.168.1.100",
    "username" : "webdev",
    "password" : "webdev"
  }
}
```

23.   http://webdevelopmentrecipes.com

We'll assume our server is located at 192.168.1.100 and that the username and password are both webdev. Remember that you can use the ifconfig command on your server's console to locate its IP address; yours may be different.

Next, we need to read that configuration into Grunt, which we can do by serializing it into a configuration variable:

static/deploy/Gruntfile.js
```
grunt.config('servers', grunt.file.readJSON('servers.json'));
```

Then we can configure the SCP plug-in itself. We define the task to copy the public folder and its contents to the /var/www folder on the virtual machine, which is where the default website for Apache goes:

static/deploy/Gruntfile.js
```
grunt.loadNpmTasks('grunt-scp');
grunt.config('scp', {
  production: {
    options: {
      host: '<%= servers.production.host %>',
      username: '<%= servers.production.username %>',
      password: '<%= servers.production.password %>'
    },
    files: [{
      cwd: 'public',
      src: '**/*',
      filter: 'isFile',
      dest: '/var/www/html'
    }]
  }
});
```

Notice that we can inject the values from our server configuration file into our SCP configuration.

Now we create a deploy task that runs our build task and then uploads the files:

static/deploy/Gruntfile.js
```
grunt.registerTask('deploy', ['build', 'scp']);
```

How to Avoid Storing Passwords in Scripts with SSH Keys

In Recipe 32, *Managing Files with Git* on page 230, we discussed how to create SSH keys. By uploading your public key to your servers, you can remove the password part of the deployment script. This is a much more secure way of scripting deployments.

Now, when we execute the grunt deploy task, our code is built and then pushed to our server:

```
$ grunt deploy
Running "cssmin:public/assets/app.css" (cssmin) task

Running "uglify:public/assets/app.js" (uglify) task
>> 1 file created.

Running "scp:production" (scp) task
ssh connect 192.168.1.100
write /var/www/assets/app.css
transfer 1/1 data
write /var/www/assets/app.js
transfer 3/3 data
write /var/www/index.html
transfer 1/1 data
ssh close 192.168.1.100
```

We can pull it up in the browser at http://192.168.1.100/index.html. When it comes time to push our code to the production server, we need to change only the login details in the script. Or we can create another target in the same script for production.

Incorporating CoffeeScript and Sass

Once you have a good deployment workflow in place, you can start working more tasks into it. For example, you could incorporate CoffeeScript, which we look at in Recipe 31, *Cleaner JavaScript with CoffeeScript* on page 221, and Sass, which we explore in Recipe 30, *Building Modular Style Sheets with Sass* on page 213, into this process quite easily, so that you can use those tools in your development process. You can set up Grunt to watch files for changes and automatically convert your Sass and CoffeeScript files to their respective formats in real time, and automatically whenever you deploy. To do that, you would install the CoffeeScript and Sass plug-ins for Grunt:

```
$ npm install grunt-contrib-coffee --save-dev
$ npm install grunt-contrib-sass --save-dev
```

You would then write the style sheet with Sass, placing it in sass/style.scss. Similarly, you would develop the form handler code in CoffeeScript in coffee-scripts/form.coffee. You would then modify the Gruntfile.js to place the generated CSS and JavaScript files into a temporary directory:

```
static/sassandcoffee/Gruntfile.js
grunt.loadNpmTasks('grunt-contrib-coffee');
grunt.config('coffee', {
    'tmp/app.js': ['coffeescripts/*.coffee']
});

grunt.loadNpmTasks('grunt-contrib-sass');
grunt.config('sass', {
  'tmp/app.css': ['sass/*.scss']
});
```

Then you'd modify the watch task so it watches Sass and CoffeeScript files for changes instead of the JavaScript and CSS files:

```
static/sassandcoffee/Gruntfile.js
grunt.loadNpmTasks('grunt-contrib-watch');
grunt.config('watch', {
  js: {
    files: ['coffeescripts/*.coffee'],
    tasks: ['coffee', 'uglify' ]
  },
  css: {
    files: ['sass/*.scss'],
    tasks: ['sass', 'cssmin' ]
  }
});
```

And then you'd modify the cssmin and uglify tasks to pull the temporary files together into the assets folder:

```
static/sassandcoffee/Gruntfile.js
grunt.loadNpmTasks('grunt-contrib-uglify');
grunt.config('uglify', {
    'public/assets/app.js': [
      'bower_components/jquery/dist/jquery.js',
      'tmp/app.js'
    ]
});

grunt.loadNpmTasks('grunt-contrib-cssmin');
grunt.config('cssmin', {
  'public/assets/app.css': ['tmp/app.css']
});
```

Of course, the build task has to change as well:

```
static/sassandcoffee/Gruntfile.js
grunt.registerTask('build', ['coffee', 'sass', 'cssmin', 'uglify']);
```

And when you run your build task, everything falls into place:

```
$ grunt build
Running "coffee:tmp/app.js" (coffee) task
>> 1 files created.

Running "sass:tmp/app.css" (sass) task

Running "cssmin:public/assets/app.css" (cssmin) task

Running "uglify:public/assets/app.js" (uglify) task
>> 1 file created.

Done, without errors.
```

This approach lets you mix regular JavaScript and CSS with CoffeeScript and Sass, which means you can use jQuery, Angular, Knockout, Skeleton, or any of the other techniques in this book in your automated build chain. Since the resulting files all end up in the public folder, our deployment task in Gruntfile.js doesn't change at all. And Grunt has many other plug-ins you can use, or you can write your own.

Further Exploration

You can investigate other tools that handle asset management and minification, such as Broccoli,[24] and other task runners such as Gulp,[25] which offers a different way to think about configuration.

To take deployment to the next level, you could investigate Capistrano,[26] a Ruby-based tool that lets you write recipes to deploy sites from version-control systems such as Git. Although Capistrano was originally designed to deploy Ruby on Rails applications, it works great for deploying static sites, PHP applications, or even software packages.

Also See

- Recipe 30, *Building Modular Style Sheets with Sass* on page 213
- Recipe 31, *Cleaner JavaScript with CoffeeScript* on page 221
- Recipe 29, *Creating a Simple Blog with Enfield* on page 203
- Recipe 32, *Managing Files with Git* on page 230
- Recipe 36, *Testing Web Interfaces with Nightwatch* on page 258
- Recipe 33, *Testing Websites on Real Devices* on page 242

---

24. https://github.com/broccolijs/broccoli
25. http://gulpjs.com/
26. https://github.com/capistrano/capistrano/wiki/

Recipe 45

Configuring a Virtual Machine with Puppet

Problem

Our team is adding a few new developers, and as senior members of the team we've been asked by our boss to help on-board them. We've been using a virtual machine for our day-to-day work and want to share that with the new developers. It would be nice to allow them to reset their development virtual machine without snapshots.

Ingredients

- Vagrant[27]
- VirtualBox[28]
- Puppet[29]

Solution

We can use Puppet and Vagrant in combination to script our virtual-machine configuration in a replicable solution.

Vagrant is a tool for building development environments that we can use to easily interface with VirtualBox without having to use its GUI. We can grab an installer from Vagrant's website.[30]

Puppet is a configuration-management tool that will allow us to define the state of the machine programatically. Since we'll be running the Puppet scripts on our virtual machine, we don't need to install anything!

Vagrant works with a variety of virtual-machine hypervisors; however, since we're already using VirtualBox in Recipe 39, *Setting Up a Virtual Machine* on page 282, we'll continue to use that.

With Vagrant and VirtualBox installed, we're ready to get started. For the rest of this recipe, we'll refer to downloaded code from this book's source code.

---

27. https://www.vagrantup.com/
28. http://www.virtualbox.org/
29. http://puppetlabs.com/
30. https://www.vagrantup.com/downloads.html

Let's start our adventure from the puppet/start directory. Inside we find two directories—puppet and site:

```
~start/
 |+puppet/
 |+site/
```

From our start directory, we run the following command to initialize the directory to work with Vagrant:

$ vagrant init

This creates a Vagrantfile file inside our folder. The file that's generated shows many of the configuration options for Vagrant. Feel free to explore the generated file and then change it to the following:

puppet/finish/Vagrantfile
```
Line 1  # -*- mode: ruby -*-
     -  # vi: set ft=ruby :
     -
     -  # Vagrantfile API/syntax version. Don't touch unless you know what you're doing!
     5  VAGRANTFILE_API_VERSION = "2"
     -
     -  Vagrant.configure(VAGRANTFILE_API_VERSION) do |config|
     -      config.vm.box = 'ubuntu/trusty64'
     -
    10      config.vm.hostname = "webdev"
     -
     -      config.vm.provider :virtualbox do |vb|
     -        vb.customize ["modifyvm", :id, "--memory", "512", "--name", "webdev"]
     -      end
    15
     -      config.vm.synced_folder "site","/var/www/site"
     -
     -      config.vm.network :private_network, ip: "33.33.13.37"
     -
    20      config.vm.provision :puppet do |puppet|
     -        puppet.options = ["--verbose --debug"]
     -        puppet.manifests_path = "puppet/manifests"
     -        puppet.module_path    = "puppet/modules"
     -        puppet.manifest_file  = "site.pp"
    25      end
     -  end
```

Let's break this file down a bit. On line 5 we're specifying version 2 of the Vagrant API. On line 8 we tell Vagrant what base box to use. Then on line 10 we set the hostname of our VM to be webdev.

In lines 20 to 25 we see some mention of VirtualBox along with options for memory and a name. These are values that normally we would configure in the VirtualBox GUI, but here Vagrant takes care of it for us.

After the section configuring VirtualBox on line 16, we see a setting to sync a folder. This line tells Vagrant to copy the site from the local machine to /var/www/site on the server.

The last section of the Vagrant file defines our Puppet configuration. Let's take a look at the Puppet files, and that'll clear up this section of code.

The starting folder structure from the book's code repository helps us out here. Puppet requires folders that we need to create: manifests and modules:

```
~puppet/
 |+manifests/
 |+modules/
```

Inside the manifests folder we create a site.pp file, which will be our main entry into our Puppet configuration declaration. This is where we'll list the modules we're going to add in a bit. Let's put the following code inside of the site.pp file:

puppet/finish/puppet/manifests/site.pp
```
Exec {
    path => "/usr/local/sbin:/usr/local/bin:/usr/sbin:/usr/bin:/sbin:/bin"
}
include aptget
include apache2
include php
```

Here we're doing a couple of things. First off, we're setting the path at which the Puppet executable can be found on the VM, and then we're defining the modules we're going to create next. We're going to have Puppet install and configure PHP and Apache. We'll also have Puppet update the server with Ubuntu's apt-get package manager.

Let's start with the apt-get module manifest, and then we'll work over to the PHP and Apache modules. Puppet requires a manifests folder inside of each module and an init.pp file inside of that. Inside the modules/aptget/manifests folder, create the init.pp file with the following contents:

puppet/finish/puppet/modules/aptget/manifests/init.pp
```
class aptget {
  exec { 'apt-get update':
    command => '/usr/bin/apt-get update --fix-missing',
    timeout => 0
    }
  Exec["apt-get update"] -> Package <| |>
}
```

We start by creating an aptget class. Next we are starting an exec block called apt-get update. By naming the method, we can invoke it more easily from other places in our scripts. In this case we're setting two properties in our exec block: command and timeout. command is the system command we want to run, and timeout is how long it should wait before it times out and fails. The 0 value that we set for the timeout disables that setting, because updating lots of packages might take a long time, and we don't want our scripts to fail when updating already installed software. The last line in our manifest is what triggers the exec block to execute. The first half of the statement tells Puppet to find an exec block called apt-get update and execute that. The second half specifies that this should be done before any package block is executed. By making sure all packages are updated and sources are refreshed, we ensure that our machine gets the latest version of all packages.

Next let's tackle our PHP installation. We need an init.pp file inside of modules/php/manifests. Add the following contents to the init.pp file:

puppet/finish/puppet/modules/php/manifests/init.pp
```
class php {
  package {
    "php5" :
      ensure => installed,
  }
  package {
    "php5-cli" :
      ensure => installed,
  }
  package {
    "php5-xdebug" :
      ensure => installed,
  }
  package {
    "libapache2-mod-php5" :
      ensure => installed,
      require => Package["php5"]
  }
}
```

We notice four package blocks in our class for installing PHP. The package block is a common tool to use in Puppet. Because Puppet can run on a variety of operating systems, package blocks allow us to specify the name of the package and let Puppet decide how to install it. In our case, we're running on Ubuntu and using the apt-get package manager by default. So Puppet will run these commands in a similar fashion to how you'd install it manually with sudo apt-get install php5. We're setting the ensure property to installed to signify that if it is installed it's good to go!

The last Puppet module we need to add is Apache2. This module has the most code in it, but you'll see that it's not all that complex:

```
~puppet/
 |+manifests/
 |~modules/
 |  |~apache2/
 |  |  |~files/
 |  |  `~manifests/
 |  |     `-init.pp
```

The Apache2 module introduces a files folder. This folder contains files related to configuring Apache. You'll learn about these as we build up our init.pp file:

```
puppet/finish/puppet/modules/apache2/manifests/init.pp
class apache2{
  package {
    "apache2":
    ensure => present,
    before => File["/etc/apache2/apache2.conf"]
  }

  service {
    "apache2":
      ensure => true,
      enable => true,
      subscribe => File["/etc/apache2/apache2.conf"]
  }
  file {
    "/etc/apache2/apache2.conf":
      source => "puppet:///modules/apache2/apache2.conf",
      owner => root,
      group => root,
      require => Package["apache2"]
  }
  file {
    "/etc/apache2/sites-available/webdev.conf":
      source => "puppet:///modules/apache2/webdev.conf",
      owner => root,
      group => root,
      notify => Exec["a2ensite webdev"],
      require => Package["apache2"]
  }

  file {
    "/etc/ssl/private/awesomeco.key":
      source => "puppet:///modules/apache2/awesomeco.key",
      owner => root,
      group => root,
      notify => File["/etc/ssl/certs/awesomeco.crt"],
      require => Package["apache2"]
```

```
      }

      file {
        "/etc/ssl/certs/awesomeco.crt":
          source => "puppet:///modules/apache2/awesomeco.crt",
          owner => root,
          group => root,
          notify => File["/etc/apache2/sites-available/webdevssl.conf"],
          require => File["/etc/ssl/private/awesomeco.key"]
      }

      file {
        "/etc/apache2/sites-available/webdevssl.conf":
          source => "puppet:///modules/apache2/webdevssl.conf",
          owner => root,
          group => root,
          notify => Exec["a2enmod ssl"],
          require => File["/etc/ssl/certs/awesomeco.crt"],
      }

      exec { 'a2ensite webdev':
        command => 'a2ensite webdev',
        require => File["/etc/apache2/sites-available/webdev.conf"],
        notify => Service["apache2"]
      }

      exec { 'a2enmod ssl':
        command => 'a2enmod ssl',
        require => File["/etc/apache2/sites-available/webdevssl.conf"],
        notify => Exec["a2ensite webdev"],
      }

      exec { 'a2ensite webdevssl':
        command => 'a2ensite webdev',
        require => File["/etc/apache2/sites-available/webdevssl.conf"],
        notify => Service["apache2"]
      }


      file { '/etc/apache2/sites-enabled/000-default.conf':
        ensure => absent,
        require => Package["apache2"],
        notify => Service["apache2"]
      }

      exec {'site-permission':
        command => 'sudo chmod -R 775 /var/www/site'
      }

  }
```

Looking at apache2/manifests/init.pp, we notice that we have both exec blocks and package blocks, and also two new block types: file and service. The file block allows us to make sure a file exists in a specific location. This is a handy tool for configuration files such as Apache2 configs and SSL certificates. The service block tells Puppet to check to see that a service exists and, in our case, is enabled.

Let's break down a file block and see what it's doing.

```
puppet/finish/puppet/modules/apache2/manifests/init.pp
file {
  "/etc/apache2/apache2.conf":
    source => "puppet:///modules/apache2/apache2.conf",
    owner => root,
    group => root,
    require => Package["apache2"]
}
```

First we have the definition of the file block, which is the final location on the provisioned machine. Then we have definitions for source, owner, and group. source is the place where Puppet should get the file from. In our case, we're getting it from the modules/apache2/files folder. Our starter code from the book's repository saved us the trouble of gathering all the config files from Recipe 41, *Configuring Secure Websites with Apache* on page 292, and Recipe 39, *Setting Up a Virtual Machine* on page 282, so we don't have to do that.

Now that our Puppet files are created, we can start our VM. We need to make sure that we cd into the start folder from our command line and then start the process with the following command:

```
$ vagrant up
```

We see a lot of output from Vagrant as the VM powers up and provisions. When it finishes, we see some output similar to the following:

```
==> default: Notice: Finished catalog run in 200.96 seconds
```

To verify that everything is working we can visit http://33.33.13.37/index.html in our browser. We see the page shown in the following figure:

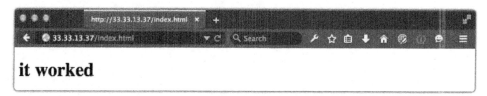

Now that we have a working web server, we can use Vagrant to do a couple more things. We can ssh into the VM with $ vagrant ssh, which is easier than remembering an IP, a username, and a password, as in Recipe 39, *Setting Up a Virtual Machine* on page 282. Typing $ exit while in the VM will bring us back to our machine. To stop the VM, we can use $ vagrant halt. Lastly, if we want to scrap our VM, we can use $ vagrant destroy.

Further Exploration

Vagrant and Puppet take our virtual-machine playground one step further and allow us to trash it and rebuild it, completely configured, in record time.

One perk of using Puppet for configuring virtual machines is we can use it to configure production and candidate machines. Also, because it's code, we can commit it to our version-control system and share it with team members. Puppet Labs[31] is a great resource for learning about Puppet and includes a search for many already created modules to add to other projects.

Also See

- Recipe 39, *Setting Up a Virtual Machine* on page 282
- Recipe 41, *Configuring Secure Websites with Apache* on page 292

---

31. http://puppetlabs.com/

Bibliography

[Bur15]   Trevor Burnham. *CoffeeScript: Accelerated JavaScript Development, Second Edition*. The Pragmatic Bookshelf, Raleigh, NC, and Dallas, TX, 2015.

[CC11]   Hampton Catlin and Michael Lintorn Catlin. *Pragmatic Guide to Sass*. The Pragmatic Bookshelf, Raleigh, NC, and Dallas, TX, 2011.

[Hog13]   Brian P. Hogan. *HTML5 and CSS3 (2nd edition)*. The Pragmatic Bookshelf, Raleigh, NC, and Dallas, TX, 2nd, 2013.

[Kle15]   Benjamin Klein. *The VimL Primer*. The Pragmatic Bookshelf, Raleigh, NC, and Dallas, TX, 2015.

[Nei12]   Drew Neil. *Practical Vim*. The Pragmatic Bookshelf, Raleigh, NC, and Dallas, TX, 2012.

[Nor10]   David Chelimsky, Dave Astels, Zach Dennis, Aslak Hellesøy, Bryan Helmkamp, Dan North. *The RSpec Book*. The Pragmatic Bookshelf, Raleigh, NC, and Dallas, TX, 2010.

[Swi08]   Travis Swicegood. *Pragmatic Version Control Using Git*. The Pragmatic Bookshelf, Raleigh, NC, and Dallas, TX, 2008.

Index

The Modern Web

Get up to speed on the latest HTML, CSS, and JavaScript techniques.

HTML5 and CSS3 (2nd edition)

HTML5 and CSS3 are more than just buzzwords—
they're the foundation for today's web applications.
This book gets you up to speed on the HTML5 elements
and CSS3 features you can use right now in your current projects, with backwards compatible solutions
that ensure that you don't leave users of older browsers
behind. This new edition covers even more new features, including CSS animations, IndexedDB, and
client-side validations.

Brian P. Hogan
(314 pages) ISBN: 9781937785598. $38
https://pragprog.com/book/bhh52e

Async JavaScript

With the advent of HTML5, front-end MVC, and
Node.js, JavaScript is ubiquitous—and still messy.
This book will give you a solid foundation for managing
async tasks without losing your sanity in a tangle of
callbacks. It's a fast-paced guide to the most essential
techniques for dealing with async behavior, including
PubSub, evented models, and Promises. With these
tricks up your sleeve, you'll be better prepared to
manage the complexity of large web apps and deliver
responsive code.

Trevor Burnham
(104 pages) ISBN: 9781937785277. $17
https://pragprog.com/book/tbajs

Seven in Seven

From Web Frameworks to Concurrency Models, see what the rest of the world is doing with this introduction to seven different approaches.

Seven Web Frameworks in Seven Weeks

Whether you need a new tool or just inspiration, *Seven Web Frameworks in Seven Weeks* explores modern options, giving you a taste of each with ideas that will help you create better apps. You'll see frameworks that leverage modern programming languages, employ unique architectures, live client-side instead of server-side, or embrace type systems. You'll see everything from familiar Ruby and JavaScript to the more exotic Erlang, Haskell, and Clojure.

Jack Moffitt, Fred Daoud
(302 pages) ISBN: 9781937785635. $38
https://pragprog.com/book/7web

Seven Concurrency Models in Seven Weeks

Your software needs to leverage multiple cores, handle thousands of users and terabytes of data, and continue working in the face of both hardware and software failure. Concurrency and parallelism are the keys, and *Seven Concurrency Models in Seven Weeks* equips you for this new world. See how emerging technologies such as actors and functional programming address issues with traditional threads and locks development. Learn how to exploit the parallelism in your computer's GPU and leverage clusters of machines with MapReduce and Stream Processing. And do it all with the confidence that comes from using tools that help you write crystal clear, high-quality code.

Paul Butcher
(296 pages) ISBN: 9781937785659. $38
https://pragprog.com/book/pb7con

The Pragmatic Bookshelf

The Pragmatic Bookshelf features books written by developers for developers. The titles continue the well-known Pragmatic Programmer style and continue to garner awards and rave reviews. As development gets more and more difficult, the Pragmatic Programmers will be there with more titles and products to help you stay on top of your game.

Visit Us Online

This Book's Home Page
https://pragprog.com/book/wbdev2
Source code from this book, errata, and other resources. Come give us feedback, too!

Register for Updates
https://pragprog.com/updates
Be notified when updates and new books become available.

Join the Community
https://pragprog.com/community
Read our weblogs, join our online discussions, participate in our mailing list, interact with our wiki, and benefit from the experience of other Pragmatic Programmers.

New and Noteworthy
https://pragprog.com/news
Check out the latest pragmatic developments, new titles and other offerings.

Save on the eBook

Save on the eBook versions of this title. Owning the paper version of this book entitles you to purchase the electronic versions at a terrific discount.

PDFs are great for carrying around on your laptop—they are hyperlinked, have color, and are fully searchable. Most titles are also available for the iPhone and iPod touch, Amazon Kindle, and other popular e-book readers.

Buy now at *https://pragprog.com/coupon*

Contact Us

Online Orders:	*https://pragprog.com/catalog*
Customer Service:	*support@pragprog.com*
International Rights:	*translations@pragprog.com*
Academic Use:	*academic@pragprog.com*
Write for Us:	*http://write-for-us.pragprog.com*
Or Call:	+1 800-699-7764

CPSIA information can be obtained
at www.ICGtesting.com
Printed in the USA
LVOW03s2019070116
469685LV00009B/44/P